CHRIST REVEALED
The History of the Neotypological Lyric in the English Renaissance

IRA CLARK

A University of Florida Book
UNIVERSITY PRESSES OF FLORIDA
Gainesville

Chapter 4 has been revised and reprinted from *ELH* (formerly Journal of
English Literary History) by permission of the publisher: The Johns Hopkins
University Press, Baltimore.

Library of Congress Cataloging in Publication Data

Clark Ira
   Christ revealed.
   (University of Florida monographs. Humanities; no. 51)
   Bibliography: p.
   Includes index.
   1. English poetry—Early modern, 1500–1700—History and Criticism.
2. Typology (Theology) in literature.   3. Christian poetry, English—His-
tory and criticism.   4. Jesus Christ in fiction, drama, poetry, etc.   5. Bible
in literature.   I. Title.   II. Series.
   PR545.T94C59   821'.04'0915   82–2696
   ISBN 0–8130–0712–7   AACR2

University Presses of Florida is the central agency for scholarly publishing of the State of
Florida's university system. Its offices are located at 15 NW 15th Street, Gainesville, FL
32603. Works published by University Presses of Florida are evaluated and selected for
publication by a faculty editorial committee of any one of Florida's nine public universities:
Florida A&M University (Tallahassee), Florida Atlantic University (Boca Raton), Florida
International University (Miami), Florida State University (Tallahassee), University of Central Florida (Orlando), University of Florida (Gainesville), University of North Florida (Jack-
sonville), University of South Florida (Tampa), University of West Florida (Pensacola).

To My Mother and Father
for giving me a tradition

Contents

Contents

Preface

When, at the turn of the seventies, I began considering how lyric poets from the early Latin Middle Ages through the close of the English Renaissance used types, I projected a set of illustrative interpretations inside a context of biblical typology (the study of Old Testament prefigurations of Christian salvation). Two primary guides at that time were Erich Auerbach's "Figura" and Rosemond Tuve's *A Reading of George Herbert*. Essays such as Victor Harris' "Allegory to Analogy in the Interpretation of the Scriptures during the Middle Ages and the Renaissance" also provided help.[1] However, it soon became notable that scholars' perceptions of typology often were at odds with each other and even more often were out of focus for much poetry after the Reformation. For understandable reasons, some scholars, such as William G. Madsen in his study of Milton's poetics, *From Shadowy Types to Truth*, saw an essentially consistent allegoresis from late church fathers through medieval exegetes to mid-seventeenth-century commentators. Others, for instance H. R. MacCallum in "Milton and Figurative Interpretation of the Bible," demonstrated significant differences between medieval Catholic and new Puritan approaches. My own studies, which began by analyzing George Herbert's use of types,[2] led me to believe that two emphases which developed during the Reformation caused profound changes that distinguish the finest sacred lyricists of the English Renaissance. Reformed straitening to stricter literal in place of allegorical biblical interpretation placed greater emphasis on types proper. Reformed Augustinianism intensified personal self-examination and identification with biblical settings, scenes, figures, and objects. The sacred English lyrics I was most interested in were devout personal lyrics based in types; the poets had embodied contemporary personae and settings inside Old Testament figures and situations so that both were illuminated by a New Testament perspective.

It seemed to me that this new form of sacred song, what I call the English neotypological lyric, was brought into existence, developed to magnificence, and exhausted in a period extending from the middle of Henry VIII's reign through the settlement of the Massachusetts frontier. Predecessors of the neotypological lyric evolved out of many poets' experiments with the expressive potential in typological allusions, devotional verse, psalmody, Petrarchan parody, formal meditation, and emblem. Its own history opens toward the end of Elizabeth's reign. The Jesuit Robert Southwell, singing to comfort himself and his congregation under threat of martyrdom and moral failure, discovered its rudimentary form. The Catholic convert William Alabaster, examining through typological analogies his capacity to face a similar fate, defined it. The early seventeenth century emblematists, charting the career of a believing soul, added self-explications through crucial scenes in a representative life, while John Donne, performing as the model converted sinner and thoroughly tried human, dramatized its persona. George Herbert laid bare the primary sacred motivations in the form and compounded its effects. His customary neotypical persona appears in some legalistic Old Testament situation complete with motifs, image clusters, and neotypical style. During the course of the lyric the speaker discovers and the reader is presumed to rediscover the beauty of providential redemption for the Old Testament type and the seventeenth-century neotype, as both are saved by the antitype. Henry Vaughan then varied the form: some of his personae expressed nostalgia over a corrupt world losing typological identification; others then followed that lament by despairing and reviving legalistic accusations of a self-damning crowd that ignored or rejected Christian redemption. The neotypological lyric disintegrated at opposite poles: the Anglican Thomas Traherne transcended it by expanding God's presence in the neotype; the Puritan Edward Taylor annihilated it by severing unique God-bearing significance from both type and antitype.

As I modified my hypothesis I initially worked through bibliographies to learn how previous interpretations of the poetry moved toward typological readings. But an increasing set of literary studies based in religious movements during the period made me jettison older references that seemed to approach but not yet discover typology. Meanwhile a surprising number of corroborations of the importance of types to English Renaissance poetry began to appear. Moreover, several scholars' ideas, including Murray Roston's "postfigurations" in *Biblical Drama in*

England, Steven N. Zwicker's biblical "models" in *Dryden's Political Poetry: the Typology of King and Nation,* and Barbara K. Lewalski's "correlative types," especially in *"Samson Agonistes* and the 'Tragedy' of the Apocalypse," anticipated and paralleled my notion of neotype.[3] In addition, Sacvan Bercovitch's bibliography of typology, which appeared first in 1970 and 1971 in *Early American Literature* and then again with a collection of helpful essays in *Typology and Early American Literature,* provided a valuable tool and corroboration.

Just as studies such as these were extending and revising the seminal discussions of typology by Auerbach and Tuve, so studies of the Augustinian revival of intense introspection by Reformers and Counter-Reformers alike, already chronicled by major influences like William Haller in *The Rise of Puritanism,* Perry Miller in *The New England Mind: The Seventeenth Century,* Helen C. White in *English Devotional Literature, 1600–1640,* and Louis L. Martz in *The Poetry of Meditation,* were also being revised and extended. In *Worship and Theology in England: From Cranmer to Hooker, 1534–1603,* and *From Andrewes to Baxter and Fox, 1603–1690,* Horton Davies describes the deepening spiritual intensity of the times, not just among Puritan and Anglican reformers but also among Anglo-Catholic humanists and Counter-Reformers. Davies particularly tells about the closer identification with biblical situations in private devotions, public worship, and sermons. And in essays such as those collected and introduced by Sacvan Bercovitch in *The American Puritan Imagination: Essays in Revaluation,* a primary motif is the impact made by covenant theology and the popular view that God intervenes in the world. Furthermore, William H. Halewood's *The Poetry of Grace* and Patrick Grant's *The Transformation of Sin* establish that the resurgence of Augustinian "guilt culture" provides ideological and aesthetic contexts important for understanding religious poetry from the period. Both Reformers and Counter-Reformers were preoccupied with the guilt of original and inevitable personal sin along with spiritual alertness to and striving after God's grace through vicarious atonement.[4] Because of studies including Martz's *The Paradise Within,* U. Milo Kaufmann's *The Pilgrim's Progress and Traditions in Puritan Meditation,* and Anthony Low's *Love's Architecture: Devotional Modes in Seventeenth-Century English Poetry,* our knowledge of introspective devotional meditation is deeper about personal practices and broader across a spectrum of practitioners from Catholics through Puritans and sectarians into mystics.

The most influential literary historian examining the relationships of these traditions is Barbara Kiefer Lewalski. And the best known arguments for the importance to English poetry of Protestant studies of types and their applications to the faithful appeared in two essays that led to a book: "Typology and Poetry: A Consideration of Herbert, Vaughan, and Marvell," "Typological Symbolism and the 'Progress of the Soul' in Seventeenth-Century Literature," and *Protestant Poetics and the Seventeenth-Century Religious Lyric*. Although the essays appeared after I had worked up my basic notions and was well through several drafts, and the book after I had essentially finished writing, the essays were in time to encourage and help me through one major revision problem. One of her central theses overlaps mine. Two Reformed alterations of traditional allegorical biblical exegesis—first, an emphasis on typological interpretation of the Bible, and second, an imperative search of Scripture to find and apply parallels to contemporary life—provided stimulus and direction for sacred poets during the period. But Lewalski's interests and mine, though very close in beginning with the same materials inside an identical context, do not coincide. First, my aims are much more limited than her wide-ranging informative presentation of Protestant theories of aesthetics, modes, genres, and styles. Even in the study of typology itself my definition is more strictly typological than her extensions into allegories and progresses; my focus is on identification with types exemplifying Christ instead of identification with Christ himself. This emphasis results from the great significance I see in the Reformed sense of a vast disparity between Christ and both types and their imitators, which she calls correlative types and I call neotypes. Moreover, my goals are more restricted in immediate subject matter and poetic form. I trace the course of a narrower poetic vein that, emanating from typology itself, seems to me to represent the quality most distinctive of, rather than her representative categorization of, the best-known seventeenth-century "personal sacred verse." Second, my aims range further in contemporary sacred lyrics and extend further back in time than do hers. I find that the new Reformed concern with and goals for typology reside within a religious movement that is not confined to Protestantism but which involves the deepest sacred concerns of many Anglican traditionalists and Counter-Reformers. Hence my choice of the modifier 'Reformed' as opposed to 'Protestant'. And I feel that much more of the heritage of these sacred lyricists is literary, carried by poetry as well as by the theological tracts and biblical commentaries Lewalski admirably documents.

My history of the neotypological lyric in the English Renaissance traces how a line of gifted, theologically astute sacred lyricists created a new kind of poem from the potential in a crucial concern of Reformed

Ira Clark

exegesis and how they successively transformed that form until they expended its potential for sacred expression. As is universally true of developmental histories, the continuity of this history of the neotypological lyric emanates from the same central features recurring throughout the lyrics written by this line of poets, whereas the distinctiveness of each poet comes not from major differences in the poetic features each employs but from the poets' characteristic emphases, their selection of certain ones out of common features, and their distinctive development of the potential. Before I can begin to trace these poets' individual contributions I must briefly distinguish how as a group they used typology quite differently from their contemporaries who continued to use it in traditional ways. Consequently, I begin with a characterizing illustration that draws parallels between a commonplace seventeenth-century Reformed theological tract and a representative seventeenth-century neotypological lyric. After a brief definition I sketch a background for my story, one I do not tell by surveying or cataloging each poem or each poet in the line. Instead, in order to discuss each poet, I first show what he understood about typology, next describe why and how he used typology generally, and finally, by focusing on a crucial theme or a significant central poem in his works, examine his contribution to the tradition.

Several institutions have given me time and aid for this history and a number of people have influenced its shape. First, thanks to the American Council of Learned Societies for a grant-in-aid to study sacred medieval Latin lyrics during the summer of 1972. Thanks to the University of Florida Humanities Council for a grant to prepare two chapters during the summer of 1974 and to the University of Florida English Department for assistance with microfilming, reproducing, and typing. And thanks to Arlene Perlette and the Florida Endowment for the Humanities for getting my first tentatively final manuscript into presentable form. Special thanks to Nicole Glover for making the reading smoother, to her and the University Presses of Florida for producing the book expeditiously, and to the Graduate School of the University of Florida for making possible the publication of this monograph.

Second, it is comforting how many have helped, perhaps embarrassing how often because of my obstinacy they have failed, to save me from myself. I owe debts to a number who made suggestions on individual parts: anonymous readers, Jackson I. Cope, Stanley E. Fish, David Locke, Arnold Stein, and Aubrey Williams. And I especially appreciate a few who have criticized the whole manuscript: anonymous readers, Richard Brantley, and most of all, John M. Perlette, whose readings, commentaries, and conversations helped me through more versions than I want to recall. In addition to those to whom this book is dedicated, I thank my daughters, Laurel and Elizabeth, for carrying on the tradition. Finally, there is an unexpressed thanks and dedication to Joanna in everything I do.

1

Christ Revealed: or The Old Testament Explained

Reformed Typology and the Neotypological Lyric

The title of Thomas Taylor's popular exegetical tract, *Christ Revealed: or The Old Testament Explained* (1635), suggests a representative definition of typology. He expands the definition in his subtitle, *A Treatise of the Types and Shadowes of our Saviovr contained throughout the whole Scriptvre*. He declares his central assumption, he would say affirmation, in the motto *None but Christ*. In opening, Taylor defines Christ as truth and grace opposed to outworn legal prefiguration, light and body instead of shadow. Mosaic law represents deadening, literal *ABC's* whereas Christian gospel is vital, spiritual learning. Typology, then, is that form of biblical interpretation which reads a faded Old Testament through the enhancing lens of the New, sees in Old Testament persons, events, and things imperfect predictions of New Testament persons, events, and things. Both covenants reveal and are revealed by Christ: the Law and the Prophets and the Writings show God's dispensations to mankind in Christ; but they differ in form and manner since they only predict the incarnate revelation of the Gospel.

Beyond employing the universal terms and suppositions of typology, Taylor's work maintains two distinctly Reformed concerns. First, he implies the disparity between type and antitype, thereby affirming both that types have independent identities and that types are dependent on Christ for ultimate value. Second, he emphasizes the personal lessons in types, asserting that types do correspond and should be applied in essential ways to the lives of believers. By implication Taylor takes for granted what his fellows stress: that the failures of types display their independent existence and their necessary reliance on the antitype, Christ. So, unlike most other Puritans, Taylor overtly writes mainly about likenesses be-

1

tween the types and the antitype rather than differences. By emphasis, like most other Reformation and Counter-Reformation commentators, Taylor uses types homiletically. After he has described a set of resemblances between an Old Testament type and its New Testament antitype, he applies these resemblances to himself and his readers. When, for example, he follows Paul's crucial comparison of old father Adam to Christ, the new father of mankind (Rom. 5), he assumes contrasts between the founder of death and the restorer of immortality. *Unlike* most Reformed typologists, he passes over the disparities to note four similarities: both Adam and Christ are sons of God; both are sovereigns over men and earth; both are married (one to Eve, the other to the Church); and both propagate mankind. Then, *like* most Reformed typologists, he applies to humanity all four lessons implied by these similarities: we should honor both, obey both, seek marriage to Christ and life, and be children of both. As we are children of the first physically, so we should strive by belief to be reborn children of the second spiritually.[1]

As a popularizer of Reformed typological exegesis who realized both the deficiencies and the personal applications of types, Taylor represents a heritage that helps us understand the neotypological lyricists of the English Renaissance. For these poets created out of Reformed assumptions about typology a sacred lyric quite distinct from typology's appearances in all earlier lyrics and even in many other lyrics of sixteenth- and seventeenth-century England. Agreeing with Reformed typological exegetes, these poets define types more rigorously than earlier poets, not variously or allegorically but integrally and literally; and they emphasize discrepancies between types and their fulfillment more than earlier poets, thus underscoring both the independent value of types and their ultimate need for the saving antitype. In addition, rather than using typological imagery for evocative reinforcement of Christian doctrine or for emotive echoes in worship, they humbly apply types to themselves to a degree of close identification, reverently present themselves as types, in the predicaments of types, in order to be saved by Christ. By strictly defining and embodying types these poets radically transformed the use of typological references in lyrics, thereby exploiting their tremendous expressive potential.

The representative minor neotypological poet and royalist churchman, Thomas Washbourne, significantly parallels Taylor. An avowed follower of George Herbert, Washbourne illustrates in his *Divine Poems* (1654) that the neotypological lyric grew out of the same concerns as those of Reformed exegetes. Like many a disciple, he provides a more useful example than his subtle and individualistic poetic mentor, since his overexplicit statements display more obvious and commonplace instructions for reading.

Washbourne's epigraph to a poem called "The Rock" is Numbers 20:11, which describes Moses in the wilderness striking the rock of Horeb and letting forth the waters of Meribah to save the chosen people. But his text is 1 Corinthians 10:4, which is Paul's identification of that rock as a type of Christ. His opening clauses thus apply not only to the type in the desert but also to the sacrificial blood and water (John 19:34) pouring out of Christ's side to save the elect:

> What wonder's this, that from Christ's side,
> Water and blood should run to cleanse our sin?
> This is that fountain which was opened wide
> To purge all our uncleannesse in;
> But this the greater wonder is by farre,
> As substances beyond the shadows are.[2]

Two essential elements clearly dominate this poem: a typological image complex governs it and the echoes of New Testament rereadings are intimately associated with its persona. A second reading reveals a more subtle but equally important element, the emotion expressed forms a psalm-like union of remorse over human failure under legalism with joy over recovery through grace; that is, dual psychic motives of both contrition for sin and rejoicing over redemption reinforce typology. These three essentials Southwell and Alabaster had drawn together toward the end of Elizabeth's reign, thereby forming the rudimentary neotypological lyric.

But the impetus for this new lyric was essentially Reformed despite the Catholicism of its first formulators. This context Washbourne insists on in his second stanza by affirming the two Reformation sacraments in their signs, water and blood: "Rather then we should faint our Rock turns Vine, / And stayes our thirst with water and with wine." The final two stanzas show sophistications which the seventeenth century added to the neotypological lyric. A persona who identifies to the degree of virtual convergence with a type explicates his own position as an exemplum, following the emblematists, and presents his personal drama, following Donne. In concluding Washbourne acknowledges his debt to the prototypical neotypological lyricist, George Herbert, when he borrows from poems clustered around "The Altar":

3

But here's another rock, my heart
Harder then adamant; yet by and by,
If by a greater *Moses* struck, 'twil part,
And stream forth tears abundantly.
Strike then this rock my God, double the blow,
That for my sins, my eyes with tears may flow!

My sins that pierc'd Thy hands, Thy feet,
Thy head, Thy heart, and every part of Thee,
And on the cross made life and death to meet:
Death to Thyself, and life to mee,
Thy very fall does save; O happy strife,
That struck God dead, but raisèd man to life.

The poem is self-explicating. The poet has converted himself into the image of one type, the rock of Horeb, in order to be chastened by the original sin of yet another, Adam, whose initiation of the fall all humankind have compounded to torture Christ. But both types have already been saved by the greater Moses. The poet has transformed himself into his typological past in order that Christ, the fountain, can mercifully accept forever his tearful contrition over failing to obey law. Washbourne's poem reflects all the centrally identifying characteristics of the English neotypological lyric, which evolved from the same emphases as distinguished Reformed tracts on biblical typology, such as Taylor's exegesis.

Identifying a new kind of poem required christening it. *Neotypological* I coined to suggest the new way a gifted line of poets presented themselves in answering a newly revived problem in sacred psychology. One Reformed dilemma was how to celebrate salvation without being damned for presumption in the midst of sin. Granting that these poets were contrite for their sins and that they fervently believed Christ assumes them, how could they portray themselves as saved by faith? Alternatively, how could they know they had done their best and that Christ had repaired their failures? They answered by presenting themselves as *neotypes*, that is, contemporary people in the predicaments of types, fully realizing in humility that Christ, the exalted antitype, redeems them. *Lyric* I extended to include a spectrum wider than the short personal song of a single singer; he might tell an embedded story, argue with, or perhaps be answered by another speaker.

The characterizing features of the neotypological lyric are first, the poets' strict definition of types, and second, their personal application of typology. First, the neotypological lyricists recognized and affirmed a

4

dual inclination in the signification of a type that has been strictly defined. Reformed theologians emphasized that an Old Testament type was real and valuable in its own right; at the same time they celebrated an Old Testament type as being invaluable for foreshadowing salvation by Christ's grace. The type exists in itself as a failure inside time. Simultaneously the type is a metaphor signifying the antitype Christ, who in transcendent eternity perfects and provides meaning to all existence. Strictly defined, then, a type is a link in a Christian rereading of history, the story of how an eternal God enters into time. The Old Testament inteprets the story of the tribes of Israel as the history of God's covenants with his chosen people. Then the New Testament reinterprets the Law, Prophets, and Writings, as faithful humanity's course inside Christian salvation: a typological person, thing, or event governed by Old Covenant law foreshadows Christ.

Second, the neotypological lyricists used this strict definition in recasting their current scenes in terms of one or more types. They recreated themselves and their circumstances in personae imitating Old Testament types—to the degree that they virtually reincarnated them. By doing so they added themselves as personae who fuse a second metaphoric link, extending the Christian reading of history through types. In these lyrics, generally the persona is a neotype. Thus he is real and valuable, although a failure, in his own time. Simultaneously he is a metaphor that signifies a type that in turn signifies the saving antitype. The interlock between the two metaphors precisely enables the neotypical persona to be indirectly, and thus humbly, yet still indissolubly linked to Christ. Such an interlocked doubled metaphor establishes the perspective of the neotypological lyric. A Reformed persona fails to recognize his salvation because he sees himself in a constricted Old Testament context. Meanwhile the poem is establishing the persona's reformation by alluding to the New Testament antitype. The persona is thereby contrite and exalted at the same time. Thus, these lyricists could devoutly sing of God entering actual people, things, and events in their own time, and of his entering into neotypes, out of their faith that he has entered time through Old Testament types and through the saving and perfecting New Testament antitype, Christ.

† † †

All typological exegetes begin by explicating those New Testament references and parallels to the Old Testament which are designed to show that Jesus of Nazareth fulfilled messianic prophecies. Paul's identification,

"And that Rock was Christ" (1 Cor. 10:4 referring to Exod. 17:1–7, Num. 20:2–14), is a central text. His typological explanation of the first and second Adam sets a precedent: "Nevertheless death reigned from Adam to Moses, even over them that had not sinned after the similitude of Adam's transgression, who is the figure [type] of him that was to come" (Rom. 5:14).

This last passage is foremost among fifteen New Testament and two Old Testament uses of the Greek *tupos* commonly cited in twentieth-century discussions of typology.[3] The word initially meant either a "blow" or a "mark left by a blow," such as the marks left on Christ's hands by the nails (John 20:25). Moreover, *type* could also mean not only the "impression" or "image," such as that on a wax seal, and "cast" or "replica," such as that of a sculpted figure, it could also mean the "die" making the mark, and even "archetype" or "pattern." In the Old Testament, Amos refers to the image (5:26) and Exodus to the model (25:40). The first of the classic passages from Romans refers to a prefigure (5:14), the second to a moral exemplum (6:17). *Type* thus remains potently ambiguous: an Old Testament type has full, substantive, inherent, and predictive values but simultaneously it is only a substantial copy of spiritual reality. The connotations of substance as both independently strong and dependently weak are echoed by *shadow*, the Renaissance English synonym for *type*; for a shadow can be either the shade that conforms to a pattern cast by something else intercepting light or the prefiguration that casts the pattern to which something else will conform.

These suggestive ambiguities deepened New Testament presentation of Jesus of Nazareth as Christ, the Messiah predicted through the Old Testament. That message which New Testament authors strived to demonstrate appears straightforwardly in Matthew's early accounts: "Now all this was done, that it might be fulfilled which was spoken of the Lord by the prophet, saying, Behold, a virgin shall be with child, and shall bring forth a son, and they shall call his name Emmanuel which being interpreted is, God with us" (Matt. 1:22–23 from Isa. 7:14); "When [Joseph] arose, he took the young child and his mother by night, and departed into Egypt: And was there until the death of Herod: that it might be fulfilled which was spoken of the Lord by the prophet, saying, Out of Egypt have I called my son" (Matt. 2:14–15 from Hos. 11:1, conflated with Exod. 4:22). In Matthew's biography Christ's life recapitulates under a new contract, that of grace, the history of the chosen people's old legal covenants with God. Thus Jesus fasts forty days in the wilderness before he ascends a mountain to deliver the beatitudes, which supersede the commandments God established when Moses stayed forty days on

Mount Sinai. Such correspondences expand from announcements that Christ fulfilled prophecy to typology, renditions showing how Christ's actions perfect prefigurations.

Types that are explicitly designated in the New Testament are traditionally grouped by people, events, and things.[4] Prominent people are Adam as father (Rom. 5:10–17 and 1 Cor. 15:45–47), Noah as covenanter (Heb. 11:7), Melchizedek as priest (Heb. 6:20–7:13), Sarah and Isaac and Hagar and Ishmael with Abraham (Gal. 4:21–31), Moses (Matt. 5–7, Gal. 3:19–29), David (Matt. 2:1, Luke 1), Jonah for three-day burial in the whale (Matt. 12:39–40 is Jesus' sole specifically typological statement). Among important events are the flood and crossing the Red Sea, both as baptism (1 Pet. 3:20–21, 1 Cor. 10:2), release from Egypt and the exodus (Matt. 2:15), and various correspondences throughout Matthew. Significant things are primarily those prominent in Exodus, including the paschal lamb (1 Cor. 5:7), the guiding pillar of cloud and fire (1 Cor. 10:2), the rock of Horeb (1 Cor. 10:4), the manna (1 Cor. 10:3, John 6:48–58), and the brazen serpent (John 3:14).

When New Testament authors were composing the Gospel as Christ's fulfillment of the Law, Prophets, and Writings, they were not creating allegory or prophecy but reinterpreting history. An important corollary follows, one which sets typology off as a mode of symbol: both type and antitype have independent historical existence. Adding to the power in their close interaction, each has a separate identity and consequence; neither relies on the other for its primary meaning.

As they were creating an evolutionary understanding of the past, New Testament authors were developing their own mode of writing from two earlier kinds of interpretation. Judaism had already used both allegory and fulfillment of prophecy in interpretation.[5] To differentiate typological interpretation from allegory and prophecy helps to characterize it.[6] Like allegory, typology displays meaningful similarities or correspondences between a former term and a latter one; in typology these terms appear in one passage from the Old and another from the New Testament. The essential distinction is that allegory neither requires nor needs to respect a separate identity for each term. Since the messages being carried are the major concern for allegorical interpretation, it is not necessarily involved with either authorial intentions or historical referents but instead with close enough correspondence between the two terms to sustain didacticism. In short, for allegory one corresponding term, usually the more important, may be an abstraction, whereas for typology each must have independent historical actuality.

Like prophecy, typology exploits the potential of essential differences between the two corresponding terms. In typology one term occurs in an Old and the other in a New Testament passage; the Old Testament term by its inadequacy or failure predicts fulfillment in the New. The central distinction between prophecy and typology, like that between allegory and typology, rests on the historical existence and importance of both the old and the new term. In typology the predicting term as well as the fulfilling one, the type as well as the antitype, must be actual and valuable in itself. Thus, typology could be seen as a fusion of Judaic prophecy and allegory that is based in actual historical referents.

Finally, when New Testament authors were writing they were creating a revisionist interpretation of history that insists on two interpenetrating planes of reality. The first plane is that of factual history, of time and the importance of things in time. But typology ultimately calls for the greater importance of an eternal plane as it is embodied in time. Thus, New Testament typology affirms the reality of God in history, of the transcendent in the individual, both in the similarities and the differences between prefigurations of Christ under old contracts and their incarnate revelation, Christ in the new gospel.[7]

Despite the fact that all typological exegetes begin with the same subject matter, evidence, and general approach, because of their assumptions and methods they can and do diverge in their final readings. Thus, critics who have seen Reformation typologists as merely appropriating or especially as extending medieval figural traditions obscure an important distinction. A literary historian like Maurice Evans, who concludes that sixteenth-century Reformers accommodating or applying Scripture to their own time virtually repeat the allegorizations of the past, disregards their emphasis on the literal, which for them included the typological but not any unconfirmed allegorical, biblical meaning. Or a statement like that by William G. Madsen, "By the middle of the seventeenth century the distinction between the Catholic theory of manifold senses and the Protestant theory of the one literal sense had, for all practical purposes, become meaningless," evades the intent of their definition and affirmation of the term *literal*.[8] The claim could seem justifiable in that medieval and Renaissance lists of Christ-types are similar and inasmuch as Protestant and Catholic commentaries often do overlap by virtue of their subject and evidence. But lists restricted to types of Christ constitute evidence that is already limited to a Protestant definition, and the two sorts of commentaries are based on different suppositions. Moreover, the convergence frequently is the result of Catholic scholars correcting and straitening their medieval forebears. The rigorous new rules applied by exegetes and popularizers among all three parties of Protestants, Anglicans, and Catholics stripped off layers of allegory. Their program of strictly promulgating the Gospel (with only a few hedged elaborations) implies a critical agreement with each other based on a critical difference from their predecessors. That important difference over how to interpret the Bible typologically is founded on a general departure from the tenets of medieval figuralists.

In their search for multileveled meanings, patristic and medieval interpreters who had started out as typologists more and more became allegorists.[9] They were tantalized by Christ's specifying only Jonah, and merely suggesting the brazen serpent and manna, as types of himself. And following Origen they perpetually cited Paul's exhortation that God "hath made us able ministers of the new testament; not of the letter, but of the spirit: for the letter killeth, but the spirit giveth life" (2 Cor. 3:6). As this apparently justifying text suggests, the history of their interpretations records with few exceptions a generally increasing predominance of allegorical readings in their catenae, those chains of interlinking glosses that extend typological readings of Scripture to doctrines, to ethics and morality, to speculation on final events, and to the blessed virgin Mary. Despite attempts to curtail the proliferation of expanding and diverging allegorizations made by Augustine earlier, by some of the Victorines in the twelfth century, by Aquinas in the thirteenth, Nicholas of Lyra in the fourteenth, and Gerson in the fifteenth, the majority expanded typology beyond recognition in the fourfold method wherein the letter teaches deeds, the allegory inculcates beliefs, the moral enforces ethics, and the anagogy indicates ends: "Littera gesta docet, quid credas allegoriae, / Moralis quid agas, quo tendas anagogia." The allegorizing spirit fostered by this common Latin tag dominated medieval interpretation of the Bible. Typology proper became a forerunner of and yielded to a maze of diffuse interpretations. In addition, the liturgy, the cathedral scenes in glass, wood, and paint, the prints in the *Biblia Pauperum, Speculum humanae salvationis, Bible Moralisé,* and books of hours, all of which made typology commonly recognized, often blurred its distinctiveness until it was submerged in widely varying allegories.

Two central tenets of the Reformers—"scriptura sola" and "literal interpretation"—precisely countered the medieval continuum of allegorizing. Accretions of allegory encrusted in commentaries, liturgies, hymns, church artifacts, and other popularizations originated from men, not God; therefore they pertained to men, not God; and Reformers had to purge fourfold allegorizations from their interpretations of the Bible.

Such a purge of allegory proportionately increased the value placed on typology, since types are specifically sanctioned as centrally embedded in the "literal meaning" of Scriptures by being announced, described, and used in the New Testament. Reformers stressing the sole authority of Scripture and Protestants interpreting it literally thus encouraged typological readings of the Old Testament. But they were not encouraging another guise for allegorizations that had accumulated in the figuralist readings of medieval exegetes. Rather, they were encouraging literal readings of legal Old Testament foreshadowings of merciful New Testament fulfillment.

Luther's transformation from a medieval biblical lecturer to a Reformed Bible explicator is instructive. His change in explicating the Psalms, from a mainly christological David to a historical one who also prophesied,[10] illustrates the new importance of strict typology. And, when in his prefaces to Scriptures he emphasized that the central principle of canonicity depends on the preaching of Christ, or that the Psalms constitute an epitome of the Bible by promising Christ, or especially in his preface to the New Testament that Christ is the true seed of Abraham and of David, he did so in a new way. He refocused attention so that the historical importance of David and Abraham and others precedes their importance as prefigurations.

Calvin's more codified position is most significant. In an important section of the *Institutes of Christian Religion* (II. 7–11) he defines the literal meaning of the Bible so that it includes typology. In addition he effectively restricts these readings to surface historical and literal interpretations of the Old Testament that include only those types confirmed by the New Testament.[11] Moreover, he is the one who sounds the charge against Origen and his allegorizing followers, a charge that reechoes through Reformed polemics. Annotating 2 Corinthians 3:6–10, he declares that no interpretation of these lines could be further from the truth than that of allegorizers, who elaborated pernicious errors in the name of the spirit rather than seeking the letter as they should have, for they thereby batted Scripture like a ball in wild shot interpretations which are sources of evil.

In England the famous early blast against old biblical allegorizers came from the Reforming Bible translator, William Tyndale. In the climactic chapter of *The Obedience of a Christian Man* (1528) Tyndale mounted a powerful attack on "The Four Senses of the Scripture" promulgated by the Catholic Church. His opening is familiar:

10

They divide the scripture into four senses, the literal, tropological, allegorical and anagogical. The literal sense is become nothing at all: for the pope hath taken it clean away, and hath made it his possession. He hath partly locked it up with the false and counterfeited keys of his traditions, ceremonies, and feigned lies; and partly driveth men from it with violence of sword: for no man dare abide by the literal sense of the text, but under a protestation, "If it shall please the pope."[12]

He goes on to describe the allegorizers' failings through their "chopological" treatments and denials of literal sense. Then he affirms literal readings. When he gives examples of figurative meanings that are literal, he favors types, because they are sanctioned and because they show particularly well how (to use his metaphor) the Bible springs from God and flows to Christ.

J. W. Blench, in his study of *Preaching in England in the Late Fifteenth and Sixteenth Centuries*, has discovered that Tyndale's indictment of conservative allegorizing preachers, the adherents of the "old learning," was justified and that it constituted one major corrective of their interpretive wanderings.[13] Another significant corrective appeared in this era when, because of the Reformers, preaching came to dominate the religious service: "some of the liveliest polemic of the Reformers is directed against Catholic allegoric glosses."[14] Furthermore, even after the first era of Reformed preachers and the temporary restoration of Catholic priests had passed, many Elizabethan preachers who advocated literal exegesis expressly used typology.[15] Such uses, of course, follow from direct scriptural sanction of types. So handbooks designed to promulgate good Puritan preaching first stress literal interpretation and then show in their discussions and examples how types abide within literal readings.

In *The Art of Prophecying* (signed 12 December 1592), an extraordinarily popular text on preaching, the Puritan William Perkins concentrates basically on the Word of God and its interpretation, which is necessary because preaching explicates and applies Scripture for the congregation. One of Perkins' initial principles exhorts preachers to always heed the literal and historical meaning of the Bible so as to emphasize that both testaments testify to Christ. He proceeds to say that the old fourfold interpretation of the Church of Rome "must be exploded and rejected," for "*There is one onely sense, and the same is the literall.*"[16] A corollary follows: even as the interpreter must diligently examine each passage by its immediate context, the context of all the Bible, and the whole analogy of

11

faith, "The supreame and absolute meane of interpretation is the Scripture it selfe." Thus, the task of collating texts that cite, repeat, or parallel each other in phrase, image, structure, and so on, takes on considerable, almost soul-saving, importance. In this view types retain potent value, as the immediately following parallel columns that correlate Old and New Testament passages illustrate. Even then, Perkins pointedly warns preachers to examine carefully the logical and linguistic contexts in which any reading is based.[17] Perkins' position is reconfirmed by another popular handbook, Richard Bernard's *The faithfull shepheard* (1607), which sets out precepts and examples designed to guide Reformed divines. On interpreting Scripture, Bernard follows Perkins' admonitions about the essential importance of and bases for literal interpretations, virtually repeating Perkins' set of parallel columns of Old and New Testament correspondences, which are essentially typological.[18]

Movement toward a stricter, literal, and therefore typological in place of figural and allegorical interpretation of Scripture was by no means confined to Protestants and Puritans. It played a major role in the Anglican Reformation. Blench has documented that even the advocates of the "old learning" were much more careful in their pulpits than earlier. In particular he cites the caution that William Peryn took in sermons at the close of Henry VIII's reign, using types and occasional prophecies but no allegories in support of his positions. By Edward VII's reign, allegorizing had disappeared from sermons.[19] Finally, while during Mary's reign some clerics reverted to old allegorizations along with church authority in matters of interpretation, for the most part these also attempted to be stricter and to rely more heavily on types proper. This tendency was carried on even by those few figures in the Elizabethan pulpits who allegorized in their personal applications.[20] According to Horton Davies this aspect of the Reformation was so successful that Anglican preachers relied most on types sanctioned by direct New Testament references.[21]

Although the chief English Protestant document in support of literal interpretation, that by Tyndale, appeared very early, that of the Anglican Reformation appeared relatively late in the movement. This was William Whitaker's *Disputatio De Sacra Scriptura; contra huius temporis papistas, inprimis, Robertum Bellarminum Iesuitam* (1588).[22] The master of St. John's, Cambridge, was also a master of theological and exegetical debate against his learned Jesuit opponent, Bellarmine. After a long and detailed argument over four controversial questions (the canon, text, authority, and clarity of Scripture), Whitaker opens the fifth, "Of the Interpretation of Scripture." Having spoken of the necessity for investigating Scripture faithfully and diligently so as to comprehend it fully, in chapter two he addresses preliminary principles for understanding some differences between Catholics and Reformers. Here he establishes major contentions between Reformers, who interpreted Scripture literally, as a single entity, and the Council of Trent, who reserved supreme authority in the Roman church in matters of exegesis and who thus relied on traditions, including some allegories. Whitaker's preliminary principles repeat three important Reformed attitudes.

The first is that there is only one sense of Scripture—the literal. After briefly tracing his view of Augustine's and Aquinas' description of one sense of Scripture, Whitaker surveys only to reject the so-called mystic senses—tropological, allegorical, and anagogical—from Origen through his Jesuit opponents. All, he charges, are guilty of severing a literal, historical outward sense from a spiritual, mystical, inward one. While he concedes that figurative interpretations can be appropriate, he claims that they can be so only when they are within the literal sense, denying "that there are many and various senses": "We affirm that there is but one true, proper and genuine sense of scripture, arising from the words rightly understood, which we call the literal: and we contend that allegories, tropologies, and anagoges are not various senses, but various collections from one sense, or various applications and accommodations of that one meaning." [23] He continues by guarding against constructions of this definition that would permit uncontrolled interpretation or allow random inclusions in the literal sense. His examples adhere to a strict standard; they are usually types. For instance, when he mentions Paul's allegorical interpretation of Abraham's wives, Sarah and Hagar (Gal. 4:24), he declares at once that they are not allegorical but typological, specifically designated within the literal sense. Not only that, he warns that even when Scripture labels something allegorical, men need to be wary of adding their own inventions. [24]

As he exemplifies this point Whitaker also discusses that potency inherent in the interaction between referents that defines a type. Citing Canaan as referring to both the country and also the kingdom of heaven, he describes the potent interpretive interaction he sees in a type: "When we proceed from the sign to the thing signified, we bring no new sense, but only bring out into light what was before concealed in the sign. When we speak of the sign by itself, we express only part of the meaning; and so also when we mention only the thing signified: but when the mutual relation between the sign and the thing signified is brought out, then the whole complete sense, which is founded upon this similitude and agreement, is set forth." [25] The relationship in types contains a dynamic, all-important revelation, which awaits discovery. Whitaker proceeds to demonstrate this power by explaining the full literal import of his examples. Here again, what is significant is that Whitaker avows the inherent historical value of the immediate referent as well as its prophetical one, a point Reformers insisted upon. And the significance which follows is that types gain tremendously in the attention paid to them, value seen in them, and power of them.

Whitaker's second principle is that only from the literal sense can one derive true arguments about biblical interpretation. When a mystical sense is part of the literal one, it exists only "when the Holy Spirit himself so teaches us." Going on to cite Hosea 11:1 ("Out of Egypt have I called my son") and Exodus 12:46 ("Thou shalt not break a bone of him") he declares two components necessary for a candidate to be declared a type: reference first to itself as an actual historical thing, and then to it as a foreshadowing of Christ. "It is sufficiently plain that the former is to be understood of the people of Israel, and the latter of the paschal lamb. Who, now, would dare to transfer and accommodate these to Christ, if the Holy Spirit had not done it first, and declared to us his mind and intention?—namely, that the *Son* in the former passage denotes not only the people of Israel, but Christ also; and the *bone*, in the latter, is to be understood of Christ as well as of the paschal lamb." [26] Whitaker is defining the full relationships that reside within the literal sense. He is also defining the power and import of typology. Plus, within these emphases he is espousing the major restriction on the standard for all faiths. He is requiring a test that is to be reiterated: the only way to know what are truly literal interpretations and legitimate types, and what are not, depends on whether or not the Bible specifically sanctions them. Whitaker's own examples are sanctioned by Matthew 2:15 and John 19:36. Whitaker goes beyond affirming this general principle when he asserts that Catholics concede it.

Whitaker also claims that the Catholics concede his third principle, "that we must not bring any private meanings, or private opinions, but only such as agree with the mind, intention, and dictate of the Holy Spirit. For, since he is the author of the scriptures, it is fit that we should follow him in interpreting scripture." [27] Given his wording, of course, Whitaker cannot be countered. What makes the Reformed position different, regardless of affiliation, is the degree of strictness in rules designed to insure that humans are aligning their literal interpretations with God's intent. Later on, in typically Reformed fashion, he lists and discusses ways by which someone should carefully seek out this literal sense: by prayer, study of the original languages, principles of rhetoric, examination of the immediate context, comparison and collation with other similar passages, contrast with opposed passages, consideration by the analogy of faith, and assiduous study of learned arguments and commentaries.[28] The all-important aims and stringent demands of such requirements become standard. Whitaker's importance rests in systematically, while still polemically, presenting points that usually appeared only as the need arose in arguments or annotations.

Two noteworthy universals appear in Whitaker's last two Reformed principles. He claims that Catholics as well as Reformers adhere to both to some extent. And his rules for seeking out literal meaning apply humanist textual principles which many Catholics as well as Reformers followed in biblical studies. In fact other preachers and commentators were affected by Reformers who affirmed typological exegesis as part of strict literal interpretation limited to specific New Testament citations. Although there continued to be famous allegorizers such as John Fisher, Blench and Davies discuss other preachers, such as Stafford and Taverner, who in the reign of Henry VIII were so imbrued with Colet's and Erasmus' "new learning" that they emphasized the literal sense of Scripture at the same time that they held steadfastly to Roman doctrines.[29] Not only were humanists from Valla through Erasmus to Grotius establishing more rigorous methods and more accurate texts, Catholics in spite of the Council of Trent's reaffirmation of an uninterrupted tradition preserved in the Roman church were deleting traditional allegorizations. In his account of Renaissance exegeses of Genesis, Arnold L. Williams concludes, "The best commentators of the Renaissance opposed the allegorizations so prevalent in the Middle Ages and among the fathers. Calvin, Luther, Pareus, and Rivetus of the Protestants and Pererius of the Catholics advanced the cause of literal interpretation, though Pererius sometimes succumbed to allegory."[30] The learned Pererius in fact provided a base for many who pared to literal glosses (which included types referred to in Scripture) by insisting upon historical veracity as well as prophecy. Thus, reforming humanists and Catholics, Reformed Anglicans, and particularly Puritans and Protestants established Bible interpretations that universally included types and discarded allegories. Out of this context rose seventeenth-century popularizers who offered scriptural interpretations to believers of all faiths.

During the seventeenth century these popularizers continued to declare that typology unlocks God's treasury or reveals his wonders in both testaments. Their familiar comparisons of the Old to the New Testament promote typology and its potent promise: dark shadows to bright substances, veiled hints to open sight, mystical promises to merciful performances, obscurity to glory, moon and stars to midday sun, shadow to body, shell to kernel or meat, letter to spirit, bone to marrow, law to love, stone to flesh, killing to life-giving, milk for babes to meat for men, honeycomb to tapers and honey, flagon to wine, garden to spices, well, and elixir.[31] Moreover, later Reformation and Counter-Reformation advocates, beyond offering suggestive comparisons and contrasts such as these, corroborated theories of typology their predecessors had defined and described through debate. Since few of the earlier combative polemicists, or practical advisers, or compiling commentators had tended to systematize their results, elaborate presentations of the details worked out through a century and a half of diatribe, sermon, handbook, and commentary came only in the middle and later seventeenth century. As excitement over literal interpretation and typological exegesis waned and that over the new criticism of Spinoza and Father Simon began, a group of Puritan, Anglican, and Separatist commentators corroborated and codified definitions and categories that heretofore they had assumed or fought over.

The Puritan Samuel Mather delivered a series of sermons in the late 1660s that form perhaps the most complete account of *The Figures or Types of the Old Testament*.[32] In the second sermon he declares two traditional purposes behind God disclosing his gospel in the Old Testament: "In regard of our Weakness" and "For his own greater Glory."[33] Human weakness in understanding requires many explanations of one truth, in absorption rate requires increasing dosage, in insight demands gradual revelation, and in drawing abstractions demands particular examples. God's glory becomes greater by a series of manifestations, by harmony between his revelation and his other works, by our inestimable gains in worth, glory, and mystery under the gospel, by the infinite plenitude of his wisdom, by his absolute liberty, and by his unique goodness. In summing up the exhaustive sermon series Mather reminds his readers of three essential points about types. But the three are one: the dispensation in types is wholly abrogated and fulfilled in the glorious revelation of the gospel of Christ.[34]

After asserting that types accommodate human weakness and enhance God's glory, Samuel Lee supplies some distinctions that a Reformed definition required: "A Type is an Arbitrary sign, representing future and spiritual matters by divine institution."[35] This idea that a sign is arbitrary leads to the conclusion that the resemblances between two historical, significant originals are artificial. But the crucial distinction between a type and other similar signs is determined by answering the question about divine institution: Is a particular Old Testament sign designated by God's decree or derived by man's ingenuity? Does it represent God's will or man's whim? Lee posits that a type can be deduced solely from Scripture; a New Testament antitype must specify its type. Finally, of course, a type must correspond both in form and in significance so that it foreshadows under legal dispensation the excellence of the Gospel.

Given Lee's by now familiar Reformed criteria for testing whether something is a type, how can a faithful expositor ascertain what God has truly implied from what man has falsely inferred? One duty for Reformation and Counter-Reformation commentators was establishing, then applying stringently a set of tests to determine whether or not God has designated some Old Testament sign as a type. This paramount duty worried Mather's editor into warning "the Reader" that many people believe Mather himself is not strict enough. The rules in most Reformed commentaries demonstrate a compelling need to affirm types, which God decreed, and deny allegories based on Bible passages, which man devised. Such a concern rests behind the Reformed and restrictive typology of the English Renaissance, as it was opposed to medieval expansions.

The strictest standard for determining whether God actually intends a type is represented by Robert Ferguson's essay on scriptural metaphor, which is part of *The Interest of Reason in Religion*.[36] Ferguson designates as types only those both readily significant and, more important, based on scriptural reference; moreover, he repeatedly warns against allegorizing. Lee, dissociating himself from Catholic practitioners, offers a more moderate, less strict, position than Ferguson. In allowing minimal speculation he hedges on whether or not he regards a candidate as typological or merely worthwhile as he describes a spectrum of possibilities. Types announced in Scripture, those forthrightly alluded to by New Testament authors, are safe. Cases almost as admissible are duplicate names. Narrative points in the Old Testament that might lead to mystical ones in the New Testament raise doubts, since the connections rest only on probability. Only questionable credence can be allowed to analogies and proportions between the two testaments, even if these seem probable; probable ones, however, might be used moderately. Lee bends the standard somewhat when he accepts as types those things which are not good in themselves but which nonetheless are approved of in the Old Testament (this is probably for Canticles).[37] Mather's rules for accepting types are less strict, though they remain Reformed. Having affirmed the encompassing importance of the question and acknowledged problems over determining if God has signified a would-be type, he unhesitatingly accepts in evidence only direct scriptural references and name permutations. But because of the infallible status and potency of true types as signs and seals, he cautiously designates parallels between several scriptural passages as proof—when they exhibit "an evident and manifest analogy and parallel between things under the Law, and things under the Gospel."[38]

A representative attitude about testing before accepting types appears in *The Mysterie of Rhetorique Unvail'd* by the pseudonymous John Smith, long believed a Catholic but probably a Protestant.[39] Early on he cautions readers not to take literal statements figuratively, and vice versa. Following the figurative passage in Galatians he discusses types under the heading "allegory." But he segregates unquestionable natural allegory that the Scripture expresses directly from "inferred" allegory that "the Scripture it self shewes not, nor makes manifest, but is brought in by interpreters." Under "inferred" come "offered" readings based on literal sense; since these are similar to analogies in faith, they are probable at best. But also under "inferred" come allegorical readings that lack foundation in literal sense; these are "inforced and wrested," and therefore totally unacceptable.

One other very important characteristic distinguishes the Reformers' attitude toward typology from that of their predecessors. Some of the earliest examiners of typology had looked mainly for similarities, correspondences, and analogies between an Old Testament type and its Gospel fulfillment. But Mather spoke for most of the later ones when he stressed that while types foreshadow similarities they also manifest disparities, primarily their own inadequacies and failures: "As there is a Similitude, a Resemblance and Analogy between the Type and the Antitype in some things: so there is ever a dissimilitude and a disparity between them in other things" in that when the antitype fulfills the type it transcends its foreshadow.[40] Throughout his elaborate scheme Mather emphasizes the discrepancy between a type and its antitype. Whether a type comes before the law (before Moses) and is individual or appears under the law and is national, it falls far short of perfection. Personal types, such as Adam before the law and David under the law, are not merely weak and imperfect, they also fail.[41] Mather provides the same kind of evidence for occasional types (extraordinary occurrences and objects like the delivery from Egypt and the brazen serpent) and for perpetual types (customary ceremonies, holy places, festivals and feasts, and priesthood).[42]

Such an emphasis on the discrepancies as well as similarities between the interacting referents in types both increases the awesome power in their interaction and also makes it easier for an adherent to identify with the Old Testament referent. The basically familiar, chronological, parallel tables of types with their antitypes in William Guild's *Moses Vnuailed* are doubly revealing. In their distinctive presentation they emphasize both central principles. The double-columned, point-by-point matchups emphasize that the first column notes "The Congruities" and the second "The Disparitie" between a type's shortcomings and the antitype's glory. This presentation acknowledges the reality at the same time that it diminishes the glory of the Old Testament; it exalts instead the New; and in the union of both it points to the expressive potential in types. Less orderly discussions and works not specifically typological also emphasize disparities as well as similarities. For example John Weemes's *Explication of the iudiciall lawes of Moses*, which describes Old Testament models for contemporary conduct, compares Solomon's wise rules of governance to Christ's, only to exhort, "here is a greater than *Salomon*."[43]

The Reformed exegetes' strict rules for accepting types and their emphasis on discrepancies between types and fulfillment established a new understanding of and potential for typology.[44] It followed from their insistence that typology resides within the literal history recorded in the Bible. It meant that types are valuable though condemned in themselves and that only when they are corroborated and fulfilled in the New Testament do they accrue wonder.

In addition, these Reformed exegetes' new understanding of typology and its expressive potential reinforced the development of the neotypological lyric in one further way. They fostered a new, more intense identification with Old Testament figures by considering types in relationship to—they would say by applying types to—their own lives. Such an argument is implied throughout the previous examples. The very fact that Mather based a series of homiletic sermons on explicating typology is noteworthy. The opening example of Reformed typology, Luther's change in opinion about Psalms, concentrated on the book of songs that forms a psychological model that is universal for Christians. The closing example from Weemes exhibits Old Testament models for contemporary life. The works of all three of these men indicate that Reformed Christians were not just looking at Old Testament figures historically; they were also scrutinizing them in order to learn how to live.

Calvin, like Luther, is characteristic in his choice of a type to apply to himself. Both follow Augustine's interest in Psalms because all three recognize that David's songs form prototypes of Christian experience. The introduction to his commentary on Psalms, "John Calvin to the godly Readers sendeth greeting," is famous in part because it is uncharacteristically personal and autobiographical. In it he establishes how important the applications of David's psychological states are for himself, just as they are for all Christians:

> Not without cause am I wont to terme this book the Anatomy of all the partes of the Soule, inasmuch as a man shalnot find any affection in himselfe, whereof the Image appæreth not in this glasse.[45]

He continues with an avowal that all griefs, sorrows, fears, doubts, hopes, cares, anguish, and turmoil of humanity find their perfect expression in Psalms, and even more importantly a further lesson is established. In Psalms the prophets "bycause they discouer all the inner thoughtes, do call or drawe every one of us to the peculiar examination of himself." Next he sets the example by applying both principles to himself: he identifies with the feelings of the type, David, and he uses the situations of the type, David, as tools for examining himself. Calvin intensively and extensively compares events in his own life to David's story as reflected in Psalms. He generally applies them to his own detriment, but he always applies them with an eye toward ultimate salvation for the type and his own humble hopes. Nor is Calvin's or the other Reformers' insistence on applying types limited to Psalms, though they most often favor and concentrate on them. In his introduction to chapter four of *A Commentarie upon the Epistle of Saint Paul to the Romanes*, Calvin emphasizes that Abraham, a notable type, is a "mirror pattern," a model of faith for the church of believers. For, while comparison to him is humbling, it does allow for a sense of righteousness being granted to the faithful.[46]

Perkins and Bernard suffice to illustrate the importance in Puritan sermons of applying literal biblical interpretations to listeners, both for their beliefs and doctrines and for their lives and behavior.[47] Citing as guides Augustine, Reformers such as Beza, and even Catholics such as Erasmus, Perkins sums up preaching in an offset conclusion. He underscores a preacher's four duties: to read the scriptural text distinctly, to interpret it by itself, to collect a few profitable points of doctrine out of its natural sense, and most significantly "To apply (if he haue the gift) the doctrines rightly collected to the life and maners of men, in a simple and plaine speech."[48] Bernard, in the fourth through the seventh chapters of Book Four of his pastoral guide, makes similar claims for the preacher's role of exhorting and putting applications into practice.

The principle that sermons should apply Scripture to the lives of parishioners was by no means confined to Protestants and Puritans. They intensified a general practice. Frequently allegorizations promoted by advocates of the "old learning" represented such accommodations. Davies notes that the sense of biblical history being reenacted in every Christian's life issues from a Pauline heritage extending through Augustine and Calvin.[49] Furthermore, such a sense is supported by lists of Bible passages cited as helps for sustaining believers under various circumstances, which can be found in multitudinous devotion manuals of the day. Also in support are the many borrowings from Catholic manuals, including those by Vives and Erasmus, which Davies finds in a host of predominantly Reformed works such as Henry Bull's *Christian and Holie Meditations* (1566 with a number of later editions) or John Norden's *A Pensive Mans Practise* (1584 with approximately 40 more editions).[50]

Reformed typology, by its restrictions to literal interpretations of the Bible alone and by its accommodating identifications, encouraged and influenced if it did not instigate a distinctive kind of lyric persona. This Renaissance neotype would not presumptuously try to imitate Christ directly as did medieval authors. Instead, the Renaissance neotypical persona could humbly embody the individuality and failure of a type, and thereby realize salvation through Christ, the antitype. In doing so the poet would be releasing and exploiting the tremendous expressive potential latent in types.

† † †

The neotypological lyric did not rise out of a context wholly dominated by polemical and exegetical texts. It rose as well from a context of broadly diverging poetic uses of types whose history and definition parallel the concerns of theologians and whose wide-ranging traditions were all readily available in lyrics. Just so, the development of typological imagery and allusion in medieval hymns repeats the historical contour of patristic and medieval typological interpretation: typology first expanded and subsequently was absorbed into other figural and allegorical schemes.[51] In hymns as early as the fourth century, types reinforced doctrine by enhancing presentations of Christian salvation; momentarily during the fifth and sixth centuries they were codified. After that, types in hymns and sequences came to be used more imaginatively and profusely but less precisely; they began to proliferate, not around Christ and the New Testament, but around Mary. The last, and best, of these hymns are Adam of St. Victor's typologically complex celebrations of Mary and

Thomas Aquinas' typologically witty and rigorous explications of the eucharist. Subsequent Franciscan affective hymns display biblical figures, such as Old Testament heroines for Mary, that are indistinguishable from allegories.

When in the thirteenth and fourteenth centuries short sacred poems changed from objective communal hymns to subjective sacred lyrics, and often from Latin to vernaculars,[52] Middle English sacred lyrics that relied on typological allusions and imagery rose out of Latin hymns. A few Middle English sacred lyrics, then, display original and beautiful typological expression, most of these adorning Mary;[53] but the majority led away from typology into allegorical elaborations like those adapted from French love lyrics. The Middle English lyricists who used typology play variations on allegorical figuralism from centuries before. So it was in strong contrast to this tradition, and out of Reformed concerns, that the neotypological lyric developed in England during the sixteenth and seventeenth centuries.

Imitative sacred versifiers in seventeenth-century England illustrate a spectrum that ranges from older medieval Catholic figural verse to the revolutionary neotypological lyric. A number repeat the sporadic allegorical allusions and expansions of medieval hymns and poems, some repeat the occasional, casual display of types common to sixteenth-century verse, a few repeat and extend the more systematic, elaborated figural references of hymnody and psalmody, and at least a couple illustrate the gains of the distinctive neotypological lyric, perhaps representing the essence of seventeenth-century sacred lyrics.

Few Protestant lyricists apart from the neotypological alluded to types. Joseph Fletcher's doggerel *Christes Bloodie Sweat* (1613) occasionally goes beyond phoenix and pelican emblems to types of Christ. For example, he writes about the waters of Meribah, the Red Sea, and sacrifices.[54] And in *Flowers of Sion* (1630) William Drummond of Hawthornden's "Hymn of the Resurrection" echoes Hebrews 10: "The law to grace, / Types to their substance yield" (129–30).[55] Sometimes these Protestants appear to be merely confused about Catholic figural tradition, as does Nathanael Richards. In *Poems Sacred and Satyricall* (1641) he manages to commingle David's and Paul's tears and to mix Abraham's faith, Jacob's strife, Stephen's charity, Joseph's life, Job's patience, Paul's purity, and Peter's penance—randomly.[56] Such confusions yielded distorted echoes of magnificently involved figural works from the Middle Ages.

Some moderately prominent lyricists did understand and follow traditional medieval allegories. These are mainly recusant celebrants of Mary. Medieval figures of Mary, such as the morning star, sea star, enclosed

22

garden, fountain, tower of David, and ark of the covenant, abound in works like Richard Rowlands' *Odes, in Imitation of the Seaven Penitential Psalmes* (under the pseudonym, Richard Verstegan [1601]) and John Braidshaigh's *Virginalia, or spirituall sonnets* (1632). At other times recusants used types of Christ. Christopher Lever writes of the "*Iacobs ladder* [we] would ascend" and of the temple in *A Crucifixe; or, a meditation upon repentance and the holie Passion* (1607).[57] Similar uses appear in the verse of a number of Laudian Anglicans sympathetic to Catholicism. Marian figures such as Moses' burning bush, Aaron's rod, Jesse's root, and Gideon's fleece, and types of Christ such as Adam, Melchizedek, Jacob's ladder, and manna show up in Charles Fitz-Geffry's *The Blessed Birth-day, Celebrated* (1634).[58] The royalist preacher and professor Joseph Beaumont produced clever if uninspired figural verse in the old manner. His lyrics like "Annunciatio B. V." can display Marian types (the Canticles garden, Aaron's rod) and associations (Maria's honey replaces Eve's gall). Once in a while, for example in "Death," he marks transition from the first to the second Adam. Occasionally he embellishes; for instance, the serpent and tree of Eden prophesy Calvary and a new paradisiacal "Garden." He shows the most originality of this reactionary group with "Newyear Day" in which he transfers a type of Christ's sacrifice, sprinkling the blood of the paschal lamb, from the crucifixion to the circumcision.

The anonymous poetaster of *Apollo Christian: or Helicon Reformed* (1617) is another apparent, somewhat lower church, Anglican who reverted to allegory though not to Marian figuralism. He exhibits one rather widespread point of confusion when he mixes anagogical interpretations, such as Palestine for heaven and Solomon's temple for the heavenly Jerusalem, with typological ones, such as Moses for Christ and manna for the Lord's Supper. He also follows the "old learning" in his sense of complete abrogation of the type, for he compares Moses, David, and Solomon's temple to Christ, in terms of chaff to grain, the old metaphor for allegory:

No miracle worth naming but his owne.
For, how farre substance shadowes doth excell,
Things done their figures set in paralell
So farre the sacred kernell of Christs deeds
The gorgeous huske of those great types exceeds.[59]

Several Anglican psalmodists and hymnodists who followed sixteenth-century predecessors by translating, paraphrasing, and being inspired by Psalms demonstrate a wavering middle way between traditional figuralists and the new movement of neotypological lyricists. These psalm and hymn writers continued to apply David's universal Christian situations and to identify with David, a type who despite his sins is through repentant faith saved by Christ. For example, George Sandys' annotated *A Paraphrase upon the divine poems* (1638) commonly applies David's situations.

George Wither's attempts to establish an Anglican tradition of hymns are especially noteworthy. At first sight, in using types more systematically as well as in applying them to members of the congregation, he seems Reformed. But in the final analysis he expands into unauthorized allegorizations. In *Hymnes and Songs of the Church* (1623) he offered versified parcels of Scripture with other ancient hymns and creeds adapted to the Anglican calendar; and in *Halelviah or Britans Second Remembrancer* (1641) he added poems personalized for special occasions, disasters and successes, relationships, and occupations.[60] Thus, he accommodated and applied Scripture to human lives around him. Indeed, in the preface to part one of *Hymnes and Songs* he cites 1 Corinthians 10 to support his claim that besides typologically predicting Christ, Old Testament songs provide profitable guides and warnings for later generations. Furthermore, at times he tends to incorporate types into some hymns so that they imply Reformed typology. In "For Saterday" (Part II, Hymn viii of *Halelviah*) the speaker explains:

This Day, the Rigour of the *Law*,
    Began to be alayd,
And, that which kept in *servile-Awe*,
    Now, makes us not afraid.
Vpon this Day, each *Jewish-Rite*,
    Both Death and buriall had.
Their *Sabbath*, was abolish'd quite,
    And uneffectual made.
For, why should we the *Tipes* embrace
    Or in their *Shades* abide,
When their true *Substance* comes in place,
    Which they but typifide.[61]

In a rough way these lines apply types personally. They further emphasize abrogation of the type: once a Christian has to some extent identified with a typological situation, through it he can recognize Christ's atonement for him. Finally echoing Hebrews 10 as well as 1 Corinthians 10, Wither reinforces his statement in the triple pun on *shade* ("foreshadowing," "insubstantial," "physical"), which urges his choir to come out of Old Testament darkness into Gospel light.

But, like many other Anglicans, Wither reverts to a pre-Reformed sense of typology. In the preface to Part I of *Hymnes and Songs* he claims that types "farre better expresse the nature of that which they mystically point out, then of what they are litterally applied vnto," and often his annotations particularly cite such predictions.[62] Furthermore, he does not stop with Reformed uses of passages like the first Mosaic song (Exod. 15), which displays a series of types from Pharaoh as the enemy to the Red Sea as baptism; his fancy roams to such instances as the tenth song, from Canticles 2, which "*seemeth to set forth the mysterie of Christ his Incarnation.*"[63]

As does Washbourne's *Divine Poems*, Christopher Harvey's *The Synagogue, or The Shadow of the Temple. Sacred Poems, and Private Ejaculations. In imitation of Mr. George Herbert* (1640)[64] also demonstrates how Reformed attitudes toward typology could affect the use of types in lyrics. Most of these poems provide precise typological allusions. His Christ perpetually fills the mediatorial office of Melchizedek in "The Priest" and his Christ, as the "sun of righteousness," glows through a veil of flesh in "The Epiphany, or Twelfth-Day." But Harvey does more than adhere to Reformed use of typological allusions. He imitates the basic form of the neotypological lyric. He particularly imitates Herbert's emblem of the human heart, which reflects God's interaction with the hearts of believers.[65] The central text is provided by 2 Corinthians 3:2–3: "Ye are our epistle written in our hearts, known and read of all men: *Forasmuch as ye are* manifestly declared to be the epistle of Christ ministered by us, written not with ink, but with the Spirit of the living God; not in tables of stone, but in fleshy tables of the heart." Paul's declaration reappropriates for the New Covenant two motifs from Jeremiah. The first is Jeremiah's indictment of mankind for sinning. His accusation is related to the typology of the ten commandments, which convict men of sinning: "The sin of Judah *is* written with a pen of iron, *and* with the point of a diamond: *it is* graven upon the table of their heart, and upon the horns of your altars" (17:1). As the horns of the altar indicate, the second is Jeremiah's promise of a more hopeful agreement. For at the same time that he accuses, he offers a pardon for humans who become remorseful over their conviction of sin: "But this *shall be* the covenant that I will make with the house of Israel; After those days, saith the LORD, I will put my law in their inward parts, and write it in their hearts; and will be their God, and they shall be my people" (31:33). By following these passages a neotypological lyricist is applying scriptural doctrine to his own faith and life in the image of the heart taken initially from Jeremiah and more emphatically from Paul's reinterpretation and reemphasis. Beyond this he is joining their dual feeling of grief over human failures combined with exaltation over human salvation, a dual movement that is akin both to that in Psalms and to the new sense of potency in a strict definition and close application of types. All declare that when human violations of a contract with God lead to remorse, the sinner is cleansed by the grace of Christ. Hence, in sinning he can humbly be comforted by identifying with salvation. And he can do so specifically through a type that effects the transformation.

The rock fountain of Horeb, an Old Testament object in its own right, also foreshadows Christ, the purifying fountain as interpreted in the New; in the interaction between the two signifieds, the type cleanses the heart. The extraordinary popularity of this type during the period indicates its emotional power for poetry. Its appearance, not just in the Good Friday service or in the continually circulating *Biblia pauperum* but even in decorating the borders of "Elizabeth's prayerbook," enhanced its value for the neotypological lyric.[66]

In "11. The Font" Harvey refers to both Zechariah 13:1 and the rock of Horeb, and then follows Herbert in creating an internal dialogue based on transforming the decalogue of stone into the gospel in the heart:

'What! Is He not the rock, out of whose side
   Those streams of water-bloud run forth?
Th' elect and precious corner-stone well try'd?
   Though th' odds be great between their worth,
Rock-water and stone-vessels are ally'd.'

                                              (11–15)

Next the persona specifically applies to himself the two Protestant sacraments traditionally signified in the flow of blood and water from Christ's wounded side; they are the signs and seals of his personal new covenant with Christ. He can be saved by identifying absolutely with a type that is saved:

Regeneration is all in all;
   Washing or sprinkling but the sign
The seal, and instrument thereof; I call
   The one as well as the other mine,
And my posterity's, as fœderal.

                                              (26–30)

The persona in the present reclaims himself as a type in the past so that he can become eternal through the antitype. He can hope to gain the promise of an endless future by imitating, indeed by trying to become, his past, because that past is typological. The poet explains with some precision if little poetry:

> If temporal estates may be convey'd
>   By cov'nants on condition
> To men and to their heirs; be not affraid,
>   My soul, to rest upon
> The covenant of grace, by Mercy made.
>
> (31–35)

The basic structure of the neotypological lyric is only echoed here in Harvey because this poem lacks the soul's agon with God and the soul's remorse, but it is clearly audible.

Harvey's "48. Inundations" provides another self-explanatory corroboration of self-consciously following a new kind of poetry, the neotypological lyric. Melding two traditions used earlier by Alabaster he conflates the type, Noah's flood, with his own contrite tears. Again, he personally applies a type to himself to the degree of identification with it, so that both are washed in Christ's blood, the antitypical flood that saves the Old Testament type and the seventeenth-century neotype:

> And when salvation came, my Saviour's blood
>   Drown'd sin again,
>   With all its train
> Of evils; overflowing them with good,
>   With good that ever shall remain.
>
> O let there be one other inundation;
>   Let grace o'rflow
>   In my soul so,
> That thankfulness may level with salvation,
>   And sorrow sin may overgrow!
>
> (26–35)

The self-explained use of the neotypological lyric structure damns the poem while it saves the poet and instructs the literary historian.

Evidence in the examples of this history of the discovery and development, achievement, and fragmentation of the neotypological lyric of the English Renaissance is suggested to corroborate by their parallels that neotypological lyricists were moved by the same impulses that moved Reformed biblical commentators to put new emphasis on typology. The commentators commended types for being specifically authorized by Scripture and therefore included in the literal meaning. This meant in turn that they were historically factual and interesting in themselves even as they failed, while at the same time they also foreshadowed the perfection of Christ their antitype. The resulting interaction between failure in themselves and achievement granted for their faith meant that when commentators or preachers applied Scripture to believers, by identification the believers could acknowledge their own self-damning failures and sins, and yet at the same time be comforted in hopes and some assurance of salvation. Moved and guided by the same set of impulses, premises, and consequent arguments about the power for salvation and its persuasive expression in types that directed Reformed commentators, English neotypological lyricists created poetic personae, neotypes, out of painful self-examinations, humble contrition, and faithful hope. Then through the progression of their poems they revealed to readers both the implications of salvation and a potent poetic matrix available in applied typological situations.

Thus, their new kind of lyric is based on a definition of typology that is specifically Reformed. Moreover, it establishes a radical unity between the poet's imitative creation and the type, a unity that far exceeds the customarily supposed analogy or correspondence, to the degree of virtual identity. These poets were unique in imitating types to such an extent that they were remaking themselves and their expression into their typological past. They were not merely discovering exempla nor were they just following models. Rather, they were consciously becoming their past in order to save their eternity; they were essentially placing themselves at the core of a saving interaction between God's eternal transcendence and history's mundane limits. They created their Christian faith around themselves in the mode of the old covenant, made themselves not the presumptuous images of God but the humble images of types, in order to be saved by the new Gospel which, they affirmed, fulfills Old Testament types and Reformed neotypes.

2

"The very state and condition of the soule"

Sixteenth-Century Forebears and the Rudimentary Neotypological Lyrics of Southwell and Alabaster

The poets who first experimented with creating personae out of types in order to reenact scenes of recovery from sin seem to have been motivated by deep psychoreligious needs stirred by the Reformation and Counter-Reformation, by Calvin and Ignatius. Influenced by the revived Augustinian awareness of original and personal sin under the intense self-scrutiny promoted and exemplified in *The Confessions*, they felt human failure and depravity to be so overwhelming that they could make no claim to imitate or identify with Christ. They realized that a chasm separated them from God in Christ and understood that to identify with him would constitute damning presumption. At the same time they had faith that Christ's infinite loving sacrifice redeems and fulfills true believers. They were torn between the terrible depression of their guilt and the exalted joy promised them in Christ's incomprehensible glory. And they vacillated between sinful individualism and saved communion.

Psalms offered major sacred and poetic models to Tudor progenitors of the neotypological lyric. Initially they offered a psychic framework for self-examination and portrayal. The printers of the old version of Sternhold and Hopkins' translation of Psalms represent the whole period when they approve Athanasius' ancient claim that "The booke of the Psalmes doth expresse after a certayne maner the very state and condition of the soule."[1] The dual motives of humbling contrition and transcending exaltation found in David's songs and the way Reformers of all persuasions applied Psalms to their congregations further supplied both spiritual and poetic forms along lines suggested by Augustine's influential *Enarrationes in Psalmos*. Ultimately, Psalms at least reinforced, if they did not suggest, using typological references in verse. Both the model and the suggestion had been transmitted by a tradition of biblical interpretation from the seminal commentaries of Jerome and especially Augustine through the revised ones of the Reformation and Counter-Reformation. The vogue from Wyatt through Sandys of poets associating with David, a prominent type as king and as celebrant who failed miserably and was saved gloriously, and of retranslating and adapting his Psalms fostered many approaches to sacred lyric.[2] When occasionally a few poets started to search out other types to compare to their Christian predicaments, the move toward one important approach began.

In order to adorn the emotional and literary model of Psalms some of these same sixteenth-century forebears of neotypological lyricists, poets from John Hall to Barnabe Barnes, reconverted Petrarchan stances, *topoi*, conceits, and image complexes for use in sacred song. When intermittent, supporting typological references on occasion became centers of attention and self-comparison for a devotional poet such as Henry Lok, the basic form of the neotypological lyric was nearing discovery. The Jesuit martyr Robert Southwell was the first to discover that basic form when he concentrated these devices in several very original poems that released the power of typological self-comparisons in order to comfort and sustain himself and his parishioners while they were facing inevitable failures of faith and nerve. The Catholic convert William Alabaster then extended Southwell's discovery when he transformed the potential of the neotypological lyric in order to intensely examine and finally understand his own soul.

† † †

The immediate psychic and literary impetus for the neotypological lyric came from poets who anglicized Psalms in the early sixteenth century.[3] Of Coburn Freer's four patterns informing Psalms, two are important here. First, "They dramatize a common psychological and spiritual pattern or present a descriptive analogue to that pattern." Psalmodists sing about the release of a universal persona from common religious predicaments. Second, "They reveal that the translators' motives have much in common with those of later devotional poets."[4] Besides private motives of pleasure or gain and public motives of edification, from the outset psalmodists seem to have written for the "Godly solace" of themselves and also of their community. By the 1530s Sir Thomas Wyatt and Sir Henry Howard, Earl of Surrey, had begun personalizing their renditions, for themselves and for others.

A characteristic development in many Psalms involves someone achieving inner strength and transcendence through weakness and miserable constriction.[5] Wyatt and Surrey counterpointed that development by welding their personal situations to David's universal ones. Introducing Psalm 102, Wyatt interpolates his personality into his immediate source, Aretino. He applies David's situations to his own life and he affirms that the mercy granted David is still available for himself. Nor is this mercy confined to the Old Testament God; it extends to the New Covenant Christ:

> Here hath he confort when he doth mesure
> Mesureles marcys to mesureles fawte,
> To prodigall sinners Infinite tresure,
> Tresure termeles that neuer shall defawte.
>
> (525–28)[6]

Wyatt's implied self-comparison to the prodigal son as well as to David permits his dual expression of remorse in an Old Testament figure and salvation in a New Testament parable. The outbursts in Surrey's translations express the same kind of potential success within inevitable failure.[7]

When making personal applications to their own souls, these translators were also serving as exempla to others, a motive to which they called attention. In commending Wyatt's adaptations of the penitential Psalms, Surrey points out that both David and Wyatt through David are magnified mirrors for morals:

> What holly grave, what wourthy sepulture
> To Wyates Psalmes shuld Christians then purchase?
> Wher he dothe paynte the lyvely faythe and pure,
> The stedfast hope, the swete returne to grace
>
> Of iust Dauyd by parfite penytence,
> Where Rewlers may se in a myrrour clere.
>
> (5–10)[8]

Besides praising David's portrayal of everyman's soul, the printers of Sternhold and Hopkins commend two other purposes of Psalms. First, like Wyatt and Surrey, they declare that the Psalms formalize one way to approach God. They further suggest the specific situations different Psalms will succor: under threat, Psalm 6; when penitent, Psalm 51; and so on. Second, and more important, they declare that Psalms express remorse for disobeying God's law precisely at those moments when Christ's charity is transforming that remorse into salvation. These two purposes moved poets to create lyric personae associated with Old Testament situations who sing about the paradoxical redemption when Christ converts humiliating sorrow into exalted joy. This moment and its double movement are the same pair illuminated by Reformed typology.

Reformed psalmodists' renditions of typology are notable for their dual expression of despair and joy. In his popular reworking of the penitential Psalms, *Seven Sobs of a Sorrowful Soule for Sinne* (1583), the amount of William Hunnis' actual translation is tiny in proportion to his rhyming commentary. Furthermore, Hunnis' versified homiletics always bring in the New Testament to correct and redeem the Old. For example, he expands the opening of the sixth Psalm almost beyond recognition:

> Euen then (alas) I shake and quake,
>   and tremble where I stand,
> For feare thou shouldst reuenged bee,
>   By power of wrathfull hand.
>
> The weight of sin is very great,
>   for this to mind I call,
> That one proud thought made Angels thine
>   from heauen to slide and fall.
>
> Adam likewise, and Eue his wife,
>   for breaking thy precept
> From Paradice expelled were;
>   and death thereby hath crept
>
> Vpon them both, and on their seed,
>   for euer to remain:
> But that by faith in Christ thy Son,
>   we hope to liue again.
>
> (St. 3–6)[9]

He continues by pointing to other types saved by Christ.

A few innovative Elizabethan poets contributed by comparing themselves to biblical characters other than the universalized David. In a poem which could have influenced Southwell's verse, the recusant Jasper Heywood likens himself not to a type yet, but to the prodigal son. After describing the prodigal's failure, he remorsefully compares the ungrateful child's waste of his father's resources to his own waste of God's free gift of grace, his own restlessness, loss of strength, and vanity. Then he prays that he too may arrive home a penitent who is welcomed and forgiven by the mercy of God the Father through his perfect son:

> Now to come home with him, and pardon pray,
> My God I say, against the heavens and thee,
> I am not worthy, that my lippes should say:
> Beholde thy handie worke, and pitie me,
> Of mercy yet my soule, from faultes set free.
> To serve thee here, till thou appoint the time,
> Through Christ, unto thy blessed joyes to climbe.[10]

Besides the universal pattern of psalmody and the association with biblical figures saved by Christ, another impetus toward neotypological lyrics appeared now: the reappropriation of Petrarchan imagery for sacred lyrics. Sacred parodists of Petrarchan devices began to challenge amatory lyrics. Not long after English courtly makers domesticated Petrarchan lyricism and booksellers promoted it in such volumes as *The Court of Venus* (ca. 1536) and Tottel's Miscellany (1557 and beyond), John Hall hastened feebly forth with *The Court of Virtue* (1565). His mission was to convert the promotion of venereal love to the propagation of Christian charity. In Hall's prologue, a dream allegory, Dame Virtue sets the moral and poetic tone:

> Suche as in carnall loue reioyce,
> Trim songes of loue they wyll compile,
> And synfully with tune and voyce
> They syng their songes in pleasant stile,
> To Venus that same strompet vyle.
>
> (p. 15)[11]

She urges Christian poets to counter love poets with "a boke of songes holy, / Godly and wyse, blamyng foly" (16). Just as important as his versification of the Apostles' Creed, Pater Noster, Ten Commandments, and various Psalms is Hall's transformation of Wyatt's "My Lute, awake," a *strambotta* bitterly describing his lady's disdain and vengefully predicting her abandonment by a fickle lover. After forsaking the "goddesse of lechery" and "praysing of the Almyghty" in imitation of David, "My lute awake and prayse the lord" establishes the rock of Christ and salvation against false Catholicism. It concludes with a prayer of faith:

Lorde graunt vs to thy worde to cleaue,
That no man other doe deceaue:
And in that zeale that I begunne,
Lauding our lorde God here I leaue,
Be styll my lute my song is done.

(pp. 171–72)

Crude as it is, the parody sets a precedent for poems, such as Ralegh's "As you came from the holy land / Of Walsinghame," that pit true charity against false lust by turning the language and imagery of profane poets against them and toward God.

Sacred poets continued to transform Petrarchan devices used to woo ladies and describe lovers' vacillations into praises of God and descriptions of contrite sinners. For the most part they began with professions of sincerity akin to those of secular sonneteers. Henry Lok, for instance, claims that his *Sundry Christian Passions, Contained in 200 Sonnets* (1593) imitate his own feelings rather than outward ornaments.[12] Besides professing sincerity, Barnabe Barnes adapts the expressions of a poetic lover's contrary passions to describe devotion and the figurative talk of being wounded by Cupid to display contrition. Both are prominent when he records his soul's warfare against the world in *A Divine Centvrie of Spirituall Sonnets* (1595) "wherin, if through secret, and inseperable combat betwixt earth and my spirite, the priuie motions, and sting of diuers wounds, as they did succeede and grieue my soule, manifested appeare."[13] In one lyric exhortation, "Optima Deo," an anonymous poet used Tasso's version of *carpe florem* to persuade readers to turn quickly to God.[14]

Beyond the forces of psalmody and sacred parody that began molding forms for the neotypological lyric, lyric uses of typology were themselves undergoing transformation during the sixteenth century. One small body of verse was in effect defining typology. Myles Hogarde, for instance, exercised considerable care when he borrowed Aquinas' hymns for the didactic "Doctrine of the Eucharist":

Christ to his disciples these wordes dyd saye
I longe to eate the pascall lambe sayth he
Wyth you my disciples for now is the daye
Of the swete bread, I praye you note and se
Howe the trueth wyth the figure doth a gre
Christe was the true lambe which the prophetes saw
Shuld truly fullfyl the Moysaical law

34

Christe eat the lambe ther as the law did will
Then to showe that that law was expired.[15]

On rare occasions a sacred poet glimpsed the culminating discovery of comparing people to types. Despite his militant anti-Catholicism, Hall one time used, in " *The complaint of Christ our sauiour*," both the complaint form and types from medieval liturgy. Christ is chastising mankind's failure to respond to his sacrifice. But the sacrifice described is not the crucifixion. Instead, the sacrifice is represented by God's chosen people repeatedly rejecting him when he recovered them—delivering them from Egypt, parting the Red Sea for them, feeding them with manna, and replacing Old Testament legalities with new covenant hope and love: "For thee I ordeynd Paradyse, / And shewde to thee my Testament, / And thou agayne dydst me despyse" (pp. 237–38).

Barnabe Barnes went farther than Hall, when in a pun he considered his speaker a type. The speaker himself becomes a lesson that "*I haue committed to the publique tipographicall Theatre of generall censure.*"[16] But Barnes did little to develop typological implications beyond adapting them to the secular world ("For Cupids darts prefigurate hell's sting / His quenchlesse Torch foreshowes hell's quenchless fire" [1. 7–8]) and discussing them dully in the twenty-second sonnet.[17]

Henry Lok was the first to come close to the neotypological lyric. He made an important decision when he considered his persona analogous to types of Christ. For by this association he extended the psalmodists' copies of David vacillating through repentance to regeneration, and he consolidated the sacred versifiers' scattered references to eucharistic and deliverance types. To open his second sonnet Lok places his speaker in the position of Jonah:

Fro out the darknesse of this sea of feare,
    Where I in whale remaine, deuourd of sin,
    With true remorse of former sin I reare
    My heart to heauen, in hope some helpe to win.

Looking at the Old Testament as a New Testament typologist, he can repent and recognize signs of salvation in the situations of both Jonah and himself. In the third sonnet his speaker suggestively compares the hopeful type of Noah's ark to himself, though the potential remains unexploited. The twentieth sonnet contains a most interesting, original comparison of his speaker to Ishmael, Hagar's bastard by Abraham. Following the specifically Reformed interpretation inaugurated by Luther, Lok has Ishmael, as a representative Gentile, saved by Christ rather than left an outcast:

> A bond man vnto sin as fleshly race,
> To whom heauen's heritage Thy lawes denaide:
> Amidst my wandring course by Thee am staide,
> And haue a promise, not to die but liue;
> Thy couenant Lord abundantly is paide,
> If grace—to feed by faith—Thou doest me giue:
> My bondage thus release, make Thou me free,
> My barren branch shall so bring fruit for Thee.
>
> (7–14)

In sonnet 76, since he sees himself sold into sin like Joseph, he correspondingly hopes for delivery out of the hell of Egypt like the tribe of Joseph.[18]

Lok brought into conglomeration several elements necessary for the creation of the English neotypological lyric. A few of his sonnets express some of the dual remorse and hope imitated by psalmodists. Many of them display the psychological and formal devices parodied from English Petrarchans. Most important, some of these are loosely linked to speakers associated with types of Christ. But Lok did not unite the three so as to effectively exploit the expressive energy available in his near discovery. The task of uniting them in a rudimentary neotypological lyric that tapped their tremendous potential for religious poetry remained for Southwell.

† † †

Robert Southwell's anguished conscience and desire to fortify the recusant congregation proved necessary in the founding of the neotypological lyric. He apparently began writing poetry to sustain himself, and then for other persecuted Elizabethan Catholics threatened with martyrdom. The rigors of Jesuit training in obedience taught him both to demand success and to acknowledge inevitable, inherent human failure, and at the same time instilled in him faith that Christ succors and fulfills those who try wholeheartedly. Southwell discovered the center of his poetry by examining his own and his parish's capacity for sacrifice. He measured both by the remorseful failures and thankful celebrations of David and Peter. For while their damning lapses were more than apparent to him, he could recognize as well how their remorse became penance through God's grace in Christ. When he identified both himself and his congregation with types, he hit upon the typological simile; when he sought to enrich his poetry he used sacred parody; when he strived for form he practiced sacred meditation. He integrated these elements in at least one masterful lyric, "Christs sleeping friends," in which he first exploited the neotypological lyric's expressive potential.

Southwell's preoccupation with Peter's failure to do his duty followed from his rigorous Jesuit training to join the Catholic underground in Europe's most powerful Reformed nation.[19] His *Exercitia et Devotiones*, written during his preparation for priesthood, reflects his dread of falling from God to damnation for lack of diligence. The seventh meditation, written near the beginning of his novitiate, strikingly records his anxiety over the possibility, perhaps the likelihood, of religious failure:

A man may have fixed his gaze upon the same colours for a hundred years, but if for a moment the light does not shine, for all his long continued vision he will no longer see them; and in like manner a religious may have remained firm in his vocation and resisted all manner of temptations and trials for a great many years, but yet if the light of grace be lost for ever so short a time, he will become so blind that what he previously abhorred as temptations of the devil he will now welcome as inspirations of the Holy Ghost. Thus it is that many, after even sixty years of God's service, have left their vocation and fallen into the gravest sins. Beware then lest God take away His light from thee on account of thy sins, and thou abandon thy vocation and being in turn abandoned by God earn His condemnation.[20]

This fear haunted Southwell through his priesthood in Rome. It appears, for example, in the sixty-second exercise, which stresses the great importance of scrupulous obedience to insignificant duties.[21] In meditating on the extraordinary occasion commemorated in the twenty-first exercise, "Reflexions on St. Luke's Day after Taking My Vows," Southwell admonishes himself to accept as absolute God's will through the Society:

Thou hast given thyself to God in such a way that for ever thou art to remain His bondsman and servant, and to have henceforth no power of willing or refusing for thyself. Whatever then may happen to thee thou must be absolutely sure that it comes by the special providence of God. Even in the most trivial matters . . . Even in matters which seem most unimportant . . . Whatever may happen we should accept from the hands of God as from a most loving father.[22]

Southwell perpetually agonizes over his assignments, worrying that he might never achieve the goal that first motivated him, the English ministry.[23]

While duty to God is paramount and dread of failing God's mission attends recognition of that duty, human failure is inevitable. As David's and Peter's lives showed, failure belies human will. Southwell's hope of God's grace repairing the inevitable deficiences of those who try is less obvious than is his despair, yet it is infinitely more important for him. In the sixty-third meditation he recalls failures of both the damned and the saved; then he prays for God's grace, because ultimately that grace segregates the two:

> Lucifer fell, David fell, the Apostle Peter also, and who am I that I should not fall? Men fell who were according to God's own heart, and shall I not fall who have served the devil, the world and the flesh all my life? Answer Thou for me, O Lord, and distinguish my cause.[24]

Southwell is torn by failures to resign his will to God's—the primary concern he acts out; but he is more taken by the potential grace of salvation—the boon he can only request God to act on.

Southwell's diligent preparation of himself, his brothers, and his congregation is indicated by his longest work, the posthumously printed *An Epistle of Comfort, to the Reuerend Priests, and to the Honourable, Worshipfull, & other of the Lay sort, restrayned in durance for the Catholike Faith* (1604?), and by his pastoral advice, *Short Rules of a Good Life* (printed soon after his execution).[25] The former argues that tribulation offers immediate comforts (though persecution indicates the nature of the fallen world, trials are granted to those God loves) and promises that Catholic martyrs will achieve a glorious future. Basically, it acknowledges dejection, which is inherent in man, and affirms exaltation, which God can grant. The latter establishes a system of methodical exercises based on accountable obedience to God and his representatives, including specific recognition of failures which are inevitable. At the same time it is filled with assurances of God's love which resurrects believers. These two motifs, joined by Southwell's emphasis on human tribulations, are supported by catalogues of examples that threaten damnation for great failures and affirm salvation for the faithful.

Southwell's poems as well are mainly hortatory. Although they do present personal identifications, even more they minister to persecuted Elizabethan Catholics. This is plain from the opening of "The Author to the Reader" that introduces the longer "Saint Peters Complaint":

Deare eie that daynest to let fall a looke,
On these sad memories of Peters plaintes:
Muse not to see some mud in cleerest brooke,
They once were brittle mould, that now are Saintes.
Their weakenesse is no warrant to offend:
Learne by their faultes, what in thine owne to mend.

Similar to the manner that David and Peter affect Southwell, both are effective examples for his persecuted congregation. And all the parish could identify not only with the traditional Mary Magdalene, the converted whore who symbolizes the church, but also with other figures who suffer remorse.[26] Another sense besides remorse, however, emanates from Southwell's biblical figures: they imply salvation. Several although failing God are nevertheless justified by Christ.

Southwell both projects himself into and exhorts his parishioners by using figures who failed to carry out vital duties even though chosen by God. The most conspicuous example is St. Peter: though he was the foremost disciple, the one chosen to establish the church, he denied Christ. In the shorter "Saint Peters Complaynte," a poem related by both manuscript position and verse form to the Gethsemane group that includes "Christs sleeping friends," Southwell imagines the saint's contrition, which is compounded by his failure in the beginning to achieve that which Christ had promised:

Was I to stay the Churche a Chosen rocke
That with so soft a gale was overthrowen?
Was I cheife pastour of the faithfull flocke,
To guide their soules that murdred thus my owne?
A rocke of ruyne, not a reste to staye:
A pastour, not to feede but to betraye.

(19–24)

The first figure recalls Jesus' pun on Peter's name as founder of the church (Matt. 16:18); but here Peter is shown to have subverted the rock of faith into one of treachery. In the second Peter recalls that his duty was to have been a traditional pastor who follows the good shepherd by caring for his flock of parishioners (as in John 10:1–18); but Peter has turned into a betrayer, a wolf not merely in the sheep's clothing Christ predicted (Matt. 7:15) but worse, in the garb of their pastor, their guardian. A number of Southwell's poems focus solely on such failings. The dirge of "S. Peters afflicted minde" is unrelieved.[27] The way Southwell adapts the imagery of the fifth penitential Psalm (102) in "Davids Peccavi" suggests that there is no hope. If "Mary Magdalens blush" hints at contrition in "Faults long unfelt doth conscience now bewraye, / Which cares must cure, and teares must wash awaye" (11–12), the poem remains comfortless.

However fallen from God's grace they may appear, Southwell chose for his exemplary failures the very people Christ raised to glory. Christ's grace, transforming human failure, brings joy out of the despair in "The prodigall childs soule wracke." At times it grants intimations of hope during St. Peter's laments. The second stanza of "S. Peters remorse," a prayer of penance, eventually does overcome the third, a plea of guilt and an acknowledgment of just punishment. In the end Peter can affirm that Christ's grace redeems the failure:

> O milde and mighty Lord,
>   Amend that is amisse:
> My sinne my soare, thy love my salve,
>   Thy cure my comfort is.
>
> Confirme thy former deede,
>   Reforme that is defilde:
> I was, I am, I will remaine
>   Thy charge, thy choice, thy childe.

Because of Peter's anachronistic sense of success, immediately after he fails and before Christ atones on the cross, his exhortation is more hopeful than despairing. The close of the longer "Saint Peters Complaint" removes any remaining doubts about whether Peter's prayer has been granted:

> Redeeme my lapse with raunsome of thy love,
> Traverse th'inditement, rigors dome suspend:
> Let frailtie favour, sorrow succour move:
> Be thou thy selfe, though chaungling I offend.
> Tender my suite, clense this defiled denne,
> Cancell my debtes, sweete *Jesu*, say Amen.

Christ's charity, even when embedded as it is in forensic diction, comforts Southwell and his parishioners. The priest and his congregation can find consolation through self-projection into biblical transformations of despair to salvation because they have faith that God's grace flows over those who are contrite after they have failed to obey him.

Affinities are clear between Southwell's belief in Christian exaltation rising out of failure and his identification with Peter, David, and the Psalms. His affinities with Reformed and Counter-Reformed typology are just as clear. His use of types as poetic devices particularly in his sequence on the Virgin and Christ has been widely recognized.[28] What has not been recognized is his originality in exploiting typological potential by placing himself with his congregation in a context so as to compare sixteenth-century men to types. When he made this intimate comparison to prefigurations fulfilled and saved in Christ, he pioneered a new form of English sacred lyric.

Southwell's interest in dogmatic delineations of typology may be suggested by a doubtful attribution, "A holy Hymme" (manuscripts entitle it "Saint Thomas of Aquines Hymne. read on corpus christy daye. Lauda Sion Salvatorem."). It is unquestionable in his adaptation of Aquinas' "Lauda Sion," "Of The Blessed Sacrament of the Aulter":

In paschall feast the end of auncient rite
An entraunce was to never endinge grace,
Tipes to the truth, dymm glymses to the light,
Performinge Deede presageing signes did chase,
Christes Final meale was fountayne of our good:
For mortall meate he gave immortall foode.

(1–6) [29]

Beyond the allusion to 1 Corinthians 13:12, which prepares for an essence/accidence presentation, Southwell explicitly establishes the movement from physical type to spiritual truth. The Passover meal foreshadows the last supper and the Easter sacrifice, commemorated in the eucharist. The ninth and tenth chapters of Paul's letter to convert the Hebrews explain how: "For the law having a shadow of good things to come, *and* not the very image of the things, can never with those sacrifices which they offered year by year continually make the comers thereunto perfect" (10:1). The poem continues to exploit Aquinan puns founded in Christian mystery and types of the eucharist.

In his own poems Southwell often refers to individual types. "Saint

Peters Complaint" more than once mentions David as a type of spiritual warrior foreshadowing Christ and tells of David's tearful contrition forecasting Peter's (277ff., 427–31). His poem refers as well to the rock of Horeb (as does "vii. His circumcision" [8–9]); just as Moses knocked twice, so Jesus' two eyes softened Peter's recalcitrant heart (439–44). In "At home in Heaven" Southwell recalls medieval and Renaissance popularizations of Samson as a type of Christ, the spiritual warrior, when he writes that in order to save us from human frailty Christ had to nestle in the flesh: "This lull'd our heavenly *Sampson* fast asleepe, / And laid him in our feeble natures lapp" (13–14).

Sometimes Southwell extended allusions to types by creating a whole poem out of strands of paradoxes and figurae. The *Ave/Eva* wordplay of "iv. The Virgins salutation" suggests the second Eve replacing the first, a topic which dates at least from early Gregorian chants; so do the second Eve and "*Elias* little cloude" (3) of "i. The Virgine Maries conception." And the figures in "ii. Her Nativity" follow Adam of St. Victor's hymns, which were widely circulated in *Elucidatorium Ecclesiasticum* by J. Clichtoveus.[30] The figures in "Christs bloody sweat," the Gethsemane poem that makes Southwell's typological eucharistic statement, provide further testimony.[31]

In addition to using allusions to types in ministering to the needs of his soul and the morale of his congregation, Southwell also explored converting Petrarchan lyric devices as well as employed sacred meditation. He sets down in a letter to his "loving Cosen" a vow to reclaim secular terrain for sacred poetic domains:

> Poets by abusing their talent, and making the follies and fayninges of love, the customary subject of their base endevours, have so discredited this facultie, that a Poet, a Lover, and a Liar, are by many reckoned but three wordes of one signification. But the vanity of men, cannot counterpoyse the authority of God, who delivering many partes of Scripture in verse, and by his Apostle willing us to exercise our devotion in Himnes and Spirituall Sonnets, warranteth the Arte to bee good. . . . I have heere layd a few course threds together, to invite some skillfuller wits to goe forward in the same.

In order to recover love poetry for sacred ends Southwell tried several means. The most obvious is parodying a particular secular lyric by changing key words, ideas, and outlines.[32] His easiest transformations were by reforming the stoicism in Sir Edward Dyer's "My mynde to me a kingdome is" to become the Christian humility of "Content and rich" and by converting a Dyer love lyric into "A Phansie turned to a sinners complaint." More originally he turned Petrarchan devices against themselves. He asks "What joy to live?" when someone is vacillating through the kind of manic-depression stemming from profane love he found described in Petrarch's *Rime* 134 and standard in English verse since Wyatt's "I fynde no peace and all my warr is done." Then he answers, as he also does in "Mans civill warre," "Lifes death loves life," "Loves servile lot," and "Lewd Love is Losse": joy comes when the lover turns from secular to sacred love. His most original adaptation was to convert common Petrarchan devices such as oxymora and conceits to express sacred love. Nor were all of his adaptations as farfetched as the address to the eyes of Christ rather than a mistress in "Saint Peters Complaint" (325–450) or as barren as the allegorical nursery of "Loves Garden grief." He presented love's emotional contrarieties in their absolute form, Christian charity, instead of in their distorted and debilitating reflection, sexual love: witness the paradoxical fiery tears of divine love in "The burning Babe." As this illustration implies, probably Southwell's most successful adaptation was converting Petrarchan love psychology so as to examine a sinful soul. In "A Phansie turned to a sinners complaint" he finds a paradigm for remorse in the forsaken lover whose dream is abused and whose poetry abuses God's gift. He transforms the lover's pangs into the Christian joy that rises out of a sinner's contrition: "Whose comfort is dismaid" becomes "Whose comfort is to rue" (2), so that the persona enacts saving penance.

Southwell employed both the conceit and the vacillation of a lover's soul in "Christs sleeping friends." The Petrarchan conceit of the poem is that of the storm-wracked ship, which floundered through English sonneteering after being launched in Wyatt's "My galy charged with forgetfulnes," his adaptation of *Rime* 189. But the threat to Southwell's soul does not come from collisions with outside objects. Rather, it comes from the speaker's remorseful projections of his vacillating sinful state, such as those opening "The prodigall childs soule wracke" or the longer "Saint Peters Complaint."

Besides imitating biblical models and parodying Petrarchan devices to express an inner analysis, Southwell sustained formal control of his poetry one more way: he adapted Jesuit techniques of meditating on one's conscience and on sacred events. Systematic meditation is clearest in the prayers to Christ on the cross by Mary and humanity in *Mæoniæ*, in the fourteen-poem sequence on the virgin and Christ, and in the smaller set on holy week written in the same stanzaic form.[33] "Christs sleeping friends" appears among Southwell's meditations on events in holy week, most intimately among the garden of Gethsemane poems. Through "Sinnes heavie loade" and "Christs bloody sweat" he reconsiders the agonies of Christ's preparations for atonement. "Christs sleeping friends" itself is divided into two initial stanzas of composition of place, three stanzas of analysis, and finally a double colloquy, the first with Christ and the second, "simultaneously a colloquy with the slumbering disciples and an exhortation to every sinner."[34]

By combining the motives, forms, and devices of religious meditation and Petrarchan parody with close association with Peter, the dominant sleeping disciple and momentary failure who thereby gave Southwell and his congregation hope, Southwell had almost found a new form of sacred lyric. By making the governing simile of "Christs sleeping friends" the type, Jonah, he was establishing the rudimentary English neotypological lyric. For it was precisely by projecting his all too human and sinful self and his parishioners into the potent interaction between a failed Old Testament type and a recovering New Testament event that Southwell opened up for himself and others a new kind of simile. By identifying their failure with a type's, they too could be redeemed by becoming identified with Christ. For the first time it was possible to simultaneously lament in humble anguish and celebrate in incomparable joy that one's very own unavoidable failures to meet the responsibilities of law and conscience were saved by Christ's dispensation of grace.

"Christs sleeping friends" retells the story of several disciples at Gethsemane while "Sinnes heavie loade" was pressing Christ prostrate until he begged relief if that be God's will, and "Christs bloody sweat" was graphically exacting his obedient sacrifice. The disciples' story is similar in all three synoptic gospels, though while Luke mentions the bloody sweat (22:39–46) he omits the names of Peter, James, and John, the sons of Zebedee, and the sequence of Christ's triple return (Matt. 26:36–46 and Mark 14:32–42). Christ had asked the three disciples to pray for delivery from temptation while waiting outside the garden; overcome with sorrow and fatigue, they failed by falling asleep; after returning twice to rouse them to renew their watch, he then allowed them to sleep before gently waking them for his betrayal by Judas.

The scene's dual message—they fail to perform their Christian duties and they are redeemed when Christ forgives them—embodies Southwell's concern with the central Christian paradox that recalls many Psalms. He can demand spiritual awareness and chastise failure, following the tradition of cockcrowing hymns initiated by Prudentius. At the same time he can demonstrate how Christ's encompassing compassion justifies men's failures, following hymns of remorse that include his own *Mæoniæ*. Southwell's concern was sanctioned by more than the obvious impact of the tale; it was supplemented by a line of Catholic exegetes conveniently epitomized in the early seventeenth-century *Commentaria* of Cornelius à Lapide.[35] According to most of these the disciples' acts at Gethsemane demonstrate not just the inevitability but even the desirability of temptation as a test of whether their faith merits reward (this, in spite of the lines from the Lord's Prayer): "Deus enim vult nos tentari, ut probet nostram fidum, & virtutem luctando augeat, meritáque & coronas nobis accersat, sed, *ut non intretis in tentationem*, ita scilicet ut illa vos occupet, possideat, dominetur."

Southwell follows the Catholic commentators by contrasting the sleeping disciples to the untiring vigilance of the powers of evil and Christ's capacity for vigilance under duress. The commentators' first contrast is the one Southwell overtly emphasizes. He warns priests to be vigilant against the powers of darkness, particularly in hard times of affliction, worry, and sorrow; to watch and pray for God's aid to avoid the fall of Judas, if not because of the danger that might befall Jesus, at least for personal salvation from the temptations of Satan's fraud: "Ecce hoc est remedium omnis tentationis, quod Christus hîc assignat; scilicet vigilia ad prævidendas & discutiendas diaboli, & hominum nos tentantium artes & fraudes: atque ad eas superandas oratio, & divinæ opis imploratio." By always staying on guard, birds avoid the snares threatened by Psalms. By being ever alert, the hook catches Jonah's great fish; that is, Christ catches Satan. Thus, following both the commentators and his own predilections, Southwell admonishes the disciples to wake up and watch for Jewish priests who, like Satan, are always prepared and alert to destroy Christ. His warnings are particularly straightforward at the end of the second and the beginning of the last stanzas. In the former he makes a harsh contrast: Christ's "foes did watch to worke their cruell spight, / His drousie friendes slept in his hardest plight" (11–12). Therefore in the latter he can exhort, "Awake ye slumbring wightes lift up your eies. . . . Arise and guarde the comforte of your lives" (37, 40).

But commentators also stress, whereas Southwell more covertly merely recognizes, Christ's understanding compassion for men. After all, they are doomed to failure under extreme duress: "Watch and pray, that ye enter not into temptation: the spirit indeed *is* willing, but the flesh *is* weak" (Matt. 26:41). As Irenaeus notes, men are incapable of bearing what Christ suffered; they escape in sorrowing sleep. Southwell follows the second of the commentators' contrasts implicitly. He shows that the disciples' sleep comes from the burden of their sorrows and sins rather than physical drowsiness. After Christ "full of feare without repose or rest / In agony did pray and watch in paine" (3–4), he finds his friends "With heavy eies, but farre more heavy mindes" (6).

The measure of God's grandeur and infinite grace (here Lapide cites Jerome and Origen) is Christ's capacity to endure temptations and burdens that flesh, mind, and spirit cannot bear. God's grace recovers human weakness. This is the message of the Gethsemane scene. Although some exegetes sense irony in Christ's final statement that the disciples need rest, Southwell prefers Christ's compassionate forgiveness: "With milde rebuke he warned them to wake" (7). Since Christ repairs men's failures, the implied, and greater, force in the poem is that his sacrifice compensates for unavoidable failures like those of his disciples.

Although it is inherent in the story itself, Southwell's message, that Christ grants mercy to those who fail while trying to carry out his commands, is more potent in the central comparison of the poem: Christ's disciples, and ultimately Southwell's congregation, are like Jonah who is a type of Christ. Southwell's *Epistle of Comfort* supplies the initial gloss. In drawing comfort from the persecutions suffered by recusants, he recalls that God's greatest tribulations are reserved for the faithful. Jonah, for example, escaped to sea rather than undertake a divine mission to Nineveh: " those whome God loueth, for that little which they haue offended, shall haue their stormes, and be cast into a sea of afflictions."[36]

Southwell does not refer directly to the typology of the whale story (Matt. 12:39–41) when he compares Jonah to Christ's sleeping disciples. Nor does he begin with Christ's reference to Jonah among the Ninevites (Luke 11:29–32). Instead, he first recalls how the putative prophet, whom God had ordered to convert the Ninevites, fled from his duty by sailing from Joppa to Tarshish. Jonah did his best not to hear God's call, by sleeping below decks through a storm God sent to rouse him. When discussing Jonah's sleep (1:5), Lapide's commentators focus less on Jonah's lack of desire and arduous voyage than on his remorseful, dejected inability to meet the demands and bear the sorrows of his calling. They compare his descent into the hold of the ship, that is, his escape into a secret, safe place, and his escape from duty by sleeping, to the sorrowful sleep of the disciples:

Partim ex fatigatione itineris, quod fecerat veniendo ex Zabulon in Joppen, partim & magis ex animi dejectione & mœrore. Sensit enim Jonas remorsus conscientiæ de fuga sua, quasi Deus illum persequeretur, puniret & comprehenderet: unde ut hos remorsus evaderet & sopiret, dedit se sopori. Mala enim conscientia parit mœrorem, mœror somnum: somnus enim mœrorem sepelit, cùm ejus cogitationem & sensum adimit. Hinc Apostoli Christo eunte ad passionem, præ tristitia sopore correpti sunt, Matth. 26.

Southwell's first comparison follows the commentators. The type who initially failed and then tried to sleep through both his failure and the rousing storm is like "these disciples [who] sleeping lie secure" (23) while stormy hatred threatens the ship of their salvation.

Southwell's second extended simile turns to another episode: Jonah among the Ninevites. Christ himself had declared that Jonah's conversion of the Ninevites damningly contrasted with the disbelief of pharisees he wanted to save: "The men of Nineveh shall rise in judgment with this generation, and shall condemn it: because they repented at the preaching of Jonas; and, behold, a greater than Jonas *is* here" (Matt. 12:41). The combination of these words from Christ in Matthew, Peter's call at Joppa to receive Gentiles into Christianity in Acts 10, and the dove (*Jonah*) as a traditional symbol of Israel laid the foundation for a typological tradition antedating Jerome. Jonah at Nineveh is a type of the promise of salvation to Gentiles. Southwell's comparison draws in the recusants. Just as Jonah's recalcitrance at offering Judaism to Gentiles caused him to evade his duty to God, so the recusants' fear of persecution could threaten their duty to Catholicism. This was an issue the poet often had to face, as he did in *An Epistle of Robert Southwell unto His Father*, who had converted to Anglicanism.

Southwell speaks powerfully to his parish when he compares the sleeping disciples to Jonah's watch outside Nineveh. After Jonah's reluctant resumption of his mission finally persuaded the city to repent, he became angry at God for not punishing the Ninevites' slowness; so he waited for their destruction in the shade of a gourd provided by God; when God's worm destroyed the plant, he railed more than before. Southwell's comparison to the sleeping disciples implies that evil in the form of a "cankered worme" took advantage of Jonah's moral fatigue ("him a heavy sleep opprest") in order to destroy his shelter (25–30). Taking the scene to be yet another exemplum of the need for vigilance against evil, he exhorts the disciples and his congregation to beware the destruction of their tree of life. But this is a misinterpretation.

In the biblical account Jonah's worm was not an agent of evil but an instrument sent by God to teach Jonah forgiveness. Jonah's anger against Nineveh and his pity for the gourd are misplaced. So God concludes:

47

"Should not I spare Nineveh?" The episode forms a lesson about mercy: God is merciful to those who sincerely repent their sins, even as he is merciful to the legalistic, recalcitrant Jonah who evaded his mission to the Gentiles. Commentaries from Gregory of Nazianzen and poems from Dracontius and Ennodius through the Middle Ages further point to God's mercy redeeming man's failures.[37] Thus, the major impetus of Southwell's comparison is not so much the need to beware of the powers of evil as it is the thanks owed to God for his merciful forgiveness of failure. Like other types, it gains force through the transformation of the old legal condemnation into the good news of salvation; it draws on the emotional impact of the relationship in the conversion.

The most assuring gospel in "Christs sleeping friends" depends on Southwell's audience recalling the popular type that is omitted from the poem while it is suggested by other comparisons—Jonah's delivery from the hell's mouth of the great fish. No commentator passed up the opportunities provided by both Matthew 12:40 and the beginning of Jonah to praise this type of Christ's descent into hell and ascent to resurrection. In Southwell's poem the message of mercy is most potently carried by an unexpressed but most familiar association.

Prefigurations in Jonah are not the only types carrying Southwell's message of God's mercy in spite of man's failure. The raging storm of "Jewish ire" (20), like the storm which menaces Jonah's ship, threatens to destroy the "barke of all our blisse" (22), thereby condemning itself also. Since both storms ultimately are instruments of God, the ship suggests a type behind the conceit of salvation. In context "barke" by rime and signification implies Noah's ark, a type of new covenant mercy in Christ and his church.[38] A more straightforward emblem of salvation is Southwell's conversion of Jonah's gourd (ivy or wild vine) to Christ, the tree of life:

> O gratious plant, O tree of heavenly spring,
> The paragon for leafe, for fruit and flower,
> How sweete a shadow did thy braunches bring
> To shrowd these soules that chose thee for their bower.
>
> (31–34)

Beyond the possible pun on *shadow*, here Southwell extends a message he explicates elsewhere by calling Christ the tree of life planted in Mary ("iii. Her Spousals" [7–8]).

The most interesting minor emblem of salvation in "Christs sleeping friends" is Southwell's final metaphor, that for "*Jonas* ivy" and tree of paradise—the "*Zacheus* tree." When the publican Zacchaeus climbed a sycamore in order to see Jesus, he clearly was climbing toward salvation (Luke 19:1–10). But commentators debated over the significance of the sycamore itself: some read it as *ficus*, a fig; others saw it as a mulberry, a combination of *siccus* (dry) and *morus* (foolish).[39] The latter must have been dear to English recusants: Lapide's annotation to Luke 19:4 specifically recalls Erasmus' punning phrase of Saint Thomas More, *Encomium Moriæ*. Perhaps alluding to a traditional recusant association with their martyr, the annotator refers to Paul's series of Christian paradoxes beginning with God's choice of the "foolish things of the world to confound the wise" (1 Cor. 1:27). The foolish mulberry becomes most wise, "Morus arborum prudentissima":

> Mysticè, sycomorus est crux Christi, ejusque doctrina, quæ Gentibus & terrenis hominibus visa est fatua, meraque stultitia, sed Zachæo & fidelibus visa fuit sapientia virtus Dei, 1 Corint. 2. Hinc & arbor vetita, è qua Adam comedens, se & posteros perdidit, à multis putatur fuisse sicus, ut dixi Genes. 2.9. Fuit utique sicus, ac fatua, quia sub modico melle & dulcedine, continuit fel & amaritiem peccati, mortis & gehennæ, quam proinde Christus expiare debuit felle & amaritie crucis & passionis suæ. Hinc múO Graecis non tantùm arborem morum, sed & cruciatum, mortem & eædem significat.

The annotator grants the sycamore eternal significance as Christ's cross, which offers the new sweet fruit of life by supplanting the tree of knowledge from which Adam ate the bitter dried out fruit of death. In culmination Zacchaeus' sycamore immediately exhorts Southwell's congregation to emulate the wise folly of the martyred English saint's vigilance and, at the same time, recalls salvation. It underscores the types that frame the whole poem.

To a degree remarkable in a pioneering effort, the design and style of "Christs sleeping friends" restate the narrative and typological dual message of exhortation to Christian duty and acknowledgement of salvation for those who truly try but inevitably fail. While the scene of Christ's agony during his friends' sleep opens and the image of the sycamore closes the seven-stanza poem with the message of salvation, the center provides comparisons of and calls to duty. Structure further balances the messages. The two opening stanzas conclude in a warning; they establish first the contrast to Christ's waking sacrifice and only afterwards the contrast to his waking foes. The central stanzas present two parallel comparisons, "As *Jonas* sayled" (the third and fourth) and "So *Jonas*" lay beneath a tree (the fifth and sixth). Again the transition (like that between the story and the comparison) is supplied by sleep. The first typological simile starts with the threat before it comes to the "Yet carelesse *Jonas*" (18) and "Yet these disciples" (23), whereas the mirror-image second typological simile begins with sleep and comes to the "cankered worme" (29) and the "envious worme" (36). As the sixth stanza extends the second simile it apostrophizes the Christ-tree, thereby mitigating the threats. Simultaneously it leads to the alarm of the final stanza: "Awake . . . Marke . . . Arise and guarde" (37–40). Southwell intertwines the paradoxical dual message of threat and hope so that mercy shines first and last.

Southwell further appears to reinforce his message of mercy by heavier alliteration and apostrophe, appropriate for God, in references to Christ. And his tense shifts centrally integrate verbal texture into the larger form. They reinforce the sense of a type transcending time, since a historical figure gains eternal moment by prophesying Christ's abolition of time's limits. In "Christs sleeping friends" Southwell's tense shifts indicate a simultaneous merging of and emerging from time. He converts into an eternity of salvation the referential gap between Old Testament prefiguration and New Testament fulfillment, which at first seems merely the use of the historical or prophetic present.

Southwell initially sets his poem in the past: Christ was "opprest" till he "did raine" blood. But he then "findes" (5) his disciples asleep. This shift to the present implies a connection with Southwell's readers, since they are threatened by both the universal malady of sin and the personal persecution that could drive them to desert Catholicism. After this single suggestion Southwell returns to the past to complete his scene. But when the similes of Jonah dominate the poem in the third through the sixth stanzas, Southwell renders Old Testament events in the past: "*Jonas* sayled once . . . [and] mute and sleeping lay" (13, 18); Jonas "Did shrowd himselfe" (26). He then takes advantage of that shift in time to place the disciples with his readers in the present: "So now though *Judas* like a blustring gust, / Doe stirre . . . Yet these disciples sleeping lie secure" (19–20, 23). Thus Southwell can call the disciples now to save "the glorie of your arbor [who] dies": "Awake ye slumbring wightes lift up your eies, / Marke" (37–39). And while he is calling them he is also now exhorting his readers to "Arise and guarde the comforte of your lives" (40). But, for Southwell and his parishioners, Christ's death for human salvation is God's predetermined interaction in the world, an eternal event redeeming historical believers for eternity.

The tense shift from two "thens" into two "nows" suggests the collapsing of past and present into the eternal referent. Southwell has once again exploited the allusive potential of both a New Testament and a recent historical association as they are directed and driven by typological identification by his manipulation of tenses just as he did by his local style, by his overall design, by his meditative structure and introspective analysis, and by his appropriation of Petrarchan image complex, conceit, and psychological portrayal. His major contribution was to demonstrate, by releasing some of the potential latent in rigorously defined and closely applied types, a new form of English sacred lyric. Though further developments, like those following from Alabaster's self-consciously and intensely applied definition and examination, were still to come, it was Southwell who discovered the rudiments of the neotypological lyric.

† † †

It seems most unlikely that William Alabaster's poetic career could have achieved the brief incandescence of his *Divine Meditations* except for his dramatic conversion to Catholicism, which wrenched him away from his family's staunch Protestantism, his Anglican chaplaincy and living, and his fiancée, and drew him into preparation for Jesuit priesthood.[40] For it was apparently during the period stretching from troubles in his theological studies (Michaelmas 1596), through his conversion, his arguments with and cross-examination by Anglican mentors, to his seclusion under Catholic care before his escape to Douay (September 1598), that he wrote the more than seventy sonnets. These intense introspections seem to be among the most personal of the neotypological lyrics; and the consequence of his self-examinations through sonnets is that Alabaster's primary attribute and contribution to the form is self-awareness and formal definition. As he looked into himself, an act he apparently repeated often in his vacillations between faiths until finally deciding on Anglicanism in 1613, he turned his considerable intellectual ingenuity toward Jesuit meditation and confession and toward Petrarchan psychology and conceits. In doing so he developed a number of intricate analyses of his poetic speaker who is identified with several types, most often the penitent David.

The vehemence of Alabaster's conversion to a new allegiance is indicated by sonnet nine cursing Luther and labeling his marriage with a nun incest and by "76. *An Invective Against Calvin*" naming him hell's minister. The depth of Alabaster's commitment is reflected in the sequence "*Upon the Ensigns of Christ's Crucifying*" and his emotional involvement with the cross. And the individual quality of Alabaster's confessions is most apparent in the "*Personal Sonnets.*" All three of these strong personal emotions precluded the kind of searching doubt and fear of his own ca-

51

pacity that is found in Southwell's journal of preparations for the priest-hood, *Exercitia et Devotiones*. Instead, this comparable record of Alabas-ter's preparation is more marked by sonnets dedicating himself to service and vowing devoted obedience to whatever religious tasks Christ re-quires of him. For example, he not only concludes sonnet "40. *To Christ* (2)" and opens its following companion by echoing Samuel's answer to God's call, "Lo here I am, lord, whither wilt thou send me?" but also closes repetitiously with, "Lord I am here, O give me thy commission." Consequently it is no surprise to discover in Alabaster none of South-well's comfort for sustaining a congregation and much less of his humil-ity in associating with types. In fact, in Alabaster's opening sonnet the speaker identifies so directly with Christ himself that it promises only a few sonnets embellished with traditional figurae, not the neotypological lyrics which follow.

Alabaster announces in the opening sonnet that he will imitate Christ's song. Closely associating with sacrifice, he recalls Christ's preparation for spiritual warfare at Gethsemane: "And when they had sung an hymn, they went out into the mount of Olives" (Matt. 26:30, Mark 14:26). After an octave description of Christ's paradoxes, Alabaster's sestet marches lyrically to an Anglican inquisition:

> Then since my holy vows have undertook
> To take the portrait of Christ's death in me,
> Then let my love with sonnets fill this book,
> With hymns to give the onset as did he,
> That thoughts inflamed with such heavenly muse,
> The coldest ice of fear may not refuse.

In the second sonnet he claims that, like Christ, he is granted a song of triumph in anticipation of his victory over suffering. The gift of song is for him a mark of grace: "To style Christ's praise with heavenly muse's wing, / Of grace and merit and reward hath store" (36. 1–2). Such a grace he recalls frequently, especially in the subordinate sequence on the mystery of the incarnation (53–67). At first Alabaster continues to follow Christ across the Cedron up to Mount Olivet and through the scourg-ings, vowing with considerable hope and perhaps a tinge of ego as well as trust never to forsake his lord as others have, and praying for aid.

But continually in such hints as the brief comparison in the second sonnet of Christ the sun/Son to the giant exulting in a race (Psalms 19:5), Alabaster is indicating in two ways the possibility of using types. One is heard in his echoes of types. The more important appears in his references to the predicaments of Peter, and especially in his association with David, a primary type whose Psalms Alabaster's language, images, and thought particularly allude to. In fact his third sonnet is based on David being a type:

Over the brook of Cedron Christ is gone,
To entertain the combat with his death,
Where David fled beforetime void of breath,
To scape the treacheries of Absolom.

(1–4)

David's flight across the Cedron during Absalom's revolt is told in 2 Samuel 15:23 and commemorated in the third Psalm. It prefigures Christ crossing the Cedron and temporarily escaping the valley of Gehenna and Moloch, both types of hell, into the garden of Gethsemane. G. M. Story's introduction to Alabaster's sonnets points out that this poem utilizes "a complex tissue of allegory and 'moralization'," for "The sonnet contains a scriptural allusion, a meditation on an incident in the life of Christ, and a reflection on the poet's own predicament, all three 'meanings' simultaneously explicit within the framework of the tradition of scriptural allegory."[41] Story's evaluation is important though misleading. It rightly emphasizes Alabaster's ingenuity and learning displayed by his use of a typological situation as well as a New Testament incident for evaluating his persona. But it erroneously considers Alabaster a medieval Catholic figuralist, which is only partly accurate.

It is true that some of Alabaster's known extravagances in figural allegorizing support such a possibility. His *Apparatus in Revelationem Jesu Christi* (1607), a scholarly interpretation of scriptural mysteries extending types, went so far beyond most Tridentines that it was proscribed as heretical and placed on the Index while he was imprisoned by the Inquisition.[42] In the tract he derives mystical meanings from Old Testament prophecies and etymologies as well as from types, relying heavily on Joseph's and Daniel's dream interpretations and on New Testament parables. In one representative instance he takes the snake God sent to destroy Jonah's gourd to be the elevated brazen serpent, a type of Christ celebrated in such popular works as Robert Cawdrey's *Treasurie or Storehouse of Similies* (1600).[43] This indicates the kind of overingenious elaboration that Alabaster was able to conjure for his sonnets such as the thirty-second, "*Upon the Crucifix* (2)," where he refers to the bunch of grapes

53

(Gen. 49:11, Num. 13, and Isa. 63:1–3) that predict Christ, the true vine (John 15:1–8),[44] and the thirty-seventh, in which he exploits Marian figures.

But Alabaster can also restrict and concentrate his poetic use of types; in the opening of his twentieth sonnet, he compares old and new Adams, as they appear in 1 Corinthians 15:21–22:

> See how the world doth now anew begin;
> Another Adam born of blessed mould
> Doth come into a garden as of old,
> Within a garden for to conquer sin,
> Which at the Garden first did enter in.

In fact, in his *Divine Meditations* he is habitually not just thorough in his applications of types to his speaker's immediate predicaments, as Story and Gardner suggest, but he is also rather strict in using them.

In closely identifying with the thorns that wounded Christ's head while meditating "*Upon the Ensigns of Christ's Crucifying*," Alabaster created a context that could stimulate figural allegory. But instead he chose to restrict and intensify this type, deriving from God's first judgment:

> The earth, which in delicious Paradise
> Did bud forth man like cedars stately tall,
> From barren womb accursed by the Fall,
> Doth thrust forth man as thorns in armed wise,
> Darting the points of sin against the skies.
> With those thorns platted was Christ's coronal,
> Which crowned him then with grief.
>
> (26. 1–7)

The speaker first recalls that primeval man was created like a cedar, called by Bateman the queen of trees. The fatal irony is doubled in the encyclopedist's claim that the good "smell of [the cedar] driueth away Serpents and al manner of venimous wormes, as the faith."[45] It could have been compounded through further allusions, such as those listed in Picinello's catalogue of significations for the cedar, which include birth and fecundity in the Virgin Mary beyond that bestowed by God's grace.[46] Rather than referring to God's judgment against Eve, however, the speaker acknowledges his own sins among mankind's thistled fields. Then Christ's crown of thorns relieves him of the thorns of sin. Guild succinctly provides the texts from both the old and the new covenants:

54

"Thornes were made a curse to the one, *Gen*. 3.17. *So were they made a crowne to the other*, Mat. 27.29." [47] What had been ironic and implicit early in the sonnet becomes dominant. Christ recovers the condemned speaker and mankind:

> but after all
> In heaven shall crown him, crowned themselves with glory;
> For with the purple tincture of his blood,
> Which out the furrows of his brows did rain,
> He hath transformed us thorns from baser wood,
> To raise our nature and odious strain,
> That we, who with our thorny sins did wound him,
> Hereafter should with roseal virtues crown him.

The failure of the type is made good by the atonement. By enduring the thorny crown of man's punishment Christ transforms his congregation into his crown of glory. The metamorphosis portrayed is still grander because believers are restored as primal spineless roses. This faintly intimates, perhaps, association with the Virgin Mary as well as with Christ's grace,[48] but it does not provide the elaboration or celebration of traditional medieval figural allegory.

Thus, Story and Gardner's term *allegory* is too figural and medieval to describe Alabaster's customary Counter-Reformed practice in his sonnets, even in the third where the speaker identifies with Peter as well as with David. This interpretation is corroborated by Lapide's notes to the account in Samuel which delineate precise parallels between the flights from predators of these two kings, of the Hebrews, and of all believers. Augustine's comparison in the *Ennarations* shows how the crux in line five of the third Psalm (through God's sustenance David can rise from sleep) foreshadows Christ's resurrection. He applies the resurrection to ecclesia; others cited by Lapide apply it to the individual soul. Alabaster applies type and fulfillment: "Go let us follow him in passion, / Over this brook, this world that walloweth" (5–6). The concluding allusion to Peter's attempt to cross the storm-tossed water to Christ (Matt. 14: 24–33) distills the essence of the poem: "Now we are up, now down, but cannot stand, / We sink, we reel, Jesu stretch forth thy hand." Both Peter's and the poet's efforts to imitate Christ fail because of lapses in faith; both therefore beg Christ's helping hand. In the third sonnet Alabaster relies on types, not allegories. This is because his self-analysis in terms of a type relies on faith in the power of Christ's interacting merciful justification. Hence, Alabaster has written a neotypological lyric.

Still, Alabaster often cleverly expands as he intensifies the application of a Reformed definition of types to the self-examination of his speaker. His ingenious elaboration appears in his use of techniques of systematic meditation and in his parody of Petrarchan psychology and conceits. Meditative techniques are particularly prominent through the middle "*Penitential Sonnets*," "My soul a world is by contraction" (15) and its sequel. Little need be said of these since the central sonnet, which is self-explicating, has been paraphrased by Helen Gardner and by Louis L. Martz.[49] The opening proposes an analogy between the poet's soul and the macrocosm; the initial analysis carries through his loving devotions, while the sun, imitating the Son, draws forth his tears; at the last, in lines approaching colloquy or answering a colloquy, he sheds tears of contrition (analyzed in the following sonnet) which become efficacious through Christ's grace.[50]

Alabaster becomes more profound than intellectually clever and elaborate when he parodies the devices of Petrarchan love psychology and the intricacy of Petrarchan conceits. His profundity is gained in large part because both the psychology and the major conceit of contrite tears are derived from the Psalms, particularly the penitential Psalms of David, the type of universal Christian experience especially identified with poets. And it is still more affecting because during the Counter-Reformation continental Catholics had created in meditations and verse an intense rhetorical and imagistic complex around tears as emblems of worship which, through contrition, simultaneously include both penance and consolation.[51] Alabaster employs this use at the opening of the *Divine Meditations*, in the speaker's explicit association with David and the Cedron crossing, as well as in the later "*Penitential Sonnets*."

Alabaster's refinement of Petrarchan erotic contrary passions into Christian agape appears frequently: in his persona cooling lawless flames by seeking the arbor of Christ on the cross (33), in his playing witty word games with blood and fire (48), and in his vacillating under the influence of sin (52). Emotional oscillations reach a climax in the sixty-ninth sonnet, "Of the Motions of the Fiend." Just as David's, or a lover's, feelings vacillate, so Satan freezes the persona into languor and burns him with lust. But by reminding him of Christ, heavenly charity transforms psychic contention into sacred *concors discordia*. The persona's love of Christ melts icy sluggishness into tears of contrition and his fear of judgment cools lust to shame. Then paradoxically, the shame, with heat from God, cools his worldly lusts, whereas the tears, with cold from God, warm his lazy heart. Of course, such operations by grace are mysteries that can only be fleetingly imagined and roughly approximated. They

56

may, however, be begged from God and confirmed on the natural level
by reason:

> O happy I if that such grace were wrought!
> Till then, shame blush because tears cannot weep,
> And tears weep you because shame cannot blush,
> Till shame from tears, and tears from shame do flush.

The conclusion on the natural level—blushes of shame rouse tears of
remorse and tears in turn rouse shame—leads the persona to contrition
and penance, which testify to the workings of faith in him as in David.
Alabaster relies on Christ's grace to convert secular love into sacred parody, thereby saving the poem and the poet, just as he affirms that Christ's
grace sanctifies the Psalms and David.

Alabaster's tear imagery operates like a Petrarchan conceit to sustain a
traditional Davidic and Christian motif wherein tears signify remorse
and purgation at the same time. Tear imagery thus confirms the Cedron
type, flowing into the dual, contrary psychic impulse of human humiliation transformed into transcending exaltation by God's grace, which
characterizes Christian interpretation of the penitential Psalms. In the
fourth sonnet the persona cannot cross the Cedron for sticking in the
sinful mire of the world:

> O shine upon me with thy blessed face,
> O rain upon me with a shower of grace,
> And dry this winter-swelling with thy love,
> And with my brooks of tears this brook remove.
>
> (9–12)

Therefore he initially prays to Christ for the water of grace; then he asks
that Christ grant him tears of contrition to purge the mire of the brook.
Both are necessary for salvation. Remorse for his failure unites with joy
over receiving grace, reconfirming the dual neotypological lyric impulse
from Psalms.

Tear conceits are especially important through the "*Penitential Sonnets*"
because they represent the persona's self-urgings: "Then run, O run /
Out of mine eyes tears of compunction" (12. 4–5); "Why should the fruit
look withered and unsound? / Is it for want of rain? It is, I know"
(13. 7–8). Such outcries resemble the sixth Psalm where David weeps till
his bed swims. Like it, they establish the remorse essential for penance,
which leads to salvation. In the eighteenth sonnet, the climax of this

series, Alabaster seems to be imitating further the Petrarchan paradoxes of Southwell's "Burning Babe." Tears and flames feed each other instead of contending: "my tears do with flame of love conspire" (3). Therefore the speaker concludes that contrition and love are heavenly and spiritual rather than mundane and physical. He weeps in love and so loves to weep:

> For love of Christ to tears mine eyes do turn,
> And melted tears do make my soul to burn,
> And burning love doth make my tears more deep,
> And deeper tears cause love to flame above.
>
> (9–12)

Contrite repentance leads in turn to purification—but it is beyond man's capability without God's help, as all commentators on the fifty-first Psalm agreed. When David asks God to forgive and cleanse him ("Purge me with hyssop, and I shall be clean: wash me, and I shall be whiter than snow" [7]), he is recognizing that his own tears of repentance merely initiate purification. The lustration which David requests, and which is required by such passages as Exodus 19:10 and Numbers 19:7, 19, can be initiated by human tears but achieved only by Christ's blood, according to Hebrews 9:13–14 and 1 John 1:7. The best known example is the penitent Mary Magdalene who, by washing Christ's feet with her tears (Luke 7:36–50), became an emblem of ecclesia and especially of love. Lapide's commentators universally applaud Christ's statements in the forty-seventh and forty-eighth verses. When Christ's grace transformed her penance into purgation, her contrition into justification, a whore turned into an exemplar: "*Quis sensus formæ absolutionis cùm absolvitur pænitens jam justificatus per contritionem.*"

In his seventy-first sonnet Alabaster proceeds by making a simile of the perspective portrait in order to describe two vantages for viewing the passion:

> When without tears I look on Christ, I see
> Only a story of some passion,
> Which any common eye may wonder on;
> But if I look through tears Christ smiles on me.
>
> (1–4)

The manuscript title, "The Difference 'twixt Compunction and Cold Devotion in Beholding the Passion of Our Saviour," is instructive. But this instruction supplies only half of the relationship as Alabaster indi-

cates in the persona's request for Chirst's aid: bend down from the cross
and cleanse my tears with your blood. Though contrition is necessary to
instigate salvation, even that contrition has to be granted by Christ:

> Then since tears see the best, I ask in tears,
> Lord, either thaw mine eyes to tears, or freeze
> My tears to eyes, or let my heart tears bleed,
> Or bring where eyes, nor tears, nor blood shall need.
>
> (11–14)

Alabaster's full theological explanation of his tear imagery appears in
the sixty-eighth sonnet, "A Morning Meditation (I)." The persona's eyes
open early one black morning to discover personal darkness, since he has
not yet thought of Christ. When he recalls the sun/Son of God, a day
figuratively begins to break in his soul. As this false predawn light breaks
out of the poet's shame, morning dew (perhaps, with the pun on Christ
being all, hinting at manna, one type of the eucharist) condenses in the
poet's tears of repentance. The light of shame and the dew of repentance
prepare him for a true dawn:

> Then let my shame a blazing morning spread,
> And from mine eyes let crystal dew be shed,
> Dew of repentance to wash out this blot,
> And shame to blush that Christ was so forgot,
> That Christ arising may wipe from my face,
> My tears with mercy and my shame with grace.

Here Christ's mercy and grace are to perfect the contrite tears of the
penitent so that the dawn is not merely for one day of the soul but, in the
allusion to the vision of the blessed in Revelation, for eternity: "And God
shall wipe away all tears from their eyes" (7:17, 21:4).

Alabaster's intensely applied association of the type David and his penitential Psalms with their joint contrition and exaltation, together with
his parody of a Petrarchan lover's oscillations, his ingenious use of the
Davidic and Petrarchan conceit of tears of contrition, and his intellectually rigorous formal meditation, all as they are being perfected by the
grace of the antitype reach epitome in his seventieth sonnet, "A Morning
Meditation (2)." Moreover, this neotypological lyric derives its power
from applying for the purpose of self-analysis still another transforming
type of Christ, the rainbow.

"The sun begins upon my heart to shine" radiates beyond the conceit
of the poet as a microcosm and the sacred pun on Son. In the first

quatrain Alabaster imagines that a prismatic cloud of feelings, passing between the persona and the Son, fragments pure light so as to display an analytic spectrum:

> The sun begins upon my heart to shine,
> Now let a cloud of thoughts in order train
> As dewy spangles wont, and entertain
> In many drops his Passion divine.

Starting from the hint (in dew) of manna, the speaker can anatomize Christ's passion that makes the antitypical eucharist efficacious. For Christ's illuminating love has been condensed, reflected, and distributed:

> That on them, as a rainbow, may recline
> The white of innocence, the black of pain,
> The blue of stripes, the yellow of disdain,
> And purple which his blood doth well resign.
>
> (5–8)

This unlikely set of colors separates into two groups, each one displaying a double message. The white, blue, and yellow, traditional for the Christian virtues faith, hope, and charity, become as well reminders of the price Christ paid in his discolored marring by physical and psychological scourgings. The black of death and royal purple of redeeming blood recall that Christ's sacrificial death was required in order for the souls of men to gain eternity. The pun on *resign* reinforces the dual impact. Christ in anguish surrenders his blood for man's salvation and Christ reveals a new covenant with mankind when he signs yet another agreement with man.

Alabaster centers on the rainbow. More than being the sign of one covenant in the series that leads to God's final agreement about man's salvation, the rainbow is a type. Commentators indulged themselves in expounding the significance gained by the rainbow when God chose it as the seal of his promise to Noah that he would never again flood the world (Gen. 9:8–17). As explicated in Lapide's collected commentaries on the thirteenth verse, God promises mankind to exchange *arcus*, his bow of wrath, for *iris*, his sign for peace; moreover, he renews this compact after each rain, symbolic of regenerative grace. Ambrose explains that the rainbow is a sign of God's mercy: "Iris, inquit, est clementia Dei, quæ quasi arcus contentus, sed carens sagitta, per adversa quæ immittit, magis terrere nos vult, quàm ferire, ut vitia corrigamus, itáque sagittas vindictæ evadamus." Augustine, Gregory, and Ticontius, according to Lapide, claim that the rainbow's semicircle suggests God's compassion and justice; they also compare the rainbow to the apocalypse.

Such readings led to examinations of the rainbow as a type, particularly as a type of Christ's new covenant. The rainbow signifies the evangels, the good news of Christ's remission of sin, and his grace which transports men to glory. The rainbow further signifies baptism. Most important, the rainbow displays the incarnate Word of God: "*iris est Verbum carne vestitum ob septem analogias.*" There are seven analogies to the Word derived from the rainbow: it displays the sun's radiation of grace; it depicts the reconciliation of the world; its two horns denote Christ's human and divine natures; it recalls Christ's heavenly origin in blue, his grace and virtue in yellow, and his sacrificial blood in red; it shoots hidden arrows of true love; it shows the pentecost of abundance in rain; its semicircle shows Christ's descent from heaven to earth and return from earth to heaven. Finally, indicating the dual force of a type, its semicircle demonstrates the imperfection of this life which is yet to be perfected by Christ in the eternal circle. Almost incidentally for commentators, the colors of the rainbow show faith, hope, and charity, by which men initiate their purgation, illumination, and perfection in Christ, paralleling Christian history from the first destruction by a blue flood to the last, by a red conflagration.

Although Alabaster invokes a complex and various type, its analytic diversity is unified by always signifying the Son's grace, as grace is forever manifested in the sunlight that creates the rainbow. At more than one of those crucial moments when Alabaster is looking for the Son of God through contrite tears, he remembers that the rainbow is a type of Christ's salvation. When, for example, he inquires into Mary Magdalen's tears over the disappearance of Christ's body (21), he concludes by seeing Christ's covenant of salvation through his own tears:

> and when my tears are done
> Mine eyes and heart shall after him pursue,
> Until his grace into mine eyes return,
> And beams reflect upon my rainbow's dew,
> And in my heart I feel his love to burn.[52]

In the third quatrain of sonnet seventy Alabaster triples the effects of seeing salvation by Christ through his soul's contrition. Devout thoughts

produce tears; through these contrite tears the visionary can see the covenant of grace in the rainbow; these mirrors or lenses that reflect God's
grace darkly until he may be seen face to face, allow poetic imitation:

> And let these thousand thoughts pour on mine eyes
> A thousand tears as glasses to behold him,
> And thousand tears, thousand sweet words devise
> Upon my lips as pictures to unfold him.

The poet's words in examining and instigating redeeming penance in his
persona imitate the Word. Like typological rainbows, they distribute for
analysis the manifold mercies of the new covenant of love and display the
sun/Son of God. All men faithfully depend on the incarnate Word.

Alabaster's capping couplet confirms his characteristic trinity.[53] Not
only does the triune meditation exercise the threefold psyche (memory,
reason, and will), all three central terms of the poem reflect the mystery
of the Trinity:

> So shall reflect three rainbows from one sun,
> Thoughts, tears, and words, yet acting all in one.

Here the poet imitates Christ indirectly, ingeniously, and most of all originally, by examining his persona in comparison to a type that displays the
mystery of the Trinity of compassion.

Alabaster's sonnets are the most fully developed self-conscious neotypological lyrics in English during the sixteenth century. His contribution lies in consistent, sustained, intensive, and intellectual self-analysis,
based on close alliance with, comparison and contrast to types. He did
not merely recognize Southwell's discovery; he extended and system-
atized it, tapping more of its expressive potential. This expressiveness
he gained through associations with the type David, the contrite sinner
purged and exalted through humiliation. It is derived from David's own
Psalms and the heritage of psalmody intensified in the Counter-Reformation. Central elements from that heritage were expanded and elaborated
by Alabaster through Petrarchan love psychology and the conceit of tears
of contrition that lead to saving purification in Christ's blood. Just as all
these elements are empowered by the interactions of dual references in
types, so his own closely applied governing types supply the ultimate
meaning and impact in his self-analysis. If he does not explicate himself

as a universal seeking soul like the emblematists, or dramatize himself in a neotype for his congregation's salvation like Donne, Alabaster did tap a considerable resource and indicated such further capabilities when he defined and examined himself through the rudimentary neotypological lyric.

3

Explicating the Heart and Dramatizing the Poet

Seventeenth-Century Innovations by English Emblematists and Donne

By the end of the sixteenth century, a number of sacred motivations had encouraged the development and integration of a cluster of poetic elements into an identifiable neotypological lyric. And Southwell and Alabaster had begun releasing some of the expressive potential in a Reformed and Counter-Reformed definition and application of types. The psalmodists' portrayal of David's typical soul had expressed simultaneous remorse for sin and joy over salvation. Some poets' gradual development of a dominant typological simile had allowed their humble sense of salvation to surface amid their mounting burden of sin. Their adaptation of Petrarchan devices for more personal portrayal of a speaker and conceits for understanding him and their application of formal religious meditation for self-analysis channeled the expression. All culminated when Southwell and his congregation derived comfort from a persona identified with a type in a neotypological lyric. And all contributed to Alabaster's extension of the lyric, that of defining and self-consciously, ingeniously analyzing himself in a neotype.

When emblematists from the end of the sixteenth through the early seventeenth centuries parsed their situation in a symbol-filled world, they expanded self-explication into the explanatory narratives of a universal believer's heart. This movement broadened audience sympathies and sometimes extended the impact of the neotypological lyric. When, on what he described as his deathbed, Donne prayed, "As the first *Adams* sweat surrounds my face, / May the last *Adams* blood my soule embrace," he was dramatizing a neotypological lyricist inside a crucial scene from that universal believer's life. Such an exemplary life and scene served to confirm the faithful and to convert others to the congregation.

† † †

Those Renaissance writers who developed English emblem books from continental models (most often writing for continental prints) were doing more than reinforcing public recognition of types and neotypological readings. They were also enhancing the neotypological lyricists' expressiveness by developing two important techniques: self-explication and narrative context. Displaying a print and then explaining its importance in a poem (with an epigram or other paraphernalia) provides one means of drawing universal significances from the particulars of the world, of understanding human and divine and especially mystical relationships beyond discrete natural things. In the interaction of their dual referents, emblems are the close kin of types. Thus, as emblem literature evolved from the discovery of Horapollo's *Hieroglyphica* in 1419 through the frequent reprinting of Andreas Alciati's 1531 *Emblematum Liber* to the adaptations of Catholic devotional emblems such as Herman Hugo's *Pia Desideria* in 1624, it nourished both poets' references and readers' responses to types.[1] As their art developed, emblematists often applied their emblems to individual ethical stances and moral crises, further expanding the tendencies of psalmody and Petrarchan parody to analyze universal psychic conditions by analogues from the world and from types. Beyond that, the emblem tradition extended this mode of self-interpretation that had developed from the use of hieroglyphics to interpret the world. Emblematists were anatomizing various individual religious scenes and states, and narrating the universal Christian's progress.

The first native English emblem book that is notable for its typological references is *Sacrorum emblematum centuria una* (ca. 1591) by the antipapal Dr. Andrew Willet. Among Willet's poems of natural emblems appears a series of thirty-one "Emblemata Typica sive Allegorica." Two extraordinary emblems are tucked into his discontinuous, commonplace discussions of Noah's ark as a type of Christ and the flood as a type of baptism (18), manna as a type of salvation (41), and Melchizedek as a type of Christ as priest, king, and judge instead of prophet (63). Emblem eight, *Ecclesia veritatis columna*, Zechariah 4:3, is instructive by the detail of its description, which perhaps resulted from the collection's lack of plates. In this emblem Willet finds one-to-one correspondences between objects and their significances so as to defend the Anglican and attack the Roman establishment:

The Church and house of Christ is this candlesticke,
The lampes doe shew forth Gods graces manifolde,

The pipes which runne oyle signifie ministers,
This oyle the spirit is, Christ is the oliue tree,
Alwaies at their neede, he readie is at hand,
As running spring his Prophets he cherisheth.[2]

Even with his extravagances, the emblematist's carefully detailed significances support the meticulous application of typological analogues to
current affairs. But this is less strictly Reformed and less significant than
the advance of his seventy-second emblem, based on Exodus 34:1. For
that emblem documents two early innovations, the association of people
with types and the representation of the heart as a type. Willet does not
merely discuss the precepts of the stony decalogue; he declares the hard
law of justice one type of the merciful promise of eternity. This initial
English allusion echoed throughout seventeenth-century emblem books.
The verse concludes with an application to the reader:

Againe I pray thee to behould,
These letters grauen in stony mould,
So God can chaunge the stony hart
And write his law in th' hardest part.[3]

This personalization is significant in that it reinforces a continuing tendency toward both the universal personalization of types and the establishment of typological scenes and stories for neotypological personae.

One follower of both tendencies in Willet is represented by the anti-
transubstantiationist Thomas Jenner. In *The Soules Solace, or Thirtie and
one Spiritual Emblems* (1626) he frequently places the type David as a universal Christian example inside the emblem tradition.[4] But the emblematist who extends the use of emblems and types into narrative scenes and
finally tells the tale of the universal, seeking Christian is Francis Quarles.

Beyond occasionally exhibiting types, Francis Quarles' exceedingly
popular *Emblemes* (1635) provides a Protestant adaptation of the continental Jesuit tradition of Hugo's *Pia Desideria* and the anonymous *Typus
Mundus* (1627). It first exemplifies individual self-interpretations, then
follows the development of a semi-neotypological lyricist's soul to tell the
story of a faithful member of the congregation.[5] Quarles' awareness of
typology is evident from quotations such as the one from St. Augustine
after the first emblem of the third book, which mentions Christ as the
sun of righteousness in a world of darkness. His most inventive semi-
typological allegory refers to the prophecy of Christ made in the promise

that Eve's seed would bruise the serpent's head. The reference appears in his description of a hart/heart panting after the brooks of God (Psalms 42:1) in the eleventh emblem of book five. Ripped by the pack, the blood draws "a Serpent, but in shape a Hound: / We strove, he bit me; but thou brak'st his back" (31–32); then the heart continues its flight to the savior.[6] Such occurrences are rare, despite Quarles' apparent promise "To the Reader," "Let not the tender Eye check, to see the allusion to our blessed Saviour figured in these Types." More often he expands these promised allusions to types into scriptural metaphors for Chirst, such as sower, fisherman, or physician.

Quarles searches further for human emblems as he reads God in natural emblems. He develops a sequence explicating a pilgrim soul searching through justice in order to find God's mercy. His major contribution— the psychological presentation of a soul looking for sanctity—does not open the *Emblemes*. It comes gradually, after initial emblems beginning with Eve and the serpent establish the theme of *contemptu mundi*. In the eleventh emblem of the first book self-presentation and explication begin to emerge from homily; through the second book, addresses to the world and personifications of virtues and vices initiate the parable of a soul's pilgrimage in search of mercy surrounded by a world of failure. Emblems early in the third book continue to portray the soul's search for the light, the life, and the way of Christ; then the tenth and twelfth emblems explicate how the dispensation of justice becomes one of mercy, in a transfer that corresponds to typology. The sixth through the eighth stanzas of IV. ii incorporate, in the epiphany to the wisemen who followed the star to Bethlehem, the type-laden story of the chosen people who followed the pillar of cloud and fire out of Egypt's hell through Sinai to the Promised Land. Finally, when in III. xiii Quarles begs salvation during his lifetime pilgrimage through a sinful world ("Draw not that soul which would be rather led; / That *Seed* has yet not broke my Serpent's head; / O shall I dy before my sinnes are dead?" [40–42]), he sets a precedent for Christopher Harvey, whose work divines a narrative through the self-explication of emblems.

Harvey's *The School of the Heart* (1647) presents an overly obvious exercise in self-explication. As with Herbert, he shows the culmination of the emblem tradition. Even though, as Rosemary Freeman has demonstrated, he appropriated most of his plates and his overall narrative scheme of separation, trials in absence, search for and return to God from the Jesuit Benedict van Haeften's *Schola Cordis* (1629), he owes his immediate source little more.[7] His real teachers, whom he has taken to typological ends, belong to the native tradition of reading the heart. It is to them that he owes his displacement of image by language, his concentration on rhetoric rather than emblem, his development of self-explication in crucial scenes that explore the archetypal story of a member of the congregation. The coda, beginning with "The Preface" to "The Learning of the Heart," explains all:

> I am a scholar. The great Lord of love
> And life my Tutor is; Who from above
> All that lack learning to His school invites;
> My heart's my prayer-book, in which He writes
> Systemes of all the arts and faculties:
> First reads to me, then makes me exercise.
>
> (1–6)

Since his heart is a novice the speaker remains with the elementary trivium instead of passing to the higher scholastics of the quadrivium. He defines "The Grammar of the Heart" as the art "Which teacheth me to write and speak mine heart" (2) truly, that is, in accord with the Bible. Thus his elementary diction, like Southwell's and Alabaster's, Peter's and David's, is made up of the sighs, groans, and tears of Old Testament contrition. Such repentance is heard ultimately, he claims, because it has no parts or particles. Instead of linguistic divisions it is resolved in the union of mercy: "What-ere my letters are, my word's but one, / And all the meaning of it love alone" (15–16). His "Rhetorick of the Heart" is the Christian plain style, that simple, inspired expression of Christ's overflowing charity:

> My rhetorick is not so much an art
> As an infused habit in mine heart,
> Which a sweet secret elegance instills,
> And all my speech with tropes and figures fills.
> Love is the tongue's elixir, which doth change
> The ordinary sense of words.
>
> (1–6)

"The Logick of the Heart" bypasses reason; faith alone in Christ's grace justifies: "My logick is the faculty of faith, / Where all things are resolv'd into 'He saith'" (1–2). As Harvey analyzes his subject matter traditionally, he affirms that Christ dissolves all old legal and historical anatomies, dispositions, and rationales in a new dispensation of mercy. His persona, then, anatomizes himself in standing for and before the congregation as their pattern of neotypological recovery.

Carrying this anatomy through *The School of the Heart* are the narrative scenes from the standard life of a member of the congregation, beginning with portrayals of original and then cumulative self-damnations in the hard, fouled heart's sins against God's ancient laws; origins thus correspond to the Law and early Writings. But before the book is a third over, such recognitions of condemnation give way to tearful, contrite purgings of the heart. By its midpoint, nurture of the heart commences. As the Old Testament tone shifts into the New, self-explanation enters the narrative. The eighteenth poem recognizes the crucial point that only acceptance by Christ can give the heart any value. This realization provides a necessary step toward "19. The Sacrifice of the Heart," which is based on the seventeenth verse of the fifty-first Psalm: "The sacrifices of God *are* a broken spirit: a broken and a contrite heart, O God, thou wilt not despise." Harvey acknowledges David's offering to be a Christian's only possible sacrifice, since the inadequate penitential offerings of bulls, calves, and lambs have been transcended by Christ's sacrifice. Covenant theology, as he explains it, is carried by types:

> Thy former covenant of old,
> Thy law of ordinances, did require
> Fat sacrifices from the fold,
> And many other off'rings made by fire;
> Whilst Thy first Tabernacle stood,
> All things were consecrate with bloud.
>
> And can Thy better Covenant,
> Thy law of grace and truth by Jesus Christ,
> Its proper sacrifices want
> For such an Altar and for such a Priest?
> No, no; Thy Gospell doth require
> Choyse off'rings, too, and made by fire.
>
> A sacrifice for sinne indeed,
> Lord, Thou didst make Thyself, and once for all.

Harvey's emphatic concluding pun, which takes in both all times and all people, reaffirms that the sole atonement is the one God himself made by mercifully abrogating old sacrificial contracts and can be granted only by him in response to a sinner's faithful self-offering.

"26. The Table of the Heart," Harvey's most notable neotypological emblem (and probably the one most owed to Herbert), offers a similar explication. It is based on the familiar transformation from God's proscriptive decalogue engraved in stone to his merciful guidance written in faithful hearts. The Geneva Bible annotation to Jeremiah 31:33, Harvey's scriptural text, examines a typological complex that attends uncommonly to Christ: "In the time of Christ my Law shal in stead of tables of stone be writen in their heartes by mine holie Spirit, Ebr. 8, 8." In Harvey's ode God didactically examines his inscription and interpretation of the heart:

3.   My Law of old
        Tables of stone did hold,
Wherein I writ what I before had spoken;
        Yet were they quickly broken:
        A signe the Covenant
Contain'd in them would due observance want;
        Nor did they long remaine
            Coppy'd again.

4.   But now I'll try
        What force in flesh doth lie;
Whether thine heart renew'd afford a place
        Fit for My law of grace.

Harvey adds Paul's admonition that the new spiritual grace is life whereas the old legalistic letter is death; and he explains that the new covenant of Christ's love once and forever abrogates the old, as a sinner signifies his faith when he sacrifices his heart.

Emblematic self-explications of the congregation's neotype continue through major moments in a representative life during *The School of the Heart*. "41. The Bathing of the Heart" examines the two fathers of mankind; "45. The Hedging of the Heart" contrasts the thorns after Eden to those before the crucifixion; and "47. The New Wine of the Heart" is based on the cluster of grapes. These are merely the most prominent ones.

Although these devotional emblems present too didactic, overly explicit explications of a persona's heart as neotypological lyrics, they did contribute to the form in three ways: by spreading neotypological recognition, by applying closer explications of universal Christian situations, and by creating crucial scenes within narrative patterns of Christian development as a context for neotypological personae. They thereby augmented the form's potential possibilities and helped set a backdrop for

Donne's dramatic scenes which personalized the neotypical persona for greater persuasiveness.

† † †

Any answer to how strenuously Donne wrestled with God, whether he followed the pattern of the types Jacob, Moses, David, or the typologist Paul, depends on evaluating Izaak Walton's account.[8] But it is no coincidence that Walton chose to apply these particular types and this typologist to Donne's life. Moreover, there is no question that Walton intended others to apply Donne's exemplary life to their own lives. Finally, it is not insignificant that in his account of Donne's choice to enter the Anglican priesthood, Walton further compares Donne's struggles to those of Saint Augustine:

> Such strifes as these St. *Austine* had, when St. *Ambrose* indeavoured his conversion to Christianity. . . . Now the *English Church* had gain'd a second St. *Austine*, for, I think, none was so like him before his Conversion: none so like St. *Ambrose* after it: and if his youth had the infirmities of the one, his age had the excellencies of the other; the learning and holiness of both.[9]

How much resemblance the conversion of Mad Jack to the Reverend Doctor John Donne bears to the transformation of the actual courtier to the real life preacher is less significant for understanding Donne's work than is the clear evidence that Donne himself contrived to present himself as leading an archetypal life. He presents himself as a saved sinner who repeated the fundamental life history of David or of Saint Augustine. And for a purpose—for he thereby established identification with and made dramatic impact on the congregations before him. At least in part he played an actor to convert them. Donne forthrightly declared that he preached about himself—as a representative of Christian remorse and, by implication, salvation:

> I preach but the sense of Gods indignation upon mine own soul, in a conscience of mine own sins, I impute nothing to another, that I confesse not of my selfe, I call none of you to confession to me, I doe but confesse my self to God, and you, I rack no mans memory, what he did last year, last week, last night, I onely gather into my memory, and powr out in the presence of my God, and his Church, the sinfull history of mine own *youth*.[10]

Furthermore, Walton testifies to Donne's universal success in accounts of those two most seeming personal and memorable sermons, on the deaths of his wife and of himself:

> His Text was a part of the Prophet *Jeremy's* Lamentation: *Lo, I am the man that have seen affliction.*
> And indeed, his very words and looks testified him to be truly such a man; and they, with the addition of his sighs and tears, exprest in his Sermon, did so work upon the affections of his hearers, as melted and moulded them into a companionable sadness; and so they left the Congregation. . . .

> And, when to the amazement of some beholders he appeared in the Pulpit, many of them thought he presented himself not to preach mortification by a living voice: but, mortality by a decayed body and a dying face. . . . His strong desires enabled his weak body to discharge his memory of his preconceived meditations, which were of dying: the Text being, *To God the Lord belong the issues from death.* Many that then saw his tears, and heard his faint and hollow voice, professing they thought the Text prophetically chosen, and that Dr. Donne *had preach't his own Funeral Sermon.*[11]

What is remarkable, as universally attested to by readers of his sermons or his *Devotions upon Emergent Occasions* or his secular verse, is that they deeply empathize and identify with Donne's dramatic self-portrayals. In fact, this attribute has come to be the axiomatic defining characteristic of his poetry generally and, since Helen Gardner's description of the "Holy Sonnets" as "an image of a soul working out its salvation," of his sacred lyrics specifically.[12] Indeed, most would agree to the confined description of his persona as a representative soul gaining Christian understanding out of original misconception. Such is the case in Donne's finest, most dramatic and seemingly personal yet universal sacred lyric, "Goodfriday, 1613. Riding Westward."[13]

This lyric has been read by Donald M. Friedman as presenting Donne's speaker recovering eternal Christian truth along erring and wayward by-paths.[14] A. B. Chambers had already explained Donne's use of meditative form; his paradoxes of falling and rising, dying and living, delimiting and transcending, humiliating and exalting, human and divine, which express Christ's sacrifice and mystery; his reinterpretation of *translatio imperii* as a revolutionary journey west to gain the east by tracing a perfect globe; and his appropriation of *stabat mater dolorosa* for saving penance.[15] Friedman shows how Donne created a persona who initially is less aware of his human predicament than either the poet or the reader, but who learns fitfully as the poem progresses. Through willful, misguided attempts at rationalization the naïve narrator discovers that he has failed to comprehend by intellectualizing. When his self-justifications become self-accusations, he realizes he must do penance; his realization signifies the presence of saving faith.

What merits further notice is that the development of "Goodfriday" parallels the double motion of the neotypological lyric. The persona has to come to terms with his own responsibility for failures, both by striving to overcome them and by begging forgiveness. At the same time he learns that his own inadequacies are inevitable and that salvation derives solely from God's grace in Christ, granted for faithful prayers. The pattern, indeed the tactic, here repeats that of Donne's other sacred lyrics, such as "Batter my heart, three person'd God." Donne is especially comforted in "Goodfriday," however, because salvation is perennial throughout God's eternal cycle—in existence before the persona's contrition. The theme of the poem appears ironically in the persona's final claim that once purged, restored, and recognized by Christ, "I'll turne my face." [16] He still does not fully understand that only his acquiescence is required; he is already in the hands of a merciful God who, by directing the sphere in the initial proposition, is turning the persona's face to the east for him. The final action in the poem does not rest with the speaker; it rests with God. Christ's hands "span the Poles, / And turne all spheares at once," thus turning the poet through the circle into perfection, precisely because his hands are "at once peirc'd with those holes" (21–22). When Donne added such a dramatic and surprising self-discovery to a neotypological lyric persona closely identified by his congregation with him and themselves, he was contributing the same essential energizing innovation to this heritage that he gave to English Renaissance lyrics of all sorts.

Although Donne is not consistent in his terminology, his preference for flexible Reformed principles of typology emerges from his discussions. For him, type can simply mean an emblem. In the verse letter "*To the Countesse of* Bedford" beginning "Honour is so sublime perfection," he refers to the old definition of God as a circle in this way: "In those poor types of God (round circles) so / Religions tipes . . ." (46–47). Alternatively, his type can mean one thing and provide an idea of another. In "Obsequies to the Lord Harrington" he hyperbolically claims that "when the labourers have / Such rest in bed, that their last Church-yard grave, / Subject to change, will scarce be' a type of [his depression]" (17–19). More restrictively it can refer to foreshadowings of future events. Each night's bed is a "*Type* of the *grave*" in his third meditation from

73

Devotions upon Emergent Occasions; torments on earth are "Types and Figures" of affliction after death; and Peter raising Tabitha is a "type" of the resurrection in his sermons.[17] But his theory of literal interpretation, which specifically includes metaphorical and typological readings, provides a definition that is considerably more restricted. Dennis B. Quinn describes how "John Donne's Principles of Biblical Exegesis" avoid both overingenious allegories and deadening literalisms.[18] He achieves a balance by insisting that literal readings are primary while at the same time explaining that much Scripture is specifically figurative—metaphorical and parabolic as well as typological.

To open one sermon Donne warns simultaneously against wandering away from the letter in Genesis and against following without deviation the letter in Revelation. In doing so he sets up axioms for a liberalized mode of Reformed exegesis:

> The literall sense is always to be preserved; but the literall sense is not always to be discerned: for the literall sense is not always that, which the very Letter and Grammer of the place presents. . . . [The Holy Ghost's] principall intention in many places, is to expresse things by allegories, by figures; so that in many places of Scripture, a figurative sense is the literall sense.[19]

In another sermon he concludes that one should not accept the figurative sense where the literal sense is sufficient by itself; but he also claims that a metaphor frequently forms the essence of a passage—witness Christ being called the gate, vine, way, water, bread.[20] In the nineteenth expostulation of his *Devotions* he is enraptured by a literal, direct God who is simultaneously figurative and metaphorical because of the "inexpressible *texture*, and *composition* of thy word."[21] What Donne does consistently is adhere to the moderately Reformed theory of the *via media* in preference to figural tradition.

Though Donne's idea of typology is freer than that of many a Reformed exegete, his uses exhibit only minor extensions of their basic attitudes. His descriptions of the movement from Jewish schoolboy parsings of the Old Testament Messiah to Christian scholarly exegeses of the New Testament Word are familiar: law to liberty, promises and prophecies and figures to Christ's personal presence.[22] Like those of the Reformers, his descriptions are based on the second father of mankind recovering the fall of the first and the seed of Eve being stung by but in turn bruising the serpent's head; his expressions include the commonplace gospel rendings of the veil and the law as well as the customary progressions, prophecy to history, type to accomplishment, old covenant to new.[23] In his sermons Donne refers to ordinary, sometimes analytically elaborated, types. Ceremonies can be types—the Mosaic law of the beatitudes, the circumcision of baptism, and Abraham's physical of Christ's spiritual circumcision.[24] Events—the flood for baptism, the angels' visit to Abraham for the Messiah, Abraham's feast honoring Isaac for the eucharist, Moses' delivery of Israel for Christ's delivery of mankind—also serve as types.[25] Objects occasionally appear: in "Expostulation 19" of the *Devotions* the rainbow is a type associated with the cloud and pillar of fire; Noah's ark is the Church; Jacob's ladder, the garment stained at the wine press, the stone of Horeb and that of David's sling, as well as the sun of justice, all are types associated with Christ.[26] The types Donne turns to most frequently are people—Adam, Abraham, Isaac as the glad son, the seed of Abraham, Melchizedek, Jacob, Moses, Solomon, Jonah, Hezekiah, and David.[27]

Donne's particular interest in people who are types, especially in David whom he considers the first Christian, indicates that he like other Reformed typologists applies types personally. His interest seems all the more personal in his identification with the shepherd/psalmodist and in his predilection for passages from Psalms as texts for his sermons. In one early sermon on the thirty-eighth Psalm he explains how David is a type of Christ serving as a model for all Christian souls, who have to live in the fallen condition inherited from Adam:

[The lines] are historically, and literally to be understood of *David*; And secondly, in their *retrospect*, as they look back upon the first *Adam*, and so concern *Mankind collectively*, and so *you*, and *I*, and all have our portion in these calamities; And thirdly, we shall consider them in their *prospect*, in their future relation to the *second Adam*, in *Christ Jesus*, in whom also all mankinde was collected. . . .[28]

The Psalms are typological—historical expressions of one man who actually lived and who also foreshadowed Christ. At the same time they are universally applicable, promising salvation to all believers, particularly Donne's auditors and Donne himself, as Christ chooses them with the type. In a later sermon discussing promises of Christ made through Old Testament figures, Donne claims that "this is *exquisita scrutatio*, the true searching of the Scriptures, to finde all the *histories* to be *examples* to me, all the *prophecies* to induce a Saviour for *me*, all the *Gospell* to apply Christ Jesus to *me*."[29] For Donne, types serve as more than personal exemplars; they can at the least be identified with.

Most important for Donne, and for his development of the neotypological lyric, is that applying types to himself is reversible. He can also apply himself to types. Joan Webber has stated that Donne used Bible events "only when they can be made directly applicable to the soul's welfare."[30] In one example he directly applies Jacob's ladder, the ark, and manna to himself; in another his congregation appears in a prayer dedicating New Chapel, Lincoln's Inn, Ascension Day, 1623; in a prayer from the *Essayes in Divinity* he requests an exodus out of his Egypt of presumption, despair, lust, and idleness.[31] Janel M. Mueller has described an additional central perception about Donne's "Exegesis of Experience," that is, his counterpointing identification with types.[32] Especially in the *Devotions* during his sickness, and particularly during his first and twenty-second expostulations, he transforms his situation into a series of biblical ones. First he translates his experience into Scripture, particularly into types. Next he explicates both his experience and the type through New Testament fulfillment. As he prays in the ninth expostulation, "thou hadst written all in the *Old*, and then lightedst us a candle to read it by, in the *New Testament*."[33] The immediacy and drama of Donne's identification with types, as he himself joins them as a self-examining exemplar, is more than apparent in his prose.

At the least significant level Donne's poetry contains sporadic references to typology, such as supplications to prophets and martyrs in "A Litanie." His lyrics based on movement from the Old Testament to the New are more interesting. The octave of a Holy Sonnet asks, "Why are wee by all creatures waited on?" Why should innocent creatures have to be sin-offerings in place of mankind? The sestet's answer, that Christ's sacrificial death saves his special creatures, humanity, turns on the perfecting atonement of Christ replacing insufficient Mosaic sacrifices of the types, bulls and goats (Heb. 10). Donne's Holy Sonnet on God's dual will, "Father, part of his double interest," is also homiletic. The first compact is the legal obligation no man can live up to, but the second is merciful redemption: "Thy lawes abridgement, and thy last command / Is all but love; Oh let that last Will stand!"

Donne's sacred lyrics gain impact when they depict discovery of personal salvation in a typological matrix. In "*Upon the translation of the Psalmes by Sir* Philip Sydney, *and the Countesse of Pembroke his Sister*" the poet ponders with considerable empathy the effective, cumulative art of their imitation. Just as David spoke for God's tongue with his own tongue, they translate David's single tongue with two. In addition, they join John the Baptist; more important, they repeat Moses' and Miriam's first hymning (Exod. 15:1–21). They reach fulfillment because in translating God's songs they themselves have been translated by God into glory. Thus, they have been restored by being inside the interaction between dual referents in typology, adding themselves as still a third referent. Moreover, others can follow their example of applying types to themselves because Reformed humanity can follow the Sidneys' Old Testament psalmody through New Testament hymnody into celebrations of eternal glory to come.

Donne's Latin emblem, " *To Mr. George Herbert, with one of my Seales, of the Anchor and Christ*," is more personal in its application. The poem opens with an acknowledgment that before his ordination Donne's seal was a sheaf of snakes. But just as he has since been sealed anew with the anchor of faith and Christ, so the sin and death of the first serpent and the plague of serpents in the wilderness have been transformed by a type, the brazen serpent. Christ's testimony (which Donne explains in one of his sermons) is recorded in John 3:14–15: "And as Moses lifted up the serpent in the wilderness, even so must the Son of man be lifted up: That whosoever believeth in him should not perish, but have eternal life." [34]

Donne's finest neotypological lyrics are striking for the same reason that his sermons are. In both he presents personally dramatic, exemplary self-portrayals through a persona so closely identified with a type that he becomes a neotype of Christ in some common seventeenth-century predicament. The tactic is prominent in "I am a little world made cunningly," a micro-macrocosmic Holy Sonnet that recalls Alabaster. In the first nine lines the persona declares that his penance is necessary, yet wonders if it is necessary to drown his little world in tears. But then he recognizes that a wholly destructive flood is impossible because God covenanted with Noah never again to destroy the earth by water and commemorated that pact by granting the rainbow a new meaning of peace and a new status as a type. When he further recalls that the world is to be destroyed by fire (2 Peter 3:10), a destruction he has all too often imitated by burning in lust and envy, he prays for the zeal of God's house to devour and heal him (Psalms 69:9): "Burne me ô Lord, with a fiery zeale / Of thee' and thy house, which doth in eating heale." Shawcross has pointed out a meaningful ambiguity in these lines. *Eating* can be a passive ("being eaten") as well as an active verbal; it thereby can refer to partaking of the eucharist, Christ's house or tabernacle, as in kenosis (Phil. 2:6–8) and the opening of John. Through this ambiguous syntax Donne is reinforcing the affirmation that faith leads to salvation by accenting a Christian paradox inherent in the neotypological structure of the poem. The poet is responsible for his acts; he must reform his own will. At the same time, he is incapable of his own salvation; he must be justified vicariously by Christ, an act symbolized in the sacrificial sacrament.

Donne's dominant neotypological lyric is "*Hymne to God my God, in my sicknesse.*" Though the poem is virtually explicated in various annotated editions, how its formal structure follows from the speaker's dramatic and exemplary identification with a type needs emphasis. He opens by preparing to move from old law to new grace, practicing God's praises on earth in anticipation of singing them in salvation, invoking the type David and the tradition of David's psalmody, just as he did in honor of the Sidneys' Psalms. As in the *Meditations*, he concludes that he himself provides his own text: "Be this my Text, my Sermon to mine owne, / Therefore that he may raise the Lord throws down." But even so, he is actually applying Scripture to himself since he is alluding in idea and reflecting in inverted syntax the Christian paradoxes of 1 Corinthians 1:26–28. Moreover, at the same time that it recalls the paradoxes of "Goodfriday" it also recalls its own second through fourth stanzas, which belong with both the *Meditations* and "I am a little world." Because flat on his deathbed he is a map, to trace his movement westward is to watch his Christian translation. His western death becomes his eastern resurrection, since the flat map actually represents the circle of perfection and eternity. This geographic, imagistic, and verbal turn is possible only because of an actual replacement that Donne's sermons, augmented by many commentaries, proclaim.[35] His persona needs to recognize that Christ's self-sacrifice must replace Adam's fall; so in the next stanza he realizes that Christ's cross on Golgotha replaces Adam's tree in Eden.[36] This emblem might appear to be merely Donne's invention, like the emblematic meanings he assigns in "*A Hymne to Christ, at the Authors last going into Germany*"; but it is not. Personal and biblical ratification comes from the flow of blood and water, which follows the traditional sweat and bloody sweat of the old and new fathers of mankind. "As the first *Adams* sweat surrounds my face, / May the last *Adams* blood my soule embrace." The sweat on the poet's brow confirms his manhood, because of God's judgment on Adam; therefore he prays for the blood Christ shed with water to reform his soul in God's image. The poet continues with the thorns type: "So, in his purple wrapp'd receive mee Lord, / By these his thornes give me his other Crowne."

Just as the "*Hymne to God my God*" forms a circle of perfection in the renewed Davidic psalmody of its opening and closing, in the poet's conceit of the little world, and in the wit of his meditative construction, so it is eternized by its sustained present tense: all mirror Christ raising the singer from death's antechamber to visionary eternal salvation. Moreover, Christ appears through its governing, double typology; both the Old Testament of Adam and the contemporary testament of the poet are vivid, vital, and potent through faith in the New Testament transformation of the interaction among all three referents. Most of all, Donne has released the energy in the multiple neotypological referents to gain more power than ever before by analyzing himself most personally and dramatically in the last, perhaps most criticial scene in the archetypal life of everyman as believer. He thereby bequeathes to the neotypological lyric heritage the last characteristic essential for the fullest exploitation of its potential, an achievement realized by George Herbert.

4

"Lord, in thee The *beauty* lies in the *discovery*"

"Love Unknown" as George Herbert's Neotypological Lyric Paradigm

The "dear and happy," close personal friendship between Donne and Herbert as Izaak Walton describes it in his life of Donne may reflect more his imagination than their historical relationship. Even so, the kinship in poetic ministry between Donne and Herbert can scarcely be questioned, and it is actually this relationship that Walton dwelt on. Although omitting discussion of a number of Donne's friends, he had to write about Herbert, "I mean that *George Herbert*, who was the Author of the *Temple*, or *Sacred Poems and Ejaculations. A Book*, in which by declaring his own spiritual Conflicts, he hath Comforted and raised many a dejected and discomposed Soul, and charmed them into sweet and quiet thoughts. . . ."[1] However, after writing Donne's biography the gentle Walton may have changed his mind somewhat about the calming effect of Herbert's poetry, though he did realize that the poet-priest had a profound effect that derived from the same fundamental, though less flamboyantly displayed, virtue as that of Donne. Herbert's dramatic, self-examining, personal portraits compel the kind of identification that made him a potent Christian exemplum for his congregation. Walton further realized that this virtue merited repeated and expanded statement in his life of Herbert wherein he prompts from the dying poet-priest's mouth this charge to his emissary, Mr. Duncon:

> Sir, I pray deliver this little Book to my dear brother Farrer, and tell him, he shall find in it a picture of the many spiritual Conflicts that have past betwixt God and my Soul, before I could subject mine to the will of Jesus my Master: in whose service I have now found perfect freedom; desire him to read it: and then, if he can think it may turn to the advantage of any dejected poor Soul, let it be made publick: if not, let him burn it: for I and it, are less than the least of God's mercies.—

Thus meanly did this humble man think of this excellent Book, which now bears the name of *The TEMPLE: Or, Sacred Poems,* and *Private Ejaculations;* of which, Mr. *Farrer* would say, *There was in it the picture of a divine Soul in every page; and that the whole Book was such a harmony of holy passions, as would enrich the World with pleasure and piety.* And it appears to have done so: for there have been more then Twenty thousand of them sold since the first Impression.[2]

However exaggerated or invented this interpretation may be, however credible Walton is about Herbert's willingness to assign his book to oblivion, there is no doubt about Herbert's strong impact on his audience. For whether readers see him as in turmoil or in reconciliation, they do feel that he is most dramatically personal in his self-analyses and believe that his situations are applicable to their own and others' lives. As a persona he is both himself and also a representative exemplum for his audience.

Herbert himself recognized the importance of this dual presentation, both as a poet and as a priest. For him, a poet becomes an intensified or supreme human being because of his divine calling to make poetic that which is every human's duty—the praise of God.[3] In "Providence" he declares that man supplies the words and hymns for concerted acts of praise by dumb creatures:

Of all the creatures both in sea and land
Onely to Man thou hast made known thy wayes,
And put the penne alone into his hand,
And made him Secretarie of thy praise.

(5–8)[4]

When the poet prays for God's help to follow his calling, he further asks that he might be "A true Hymn," "*Loved*" penned by God. The poet as a performer becomes the interpreter of the text of himself. While regathering the shards of his heart, which has been shattered by affliction, the persona of "Jesu" parses his own mystery of both remorse and relief, in a dual way:

When I had got these parcels, instantly
I sat me down to spell them, and perceived
That to my broken heart he was *I ease you,*
And to my whole is *JESU.*

(7–10)

Most significantly, these lines suggest that self-presentation is not wholly possible, a suggestion that is borne out by the similar self-presentation of a priest.

The priest's role parallels the poet's as an exemplary human being. He, too, is God's amanuensis creating and interpreting the text of himself. To open the thirty-third chapter of *A Priest to the Temple*, Herbert declares that "The Countrey Parson's Library is a holy Life," for the sake of his own soul and especially for the sake of presenting a model for his parish. Though the task is a demanding one, the poet-priest can take comfort in God revealing himself perfectly through mundane vessels as in Herbert's advice from "Perirrhanterium":

> Judge not the preacher; for he is thy Judge:
> If thou mislike him, thou conceiv'st him not.
> God calleth preaching folly. Do not grudge
> To pick out treasures from an earthen pot.
>
> (427–30)

Herbert's defense both here and in the similar dilemma of "The Priest-hood" draws on Paul's defense along lines suggested by an old metaphor:

> For we preach not ourselves, but Christ Jesus the Lord; and ourselves your servants for Jesus' sake. For God, who commanded the light to shine out of darkness, hath shined in our hearts, to *give* the light of the knowledge of the glory of God in the face of Jesus Christ. But we have this treasure in earthen vessels, that the excellency of the power may be of God, and not of us.
>
> (2 Cor. 4:5–7)

Herbert extends the principle that by the merciful sacrifice of Christ, God can employ quite individual priests to manifest his providence.

"The Windows" displays how a poet-priest can be important as himself at the same time that he is an emblem perfected by Christ, providing a universal lesson. A priest begs God to reveal how to preach the holy word because, like an uneven and irregular stained glass, he is leaded into place. The poet's answer, granted by Christ, reveals that both the window and the poet-priest are glorified by God's grace displayed in the light of the sun/Son shining through the colored glass of the one and the imperfect life of the other. Christ's light perfects the thinnest and most wan portrait or life until it can move the souls of beholders. The persona is at once himself portrayed in the sinful drama of an individual life and also an exemplary text and interpreter to the degree that God is seen through him. The movement of metaphor in this poem is so close to that in a neotypological lyric that it merely needs mention. It releases the potential expressiveness of multiple referents by identifying the window's value both as inherent in itself and as granted by the sun's light. All it lacks is the context of a seventeenth-century neotype identifying with a type in order to become part of the interaction with the antitype.

The release of powerful expression in "Aaron" does not derive from Aaron as the founder of an order of priests, who in bejeweled and brilliant glory raises the dead to harmonious chimes, but rather from Aaron as the type whose seventeenth-century neotype, even though dressed in contemporary and contrasting defective darkness, sins, and discordant passions, can also bring sinners to salvation. Both the antitypical redeemer and head of the frail church are capable, being made perfect by Christ:

> Christ is my onely head,
> My alone onely heart and breast,
> My onely musick, striking me ev'n dead;
> That to the old man I may rest,
> And be in him new drest.
>
> So holy in my head,
> Perfect and light in my deare breast,
> My doctrine tun'd by Christ, (who is not dead,
> But lives in me while I do rest)
> Come people; Aaron's drest.
>
> (16–25)

Here a personal neotype is claimed to be an effective poet-priest, precisely because he has entered the reaction between a type and the antitype. Herbert is perfecting the neotypological lyric by showing the expressive potential of a persona confessing so as to present both a self-dramatizing portrait and an exemplum, fulfilling the form that had been developed from psalmody through Donne out of the Reformed definition and application of typology.

Repeatedly in *The Church* readers observe how a persona who, wrestling with his own situation and contending with God in his life, only fitfully and imperfectly discovers that he himself is a contemporary neotype of Christ, almost a reincarnation of some type of Christ. Herbert often places his persona in typological situations with traditional allusions, imagery, and diction. During a dramatic, self-portraying lyric the persona sometimes senses implications of redemption through Christ, but more often he fails to do so until he belatedly discovers that God's providential prophecy is inevitably fulfilled for him. The persona ultimately discovers the beauty of God through Christ's recovery of types. Herbert invites his reader to look through his neotypical persona in neotypological settings and rediscover the beauty of God.[5]

This paradigm shows Herbert compounding the dual emotions of a soul's simultaneous remorseful humility and grateful exaltation with the vacillations of a lover's psyche, as these derive from the form itself. So it is that throughout *The Church* the personae, and Herbert's readers, are repeatedly surprised to discover God in the least likely, often seemingly impossible places precisely because, though man often forgets, God's beauty and providential mercy are nonetheless everpresent. This paradigm provides the impetus behind most of Herbert's lyrics, many of which are not directly neotypological as well as those that are. And this paradigm would seem as well to follow the same concerns as Reformed typology's strict definition and close application to contemporary scenes that formed the contexts and possibilities of neotypological lyrics such as "Aaron," or "The Altar," "Decay," "Sion," "The Bunch of Grapes," or "Love Unknown."

The impact Herbert seeks in his neotypological lyrics can perhaps be conveyed best by focusing, within the context of *The Church*, on one masterful lyric, "Love Unknown." Because it lays bare Herbert's strategy for the beautiful discovery of God's merciful provision for humanity and because in context it also represents a most complex reinforcement of the expressive potential in the neotypological lyric, "Love Unknown" provides a paradigm of the deep, dual, sacred motivations and motifs, the situations, and the poetic techniques in the form itself. Perhaps it also demonstrates what is most characteristic of all Herbert's lyrics.[6]

† † †

Since Rosemond Tuve's brilliant *Reading of George Herbert*, no one has been able to comment on his lyrics without at least acknowledging that typology is fundamentally embedded in them. That acknowledgment appears not only in typological annotations so predominately that C. A. Patrides' edition includes a special "Note on Typology" but also in closely related studies such as those of Herbert's emblems, which assume some types and extend our knowledge of others, as well as in theories accounting for Herbert's aesthetics founded in typology such as H. Andrew Harnack's "George Herbert's 'AARON': The Aesthetics of Shaped Typology."[7] However, it is universally acknowledged that typology is a prominent if not the dominant concern in any discussion of Herbert's works.

Tuve's own identifications and discussion, based on references she and Hutchinson discerned, show clearly that Herbert used types for specific occasions. "The Sacrifice" alone displays the types of Adam and the thorns, of Moses, the paschal lamb, manna, and the rock of Horeb, and of the bunch of grapes. The old and new Adams are alluded to in such poems as "Easter," manna in "The Collar," and the rock heart in "Sepulchre." Personal types appear such as Melchizedek in "Peace" and Samson in "Sunday," and both inanimate and human forerunners appear in "Decay." These and others are repeated and extended in Herbert's Latin poetry, such as "Velum scissum" and "Petrae scissae" from *Passio Discerpta*. Types thus form a general context for each of Herbert's poems.

But Tuve does not stop at general or incidental uses; she goes on to note that a number of Herbert's lyrics are dominated by specific types. "Jesu" returns to the rock of Horeb and the emblem of the stone heart. "Love-joy" is governed by the bunch of grapes. And the allegory of "Sighs and Grones" follows from types based in the physical and spiritual wanderings of the chosen people. For these, medieval figuralism supplies an adequate context.

However, a closely related poem, which Tuve discusses fully, requires more specific and detailed, indeed Reformed, definition and application. In "The Bunch of Grapes," Herbert applies closely defined types to his persona and contemporaries so that both may become part of the reaction between type and antitype, fully exploiting the expressive potential in multiple referents. The speaker imagines himself following the detours, backtracks, and backslidings of the chosen people as they seek the Promised Land only to end at the Red Sea again:

> For as the Jews of old by Gods command
>   Travell'd, and saw no town;
> So now each Christian hath his journeys spann'd:
>   Their storie pennes and sets us down.

(8–11)

He continues by acknowledging that both his own and his era's failures are made up of intimately related imitations of human failures under law, even while those chosen are directed toward God. He then can beg the hoped-for success of their final journey, as these types are exalted into transcendence by the antitype:

> Then have we too our guardian fires and clouds;
>   Our Scripture-dew drops fast:
> We have our sands and serpents, tents and shrowds;
>   Alas! our murmurings come not last.
>   But where's the cluster? Where's the taste
> Of mine inheritance?
>
>   (15–20)

What the speaker requests here is not limited success or failure, whatever the intrinsic worth of his referents in the Old Testament and the seventeenth century, but rather to be granted worth through still another referent, through the antitype that fulfills the type. He seeks the salvation of the individual and the representative, Reformed neotype placed in the interaction between type and antitype. As he follows failure and remorse, so he also would be one with exaltation and joy.

Such neotypological lyrics as "The Bunch of Grapes" and many of Herbert's related poetic references and designs need the more defined context of "The H. Scriptures. II." Here the speaker vows that human destinies are transmitted neither by tea leaves nor by stars but by the message of eternal salvation for Christians found in both Old and New Testaments:

> This verse marks that, and both do make a motion
>   Unto a third, that ten leaves off doth lie:
>   Then as dispersed herbs do watch a potion,
> These three make up some Christians destinie:
> Such are thy secrets, which my life makes good,
>   And comments on thee: for in ev'ry thing
>   Thy words do finde me out, & parallels bring,
> And in another make me understood.
>
>   (5–12)

If biblical types form the true constellation for interpreting, "The H. Scriptures. II." further implies that the proper astrology is to read the single star of Herbert's neotypology. For it is through the book of the soul that people can immediately apprehend revelations in widely separated biblical passages. Thus, Christ saving the neotypical persona is a contemporary act taken into the interaction between type and antitype, between Old and New Testaments.[8] Its expressive power derives from the specifically straitened and Reformed definition and application of typology that was discovered and developed through the neotypological lyric tradition.

Ultimately Herbert's essential perspective is Christ's revelation of this set of interactions. It is found in "Justice (II)" because the "Afflictions," "Mortification," and "Grief" of remorse and contrition become exaltation in and by Christ. In "Justice (II)," *scale* is both a pun on *scala* recalling the type, Jacob's ladder, and an association with the bucket and well of the goddess Fortuna. It comes to be seen not as an engine of condemnation under legal contract or testament but as a means of climbing up from this world, supported by the good news of Christ's mercy.

Herbert's perspective and a viable reading method are established by "Faith." When this poem opens the persona's sense of blind law and hunger for God's will are absorbed by his faith in Christ's appeasement of justice and his communion through the eucharist. He next applies the typological prediction of Christ in the Genesis sentence on the serpent. At the climax his faith in the birth of the new Adam removes his sense of sin and death inherited from the old:

> Faith makes me any thing, or all
> That I beleeve is in the sacred storie:
> And where sinne placeth me in Adams fall,
> Faith sets me higher in his glorie.
>
> If I go lower in the book,
> What can be lower then the common manger?
> Faith puts me there with him, who sweetly took
> Our flesh and frailtie, death and danger.
>
> (17–24)

In the last stanzas he applies typological salvation by faith to himself as a neotypological everyman whose darkness is relieved by the light and grace bestowed on him in order that the sun/Son might be revealed in him:

> When creatures had no reall light
> Inherent in them, thou didst make the sunne
> Impute a lustre, and allow them bright;
> And in this shew, what Christ hath done.
>
> (33–36)

This process in "Faith" describes a precise way of reading all neotypological lyrics, but it especially describes those refined by Herbert into the uncomprehending self-examinations of the dramatic and personal, yet universal and exemplary personae of many of his lyrics. These lyrics follow the paradigm that reveals, at their most complex and subtle, the motivations and poetics of the fulfilled form. One such is "Love Unknown."

† † †

"Love Unknown" is a simply rendered, fantasized dialogue in which a persona tells an anonymous friend about a series of confrontations with his landlord, God. Each time he had tried to please the landlord he was painfully thwarted: when he brought his landlord a dish of fruit centered by his heart, like Cain's his offering was ignored and his heart was scoured; when he presented a sheep, unlike Abel's his sacrifice was ignored and his heart was scalded; when he tried to recuperate and begin anew, like Christ's disciples during the bloody sweat his rest was haunted. At the close of each pathetic description the Friend laconically points out that the persona has failed to recognize how the landlord is redeeming him. Finally the Friend explains:

> For ought I heare, your Master shows to you
> More favour then you wot of. Mark the end.
> The Font did onely, what was old, renew:
> The Caldron suppled, what was grown too hard:
> The Thorns did quicken, what was grown too dull:
> All did but strive to mend, what you had marr'd.

However fully the persona finally understands what the Friend's summation teaches, this explicit concluding moral reconfirms for readers that God saves the sinning speaker. For Herbert's tactic is for readers to rediscover psalmody's dual motivation of humiliation and exaltation generated from the potential in a Reformed definition of types applied to life and carried through the contemporary neotypical persona and situation. Herbert's neotype has become part of the reaction within the multiple referents to Old Testament types and their New Testament antitype in such a way that he can, during humiliating remorse over his personal responsibility for sin, still celebrate his salvation by Christ. And Herbert has achieved this through a beautiful complex of neotypological motives and motifs, situations, imagery, and style that fully exploits the expressive potential of typology.

Herbert particularly mastered that heritage of neotypological lyrics which followed psalmody's dual spiritual forces of personal humiliation and universal Christian exaltation that emphasize the personal predicament of sin and the fulfillment of everyman deformed in Adam and reformed in Christ.[9] "Love Unknown" follows Southwell's "The Burning Babe" whose breast is the furnace of affliction which tempers, whose fuel the thorns which enliven, whose bath the font which cleanses Herbert's heart. The neotypical persona of "Love Unknown" specifically renders a new version of the fifty-first Psalm.[10] He follows both of David's movements. He first begs that God purify his heart: "Purge me with hyssop, and I shall be clean: wash me, and I shall be whiter than snow. . . . Create in me a clean heart, O God." Then he realizes that rendering his contrite heart for purgation is the sole sacrifice acceptable to God.

"Love Unknown" reflects primarily the fifty-first Psalm as it rests inside the New Testament because it indicates man is not capable of making the sacrifice necessary for redemption. Both Protestant and Catholic commentators, particularly in their notes to the fourth, seventh, and ninth verses, discuss Adam's original sin and everyman's absolution by the blood of the second Adam. Their reading was disseminated by such popular biblical aids as Ainsworth's:

> He applieth the washings used in the Law, (*Lev.* 11. 25. 32. *Exod.* 19. 10. *Num.* 19. 19) to the spirituall washing from sinne in the bloud of Christ, *Rev.* 7. 14. I *Joh.* 1. 7. . . . [Sprinkling and cleansing] was the last part of the purification of the uncleane, here used to signifie the ful cleansing from sinne by the bloud of Christ, *Heb.* 9. 13. 14.

Herbert follows the dual Christian interpretation of the Psalm in all three emblems: the first direction is the penitent believer's self-sacrifice; its vector is absorbed into the second, Christ's sacrifice that purifies and saves all believers. The movement from law to grace in the typological exegesis of the fifty-first Psalm and the poem stimulates a similar dual response. The persona must recognize his own failures and need for self-sacrifice; in the process he must realize his contrition is justified solely by belief in Christ's sacrifice.

Each of the three scenes described by the persona of "Love Unknown" sets him in a typological situation. The first establishes the terms: when the persona offers his landlord a dish of fruit, the landlord's servant, knowing that the offerer must be the offering, seizes the persona's heart. As in the Psalm, what is acceptable is a heart painfully cleansed by that dipping, dying, washing, and wringing which extort tears of contrition. Herbert's reiterations about the necessity of painful, tearful purgations culminate in his advice during "The Water-course":

> But rather turn the pipe and waters course
> To serve thy sinnes, and furnish thee with store
> Of sov'raigne tears, springing from true remorse:
> That so in purenesse thou mayst him adore,
>
> Who gives to man, as he sees fit, $\begin{cases} \text{Salvation.} \\ \text{Damnation.} \end{cases}$
>
> (6–10)[11]

From his limited perspective the persona sees himself under extortion. But with the Friend the reader recognizes the message of salvation in that ceremonial font where the persona's heart is washed in blood streaming from the side of a great rock. Here again is the rock of Horeb. It is as difficult not to see emblematic salvation in the persona's description here as it is in Christ's complaint in "The Sacrifice": "They strike my head, the rock from whence all store / Of heav'nly blessings issue evermore" (170–71).[12]

Herbert frequently acknowledges both the necessity and opportunity for Christ to purify believers beyond the legal purgation that the servant exacts from the persona of "Love Unknown." "Ephes. 4. 30." provides a central confession:

> Then weep mine eyes, the God of love doth grieve:
> Weep foolish heart,
> And weeping live:
>
> .   .   .   .
>
> Yet if I wail not still, since still to wail
> Nature denies;
> And flesh would fail,
> If my deserts were masters of mine eyes:
> Lord, pardon, for thy Sonne makes good
> My want of tears with store of bloud.
>
> (7–9, 31–36)[13]

Transit from the first to the second emblem in "Love Unknown" is supplied by tear imagery associated with "Marie Magdalene" generally acknowledged in the Renaissance to be the woman who anointed Christ's feet (Luke 7:36–50). Attempting the impossible by trying to clean the feet of the undefiled Christ, paradoxically she washed away her own multitudinous sins with her tears. The persona of "Love Unknown" must learn what readers recognize: when with her tears she was "washing one, she washed both" (18). Eucharistic associations evident in the blood streaming from the rocky fount are familiar.

The central scene described by the persona of "Love Unknown" presents the most complex typological situation. After his heart has healed, the sight of a huge furnace with a boiling caldron stirs him to offer his landlord a sacrificial lamb; but the servant hurls the offerer's heart into the pan. First (as with Donne in "Batter My Heart") the persona must acknowledge his personal responsibility for sin and the necessity of his painful purification. Then (as with Southwell in "The Burning Babe") he must acknowledge Christ as the ultimate furnace of purification.[14]

The anguished persona of "Love Unknown" fails to recognize that his heart is being purified. Since he views God as arbitrary he fails to recognize, much less pray for, the descent of God's purgative fire as Herbert does in the opening of "Love II":

> Immortall Heat, O let thy greater flame
>   Attract the lesser to it: let those fires,
>   Which shall consume the world, first make it tame;
> And kindle in our hearts such true desires,
> As may consume our lusts, and make thee way.[15]

The persona of "Love Unknown" feels he has been cast into that formulaic hell, the "iron furnace of Egypt" from which God delivers his chosen (as in Deut. 4:20; 1 Kings 8:51; Jer. 11:4). Even more debilitating is his sense of having been judged wanting. Such is the charge when Dr. Willet applies Ezekiel 24:11, 12 "To the english Papists" in his nineteenth emblem. Willet contends that God's wrath will burn to ashes the flesh of those now boiling in the brass caldron. Similarly Herbert's persona identifies with the harsh vision of Ezekiel who sees in the furnace of Jerualem not ore but castoff slag:

> Son of man, the house of Israel is to me become dross: all they *are* brass, and tin, and iron, and lead, in the midst of the furnace; they are *even* the dross of silver. Therefore thus saith the Lord GOD; Because ye are all become dross, behold, therefore I will gather you into the midst of Jerusalem.

> *As* they gather silver, and brass, and iron, and lead, and tin, into the midst
> of the furnace, to blow the fire upon it, to melt *it*; so will I gather *you* in
> mine anger and in my fury, and I will leave *you there*, and melt you.
>
> (22:18–20)

The persona senses that this is the destructive furnace to which Jesus assigns those he rejects (Matt. 13:41–42, 49–50), instead of the Isaiahan purificatory furnace of affliction: "Behold, I have refined thee, but not with silver; I have chosen thee in the furnace of affliction" (48:10). Although Catholic and Protestant commentators recognized the difficulty in interpreting whether the elect are purified in a silver furnace, in silver, or like silver, most choose the simile and claim that the dross of sin is smelted out of the chosen. Cawdrey follows this trend: affliction amounts to God purging his children like a goldsmith does gold, by placing them in purifying fire.[16] Several Catholics cited by Lapide further consider the purgation a reference to Christ abrogating legal condemnation.

The heart scalding in a pan calls to mind flesh seething in a caldron, an image that is often interpreted as signifying replacement of the old law and expanded as forecasting the eucharist. To Catholic and Protestant commentators alike, this image from Ezekiel's visions (chapters 11 and 24) indicates a soaring out of flesh pots into spiritual realms. The Westminster Assembly annotations to the twenty-fourth chapter offer alternatives. The pot can either soften and save or punish and annihilate, depending on the nature of the flesh:

> The pot is Jerusalem; the flesh and fat pieces, are the chief, the richest, and
> the noblest that are in her; the fire are Gods judgments, by which he would
> have humbled, and mollified his peoples hearts, to bring them to repen-
> tance; but that having taken no effect, by reason of their obstinate re-
> bellion, he would convert those Judgments, into a total consumption.

While the persona of "Love Unknown" senses the latter, still other commentators point to hope beyond that of the Presbyterians. The eightieth emblem of Georgette de Montenay's polyglot, *Monumenta emblematum. Christianorum virtutem or A Booke of armes or remembrance, wherein ar one hundred godly emblemata* (1619), pictures God's hand above a caldron over an altar furnace. The poem explains that as precious metals are purified by a goldsmith so sinners are purified only by Christ.[17] And Lapide's commentators claim that beyond its demand for penitential purgation, Ezekiel's vision alludes to the "Moab olla spei meæ" of the fifty-ninth (sixtieth) Psalm. The line is a figurative call for the victim, Christ, to transform flesh, men, from the pot of hell to spirit: "id est, Tuth Moabitis est progenies mea quam spe concepi, nam illa pariet Christum."

A stronger sense of salvation derives from the allusion to the pots at the feast of tabernacles in Zechariah's apocalyptic segregation of believers:

> In that day shall there be upon the bells of the horses, HOLINESS UNTO THE LORD; and the pots in the LORD's house shall be like the bowls before the altar. Yea, every pot in Jerusalem and in Judah shall be holiness unto the LORD of hosts: and all they that sacrifice shall come and take of them, and seethe therein.
>
> (14:20–21)

Lapide's commentators explain both mortification of the body and the eucharistic type commemorating Christ's sacrifice which renders mortification efficacious. The sacrifical flesh seething in the bowl combines the odor of incense, the libation of wine, and the blood of the victim. These foreshadow eucharistic symbols of Christ's aroma, flesh, and blood, which supplant legal exaction and purify gold and silver drawn from the pots of Egypt, "in quibus vel sacrificatur caro & sanguis Agni immaculati Christi Domini, vel aliquod ministerium huic sacrificio exhibetur." Such is the model of mortification and penance necessary for instigating Christ's charity:

> *Fit ex lebete phiala,*
> *In vas translata gloriæ,*
> *Ex vase contumeliæ.*

This verse from Mary Magdalene's song of the transformation of the vessel, *ecclesia*, is explicated by Lapide's exegetes. The blood and flesh of Christians seething in the caldron of mortification are transmuted into sweet spirits rising to God from the eucharistic golden vessel: "Sic enim Magdalena, quæ peccatrix erat lebes ignominiæ, pœnitens facta est phiala gloriæ." Thus a second eucharistic reference confirms the presence of "Love Unknown" among poems like "The Bunch of Grapes," in which a speaker mistakenly bemoans as irredeemable the situations that should be understood to include saved types.[18] Transition from the first to the second emblem in "Love Unknown" is also formed by Mary Magdalene imagery. Through it readers see both that the purgation of the nearsighted speaker is necessary for him to become a contrite offering and that his sacrifice becomes valuable when it is absorbed into Christ's. Mary Magdalene's association with the disciples leads into the final emblem of "Love Unknown."

The final scene described by the persona of "Love Unknown," like the first, is set in a simple typological situation. Its impact is compounded, however, by being set in the New Testament as well. When he has escaped, the persona retreats homeward in order to recover from the exhausting affliction he construes to be rejection. There he discovers thorns of thought which torment him into watchfulness. He is forced to follow Paul's exhortation to remain vigilant for the sake of being saved: "Let us not sleep, as *do* others; but let us watch and be sober" (1 Thess. 5:6).

The requirements necessary for the persona here are the same as Southwell expresses in "Christs sleeping friends" and those underlying "The Sacrifice" (29–36). First is the demand for vigilance against God's enemies; second, the need to recognize humanity's inevitable failure to withstand satanic stress; and third, the necessity and availability of Christ waking men and enduring the afflictions of their sins. The typological message is that Christ's thorns punish the persona by law and spur him by grace. Even though the persona recognizes only sacrifice, the thorns are types which signify salvation by Christ here just as they do in Herbert's juxtaposition of men's failures ("thorny all their crowns" [178]) and Christ's recovery ("on my head a crown of thorns I wear" [161]) in "The Sacrifice."[19]

Each emblem then of "Love Unknown" alludes to a type demonstrating, in order, first that each believer is legally required to sacrifice his contrite heart to God, and second that his action fails unless Christ's sacrifice absorbs his. The persona of "Love Unknown" understands neither. Because he feels that God is being arbitrary he cannot recognize anything beyond his own anguish. Readers, however, because Herbert shows them the potential dual religious motivation and referents in types applied to contemporary life, can interpret the typology of these emblems through the persona. They are to discover the beauty of God through the neotype's remorseful self-offering as it reveals his salvation by the antitype.

Although the potent expression of Christianity is available for discovery through types, Herbert's complex art exploits its beauty as he develops and expands the patterns of the neotypological lyric heritage through the image matrix of *The Church* and intensifies them in the immediate rhetoric and style of each poem. The image cluster most important to "Love Unknown" centers on the persona's heart, a familiar type and neotype throughout this lyric heritage. Moreover, it is specifically God's offering, text, and dwelling in *The Temple*.[20]

The heart is specifically "An Offering." In this poem a single repentant heart prepares to celebrate the eucharist which will rectify its failings. The threefold reception of the heart's contrition, signifying justification by faith, reaffirms Herbert's belief that the heart is the sole offering acceptable to God. This metaphor makes up part of the typological reading of the fifty-first Psalm

The second metaphor for the heart central to "Love Unknown" is that it is a text already or yet-to-be written by the hand of God. In "Good Friday," Herbert wants to know how to calculate Christ's grief. Having discarded as inadequate the number of Christ's foes, the stars, and fall leaves, he considers counting the hours of his own life eternally redeemed by the sun of Christ's sufferings and then his own multitudinous sins with their multiplying sorrows that Christ has repaired. Finally he hits upon calculating by his heart blood which Christ's sacrifice has regenerated:

> Since bloud is fittest, Lord, to write
> Thy sorrows in, and bloudie fight;
> My heart hath store, write there, where in
> One box doth lie both ink and sinne.
>
> (21–24)

By thus calculating Christ's sacrifice the persona hopes to scour sins out of his heart so that the writings of grace in it will be legible.[21] That heart which the Friend in "Love Unknown" reads as foul until cleansed, hard until tempered, and dull until regenerated is preparing for the New Testament engraving to replace the stony decalogue.

The third metaphor for the heart, that it is Christ's special dwelling, follows from Paul's request "That Christ may dwell in your hearts by faith" (Eph. 3:17). Herbert chastises any heart which ought to be open to Christ but has become a chilled, flint "Sepulchre" by excluding Christ while lodging sins. Even though hard hearts metaphorically stone him like the persona of "Love Unknown" who tries to keep him out, Christ persists in making them suitable habitations:

> Yet do we still persist as we began,
> And so should perish, but that nothing can,
> Though it be cold, hard, foul, from loving man
>   Withhold thee.
>
> (21–24)[22]

All three metaphors for the heart repeat the message of "The Altar": the persona of "Love Unknown" must offer his contrite heart so that Christ can remake it.[23] In "The Altar" God's hand gathers together broken pieces of heart (a shattered offering, a scattered text, a demolished house) to be sanctified by Christ's sacrifice. In "Love Unknown" the Lord prepares the heart, cleans it of the pollution revealed by law as in "H. Baptisme (I)," softens it from the hardness of a pharaoh as in "Grace," quickens its "Dulnesse," and mends its mortal flaws like he repairs the rime in "Deniall."

God's actions on the persona's heart in "Love Unknown" are profitably read in *The Church*'s context of contracts between man and God, for these belong to a tradition that emphasized mankind's legal predicament which must be understood for full appreciation of the grace of God's mercy. Contract diction forms the necessary Old Testament condition of a type in itself before access to New Covenant redemption in reference to the antitype. And it is specifically applicable to everyman's problem of responsibility in every age and essentially to every neotype. One such contractual image for Herbert's persona—ground leased from God, tilled by man, and nurtured by charity—appears often in *The Church*.[24] Usually a speaker bemoans first his obligations under the contract and later his failure to discharge them. The obligations are more critical since failure, granted original sin, forms a condition of existence.

"Redemption" sets the pattern. A tenant, dissatisfied with his old lease, seeks his landlord; failing to find in heaven the incarnate lord who has descended to repossess earth, the tenant returns to search the world; at last he finds the lord being crucified and learns of a new lease. God had already arranged to grant the suit whenever the tenant realized his need, a realization that signifies justification by faith. The text for "Redemption" is Paul's description of Christ "blotting out the handwriting of ordinances that was against us, which was contrary to us, and took it out of the way, nailing it to his cross" (Col. 2:14).

Revelations to personae and reassurances for readers that the search for a new compact of redemption overrides human shortcomings and failures are a surprise in Herbert. His even more surprising reassurance, however, is that the landlord also plays the role of the tenant. He is the one who abides by the agreement, pays the penalty of death for man's original sin, and continues to stand as supreme ally for each Christian. In "Assurance" a persona attacked by doubts laments that either his compact with God was false from the beginning or he has been deceived since. Worst, he must plead guilty to accusations of failure and sin. Only after his plea can he recognize that the Lord has not only formed the league, the Lord has also assumed his part:

> But thou art my desert:
> And in this league, which now my foes invade,
> Thou art not onely to perform thy part,
> But also mine; as when the league was made
> Thou didst at once thy self indite,
> And hold my hand, while I did write.

$$(25-30)^{25}$$

God, by Christ adopting the humanity of the tenant in addition to the deity of the landlord, has taken Old Testament legality into New Testament grace.[26]

Throughout his poetry Herbert relies on the terminology of the landlord assuming the debts of the tenant, Christ paying human scores with his scourging to emphasize Christ's sacrifice for mankind. But such expressions for Christ redeeming sins by spending his sacrificial blood did not come directly from legalistic, commercial diction and imagery. They had been transformed through psalmody.[27] The source reconfirms, once again, how Herbert amplifies the potential expressiveness of the neo-typological lyric.

Three references in "Love Unknown," the first and last framing the persona's tale, establish contractual language which expresses the paradoxical dual motives and motifs that drive the poem. The poem opens with the persona telling a Friend about his ambiguous lease: "A Lord I had, / And have, of whom some grounds, which may improve, / I hold for two lives, and both lives in me" (3–5). The pun on grounds alludes to two crucial ideas. The heart is land leased from God, tilled by both the Christian and his God for two lives—the Christian's continued existence now and hereafter and his responsibility for gaining the hereafter. "Of whom some grounds, which may improve" implies in addition that God's contract depends on the actions of the tenant. Though characteristically pained and confused by his lack of comprehension, the persona does not seem to know what these conditions are. In the second reference the persona admits to inevitable failure to meet the terms of the lease. At the same time, however, he glibly admits that the contract will be resolved in mercy: "I did and do commit / Many a fault more then my lease will bear; / Yet still askt pardon, and was not deni'd" (19–21). The final framing reference punningly twists legal into commercial diction. The persona is beginning to grasp the conditions of the contract just before the Friend is to reveal them: "But all my scores were by another paid, / Who took the debt upon him" (60–61). He is acknowledging both his inability to repay the debts of sin and his grateful acceptance of Christ's reimbursement, in the same manner of a typological and neotypological reading. He must further realize the price Christ pays, understand the pun on scourging that accompanies Christ's removal of our "scores." This legalistic/commercial reading of "Love Unknown," founded on the terrain of *The Temple* as it extends psalmody, returns to the paradigmatic motives and motifs of Herbert's neotypological lyrics.

During the course of many a Herbert lyric a neotypical persona discovers and the reader is supposed to rediscover through that persona's obtuse search the beauty of God's grace as his new covenant replaces the old. Such a discovery is made through the expansive context of the image matrix of *The Church* as Herbert repeatedly exploits the expressive potential inherent in these transforming neotypological scenes with their image and diction clusters. Discovery is also achieved through the intense immediate context of each poem. For Herbert masterfully exploits techniques of style that descended to him from the neotypological lyric heritage, techniques that dramatize the oscillations of a very human, contemporary Christian soul.

Herbert's puns on "grounds" early and "scores" late in "Love Unknown," which stylistically hint at the soul's vicissitudes in discovering the beauty of being a type, are reinforced by other morally significant puns. The wringing of the heart that "enforceth tears" (18) refers not only to forceful extortion but also to moral strengthening. And the "tender" of the heart (33) refers not only to the persona offering but also to God softening.

Several opening indirections in "Love Unknown" create a sense of ambiguous uncertainty in the persona who claims salvation by rote but does not seem to understand it. Having invited the Friend to sit down and listen to his plight, he adds:

> And in my faintings I presume your love
> Will more complie then help.

> (2–3)

The persona's whole sentence indicates that he anticipates the Friend's love will consist more of polite concern than genuine comfort. "I presume your love," however, suggests a forceful ambiguity since it forms a complete subsentence stopped by the conclusion of the verse line. This ambiguity strikes at the center of the poem, for the persona's failure is his presumption of God's love. By taking God's love for granted he fails to recognize the active faith that is necessary for him to be granted God's love. In order to present his contrite heart in a justifying act of faith, he must first discover God's beauty. Herbert has called attention to the crux of this as well as many of his other poems.

"Love Unknown" belongs to Herbert's set of poems that have been called double fictions.[28] These take the form of a dramatic dialogue/agon during which a speaker carries on a vociferous argument against God only to later realize his total dependence on and gratitude for God's saving sacrifice. Most often, as in the well-known "The Collar," the rebel wages his combat against God in multiple typological puns.[29] In "Sion" for example, while God's living, threadbare, New Testament temple in the heart is replacing the moribund splendor and glory of Solomon's temple, the speaker recognizes God's counterattacking victory:

There thou art struggling with a peevish heart,
Which sometimes crosseth thee, thou sometimes it:
    The fight is hard on either part.
    Great God doth fight, he doth submit.
All Solomons sea of brasse and world of stone
Is not so deare to thee as one good grone.

                             (13–18)

Participants in such poems come to defeat at the hands of God in order to achieve their own paradoxical victory—surrender to Christ's passion, as in "The Reprisall":

Couldst thou not griefs sad conquests me allow,
    But in all vict'ries overthrow me?

    Yet by confession will I come
Into thy conquest: though I can do nought
Against thee, in thee I will overcome
    The man, who once against thee fought.

                             (11–16)

The landlord requires that the persona in "Love Unknown" surrender his contrite heart. When he does he will finally recognize his original, unintentional pun on "faintings"—his dejected swoons and his feints, mock blows that God counters.

Herbert's dialogue/agon, in which God (or the Friend) corrects the rebellious persona in order to save him, seems to be accomplished through examination and expansion of *metanoia* or *correctio*, the rhetorical figure of "setting right." In *The Arte of English Poesie*, George Puttenham describes the figure in terms important for the set of correcting poems to which "Love Unknown" belongs:

> Otherwhiles we speake and be sorry for it, as if we had not wel spoken, so that we seeme to call in our word againe, and to put in another fitter for the purpose: for which respects the Greekes called this manner of speech the figure of repentance: then for that vpon repentance commonly followes amendment, the Latins called it the figure of correction, in that the speaker seemeth to reforme that which was said amisse. I following the Greeke originall, choose to call him the penitent, or repentant.[30]

It is critically significant that Puttenham returns to the primary Greek meaning of the figure—*the repentant*. For *the repentant* emphasizes imitation, as most rhetorical figures are categorized reflections, of a psychic condition. Furthermore, this psychic condition is also a primary sacred condition. In describing a rhetorical figure Puttenham is discussing a crucial event for the Christian psyche, and he is emphasizing that *the repentant* reflects the personal anguish of recognizing sin as well as the necessary responsive afterthought correcting it. Herbert's extension and probe of *the repentant* (what might be called Herbert's repentant) linguistically intensifies what are apparently personal statements that also reflect a set of universal Christian states. A speaker is thus simultaneously individual and exemplary when he discovers God's New Testament in his neotypical status by learning from Old Testament afflictions to repent and so correct his faith. Therefore, style which makes the person repeats patterns God has created and Herbert utilized to save people.

Herbert's syntactic repentant compels the neotype to discover God's ever present beauty and mercy while it urges the reader to discover how God disabuses all who listen of their presumption. Each of the three scenes that the persona describes follows the same pattern. When he tried to serve his landlord he was thwarted. The syntax of "I . . . But he" forming each emblem precisely mirrors the emblem: "I brought a dish of fruit . . . But he / . . . Lookt on a servant"; more expansively, "I went / To fetch a sacrifice . . . But . . . the man, / . . . slipt his hand"; and yet more subtly, "But when I thought to sleep out all these faults / . . . I found." The concluding discovery is no accident.

Herbert's repentant is even more important to the persona and his Friend's dialogue than it is to their syntax. At the moments when the persona is striving hardest to gain understanding and sympathy, he is mildly rebuked for misrepresentation by the Friend; as he is corrected for willfulness, he is made to repent for self-pity. His initial impression is anguish over God's repeated reprimands. He himself forewarns that his story is sad. In relating each scene he interrupts the flow of frequently run-on iambic pentameters by gulping out a monosyllabic dimeter lament/refrain:

(I sigh to say)
(I sigh to tell)
(I sigh to speak)

His pain drives him to seek sympathy for what he perceives to be a predicament. Frequently his plea takes the form of interpolated relative clauses colloquially modified and expanded: he tells of the grounds "which may improve" (4), the sacrifice "which I did thus present" (31), the hope of rekindling God's love "which I did fear grew cold" (32). Each more nearly begs sympathy than explains his position. None, however, is so obvious as his appeals to the Friend for understanding. In his overplayed, parenthetical, relative clause at the climactic moment in the first scene, he makes a hyperbolic claim about the Friend's knowledge: the servant who cast his heart into the font knows God's eye "Better then you know me, or (which is one) / Then I my self" (10–11). Shortly thereafter he claims to understand his impasse with God (though he fathoms no method in it) and summons the Friend's support: "I well remember all, / And have good cause" (15–16). At the climax of the second scene he cries out demanding that the Friend commiserate because the servant threw his heart into the caldron: "My heart, that brought it (do you understand?) / The offerers heart" (36–37). In the final episode when he cannot rest because of the mental thorns, he despairingly laments and presumptuously claims to understand what he clearly does not:

Deare, could my heart not break,
When with my pleasures ev'n my rest was gone?
Full well I understood, who had been there.

(52–54)

Because the Friend does comprehend contrition and salvation in the three typological situations, he becomes a teacher who corrects the persona's misinterpretations:

Your heart was foul, I fear.
Your heart was hard, I fear.
Your heart was dull, I fear.

The Friend's three monosyllabic, formulaic corrections, each a conclud-ing line, forcefully answer the persona's laments and teach him to reap-praise his situation. The Friend denies that the landlord is arbitrary; he blames the persona. The pattern consisting of the persona's interpreta-tions followed by the Friend's corrections, like the pattern of the scenes themselves, ultimately creates penitence.

Herbert's repentant encompasses still more than the persona's plea for sympathy and the Friend's determination of true fault and saving pen-ance. Besides individual contrition and personal humiliation, typology and correction signal the universal rejoicing of exaltation in the transac-tion. Thus it is a peculiarly Christian expression not of just a single but of several diverse, even contrary emotions. So the persona concludes each scene with another similar formula that is integral to his developing un-derstanding. He begins each summation with an admission of guilt, an "indeed," which leads to a "but" counterclaim of license. This device imitates Christ encompassing and restoring types. Even though his the-ology is impeccable, the persona fails to genuinely understand his own statements. At first he remains presumptuously complacent. To the Friend's first charge he responds disarmingly that God forgives contrac-tual failure:

Indeed 'tis true. I did and do commit
Many a fault more then my lease will bear;
Yet still askt pardon, and was not deni'd.

(19–21)

To the last he replies comfortably that Christ redeems his debt: "Indeed a slack and sleepie state of minde / Did oft possesse me. . . . But all my scores were by another paid" (57–60). To the central charge, that his hard heart must be softened to demonstrate the faith which justifies salvation, he answers with almost blasphemous complacency:

Indeed it's true. I found a callous matter
Began to spread and to expatiate there:
But with a richer drug then scalding water
I bath'd it often, ev'n with holy bloud.

(38–41)

102

Although the speaker's answer is couched in eucharistic terms, he fails to realize that without heartfelt contrition the eucharist lacks efficacy. Nevertheless, because Herbert presents God's grace as operative despite the persona's hard-headed if not hard-hearted recalcitrance to read neotypologically and so do penance, he is blessed in his ignorance. Herbert demonstrates God's grace by forcing his persona out of presumption into penance—a spiritual achievement attained through the syntactical and rhetorical pattern of a poem that points toward exaltation in God's grace through the antitype.

Even the overall structure of "Love Unknown" is formed on Herbert's repentant. Its first sixty-one lines are devoted to the persona's blind reading of a supposedly unwarranted punishment, the last ten to the Friend's revelatory correction establishing proper blame, initiating penance, and asserting salvation. The Friend first counters in single lines each of the persona's drawn-out emblems and excuses; his subordinate relative clauses (the three "whats") demolish the persona's long, begging rationales. Then he succinctly concludes.

One final aspect of Herbert's repentant makes a last, new correction: a correction in time reforms types from the past and neotypes in the present by uniting them with the eternal antitype. The persona begins both his story ("A Lord I had, / And have" [3–4]) and his first self-justification ("I did and do commit" [19]) with temporal corrections. The movement extends with each new correction throughout "Love Unknown": the persona begins to sense the exaction of his penance as he still feels the wringing of his heart ("the very wringing yet / Enforceth tears" [17–18]); then he claims to perpetually apply for God's pardon, and always to receive it ("Yet still askt pardon, and was not deni'd" [21]). In explaining the eucharist he notes that a friend enters the wine *for good*, both for virtue and forever. And in explaining the redemption he implies his recovery of debts to come as well as those already made good. The Friend's concluding revelatory correction envelops the past in order to redeem the persona's past tense recollections in God's ever-present concern:

For ought I heare, your Master shows to you
More favour then you wot of. . . .

. . . .

Wherefore be cheer'd, and praise him to the full
Each day, each houre, each moment of the week,
Who fain would have you be new, tender, quick.

103

Thus, Herbert has designed his poem to dramatically reveal to the reader the discovery of God's beauty by the persona. That discovery appears universally and extensively in the neotype's interaction in the enriched potential of being placed between the full scenic, imagistic, and linguistic context of an Old Testament legal type and its recovery by the New Covenant antitype while it is reflected personally and intensively in the rhetoric and style of the individual Herbert repentant. But, of course, for Herbert these are all appearances, reflections, representations. For Herbert full revelation comes solely from God: God's revelation provides the only way any person is able to see a personal or a representative status and recognize an exaction of penance, just as his revelation of grace in the Gospel is what makes possible typological interpretations of Old Testament legalism. The Friend's terse corrections throughout "Love Unknown" cumulatively reveal the persona's exegetical shortcomings and lead him to understanding. Finally the Friend reveals straightforwardly the types for the three emblematic scenes. Revelation comes in a conclusion reminiscent of the miraculous closings in a number of Herbert's poems.[31]

In addition to the reflection of revelation in "Love Unknown," vision appears when the Friend advises that the landlord "shows" favor and commands "*Mark the end.*" The entire passage belongs to a host of acknowledgments in *The Temple* that refer to John's accounts in which Christ miraculously cures the physically and spiritually blind.[32] Herbert's aptest text is "The H. Scriptures. I":

> This is the thankfull glasse,
> That mends the lookers eyes: this is the well
> That washes what it shows.
>
> (8–10)

The dual reference to 1 Corinthians 13:12 ("For now we see through a glass, darkly; but then face to face") and to Johannine symbols of Christ as a well of purgation and restorer of sight helps explication. Such a revelatory reflection of God can be read in the threefold gospel granted by Christ—in Christ himself, in the document itself, and in mankind, ourselves. However, it is read more fully in the interaction of the three, as the expressive potential in types defined and applied in a Reformed manner personally and universally.

"Love Unknown" reveals a vision granted by the only Friend who can grant such miracles, Christ.[33] This is clear in part because Christ, who knows the persona infinitely well, reveals him; and in part because Christ, who slips into the eucharistic chalice for good (43), is the only friend identified in the poem. It is clear in the main because it joins other references Herbert makes to Christ, his "Friend." The Friend who tells all at the end of "Love Unknown" is the same Friend who tells the persona to copy out charity inside himself in the conclusion of "Jordan (II)"; the Friend who chastens the persona is the same Friend who prunes away sins in "Paradise" (13); the Friend who interprets the contract to the persona is the same Friend who carries messages to the landlord in "The Bag" (36–39); the Friend who steals into the sacred wine is the same Friend who writes "Sunday" with his blood (3–4) and dispatches grace in "The H. Communion." The Friend in "Love Unknown" proves to be the friend beyond all others who, recrucified by the "Unkindnesse" of the complacently presumptuous, still saves them.

"Love Unknown" teaches its persona to see himself as a new Christ type in precisely the same situations with their attendant imagery and diction as Old Testament Christ types that are fulfilled and redeemed. Since he has lacked sensitivity to what Christ endured in order to redeem sins under the law, the persona is corrected by the syntax and style of the Herbert repentant reflecting his intense oscillation and simultaneously reforming his notions and requiring him to do penance for his complacent presumption of salvation. Here he learns corrective penance under the tutelage of Christ who, by atoning for humanity, grants the faith that justifies man. The expressive power in "Love Unknown" derives from multiple referents that seem to be ever present. In "The Holdfast" Herbert's persona tells how a person paradoxically becomes more himself by belonging to Christ:

> But to have nought is ours, not to confesse
>   That we have nought. I stood amaz'd at this,
>   Much troubled, till I heard a friend expresse,
> That all things were more ours by being his.
>   What Adam had, and forfeited for all,
>   Christ keepeth now, who cannot fail or fall.
>
>   (9–14)

Another identity is revealed in this passage. As well as becoming more personal, in part by assuming the first person plural, Herbert's speaker also becomes the universal representative of those to whom Christ reveals himself. If everyone inherits Adam's original sin only those who are chosen by and who choose Christ and salvation are true everymen, contemporary neotypes whose existence and fulfillment together with Old Testament types rest in Christ. Thus Herbert would teach the reader of "Love Unknown," of his neotypological lyrics, of many of his other best-known lyrics, and of neotypological lyrics as a form, to learn about God's love by reading a contemporary neotype just as he would read an Old Testament type. He should see in the neotype an independent being everlastingly meaningful through the lens of Christ. He should perceive the neotype enduring the individual agony of failure under the law at the same time he is exulting in the transcending joy of deliverance from that law by grace. Herbert teaches his audience to read through the persona typologically inside three principal contexts—his neotypological situations, emblems, and diction; his extended symbolic matrices in *The Church*; and his immediate, intensive rhetoric and style in his own version of the repentant. All three emanate from the neotypological lyric heritage which aims at portraying the discovery—by the most personal a persona and the most universal a Christian—of God's beauty in redemption so as to stimulate the reader's rediscovery of God's beauty in the neotypical persona. Herbert's neotypological lyrics thereby represent the fullest exploitation of the expressive potential for poetry of the Reformed strict definition and personal application of types. Furthermore, his poetry achieved a personal and universal, expressive paradigm that successors reinterpreted, expanded, and exploded.

5

"The Rain-bow" of Wrath

Henry Vaughan's Nostalgia over Spurned Typological Mediation and the Antipodal Neotypological Lyric

The opening of the first edition of Henry Vaughan's *Silex Scintillans* (1650), *"Authoris (de se) Emblema"* is founded on the typological stone heart. The opening of the augmented edition (1655), "The Authors PREF-ACE to the following HYMNS," rejects secular verse to promote "sacred poems and private ejaculations" inspired by George Herbert.[1] Together these rouse anticipations of neotypological lyrics to follow. And, after several dialogues between body and soul about death followed by medi-tations on judgment day, a cluster of neotypologically aware and in-formed lyrics seems to confirm those anticipations. Consequently, some critics have used applications of Scripture and of types to personal life to interpret a number of Vaughan's poems.[2]

Vaughan encourages such readings when in his preface he goes beyond the notion of converting secular to sacred poetics, found prominently in Hall's and Southwell's prefaces and Herbert's verse, to that of rejecting the follies of secular poets. The reward anticipated for exchanging *"vain* and *vitious subjects*, for *divine Themes* and *Celestial praise"* that will turn others to righteousness is conversion into eternity.[3] In making such a claim he is acknowledging the example of and debt he owes to his major poetic mentor, George Herbert, who through *The Temple* moved him to deepen his religious commitment:

> The first, that with any effectual success attempted a *diversion* of this foul and overflowing *stream* [of corrupting verse], was the blessed man, Mr. *George Herbert*, whose holy *life* and *verse* gained many pious *Converts*, (of whom I am the least) and gave the first check to a most flourishing and admired *wit* of his time. After him followed diverse. . . . He that desires to

excel in this kinde of *Hagiography*, or holy writing, must strive (by all means) for *perfection* and true *holyness*, that a *door may be opened to him in heaven*, Rev. 4. 1. and then he will be able to write (with *Hierotheus* and holy *Herbert*) A *true Hymn*.

Vaughan is not just following the master of the neotypological lyric; he is promoting one of the chief characteristics of the verse form by applying Scripture to his own life.

Vaughan is signaling as well that his foremost mentor in *Silex Scintillans*, regardless of where he learned his technical skills, is George Herbert.[4] And the twenty-six titles he appropriated from *The Temple*, the more than sixty poems that quote and refer to Herbert's lines, not to mention the words, puns, and ideas he borrowed from Herbert, attest to this influence, particularly in the first part of *Silex Scintillans*.[5] But the major lesson Vaughan emulates from Herbert amounts to more than merely applying Scripture to himself and his own life, in a line of Reformed applications that follow from Augustine, Erasmus, Donne, and Herbert. Vaughan follows these exemplars and emulates Herbert by displaying his own life as an exemplum for a potential readership of Anglican believers:

> To effect this [being himself and being able to write true hymns] in some measure, I have begged leave to communicate this my poor *Talent* to the *Church*, under the *protection* and *conduct* of her *glorious Head:* who (if he will vouchsafe to *own* it, and *go along* with it) can make it as useful now in the *publick*, as it hath been to me in *private*.[6]

This doctor felt called to be a physician of the soul. Even more than the others, who had their own pastorates, he needed to create a congregation of readers of *Silex Scintillans*.

Vaughan reconfirmed his own commitment through observing another poet apply Scripture successfully, for the sake of the congregation as well as the sake of the poet. Now Vaughan wanted to follow by creating through his own verse a life that would be doubly consecrated and made effective by Christ. Such a dedication seems the inspiration for the opening of "The Match," which appears to be, because of its echoes, diction, and thought, both from and for George Herbert:

> Dear friend! whose holy, ever-living lines
> > Have done much good
> > To many, and have checkt my blood.

It is not so much, then, the acclaimed fact that *Silex Scintillans* is filled with biblical references that leads to the expectation that types play an important role. It is even more than Vaughan imitating Herbert. It is most his application of Scripture to his own life as exemplary both for himself and for others. Nor was the tradition that led to Herbert, the latest of renowned Christian exemplars, Vaughan's sole promise of the rewards of applying biblical contexts and typology to himself and his time. When he writes about his bereavement after the death of his younger brother William or his wife Catherine has left only vestiges of comfort, he also acknowledges their neotypical guidance:

Joy of my life! while left me here,
    And still my Love!
How in thy absence thou dost steere
    Me from above!

.   .   .   .   .   .

They are (indeed,) our Pillar-fires
    Seen as we go.

                                 (1–4, 25–26)

Here he is following, nostalgically, the precedent of such writers as Cawdrey who compared the elect as neotypes to a type in order to show examples: "As the cloud did guide the *Israelites* through the wildernesse to the land of *Canaan*: So the faithful now are to be guided to the heauenly *Canaan*, by the Examples of good men that haue belieued in God before vs, and haue walked the straight way to life euerlasting. *Heb. 12,1.*"[7]

The main direct evidence of Vaughan's faith in applying biblical passages to his own life and to the lives of the people and nature around him is found near the end of the augmented edition of *Silex Scintillans*. Here he begins a paean to the Bible by affirming in "The Agreement" that though he had known it before, he had forgotten the exalting significance of the Bible in his own life; but he has recovered it by God's grace:

O beamy book! O my mid-day
Exterminating fears and night!
The mount, whose white Ascendents may
Be in conjunction with true light!
    My thoughts, when towards thee they move,
    Glitter and kindle with thy love.

                                 (13–18)

His exalted state is achieved when he realizes again that "Each page of thine hath true life in't, / And Gods bright minde exprest in print" (23–24). But it is achieved when, and only when, after an earlier condition of uncomprehending ignorance or forgetfulness, he has applied the Bible to himself and to life. Only then can the praises and comparisons of the rest of the poem, or those of the last two poems before "L'Envoy," appear. "The Book," through its emblematic physical makeup, provides a reflection of the true and whole meaning of biblical application: it both includes and applies to all creation, particularly those people who have been redeemed:

> O knowing, glorious spirit! when
> Thou shalt restore trees, beasts and men,
> When thou shalt make all new again,
> Destroying onely death and pain,
> Give him amongst thy works a place,
> Who in them lov'd and sought thy face!
>
> (25–30)

"To the Holy Bible" bids farewell by praising and thanking "lifes guide."

Significantly, these poems are not typological. In fact, they make no typological references. However, a similar, less straightforward poem in the first edition does contain typological references and is typological to a degree. "H. Scriptures" begins like these last poems, and like several of George Herbert's, by addressing the Bible in a series of appositive metaphors. However, in the middle of the first of its two stanzas are two important typological references, to manna and to a rock. Each shows the Bible to be "The Key that opens to all Mysteries, / The *Word* in Characters, God in the *Voice*" (7–8). First the speaker establishes both the historical referent and the ultimate reference to grace's abrogation of law that make them typological. Then he concludes by applying and explicating the familiar stone heart emblem for himself:

> O that I had deep Cut in my hard heart
>   Each line in thee! Then would I plead in groans
>   Of my Lords penning, and by sweetest Art
> Return upon himself the *Law*, and *Stones*.
>   Read here, my faults are thine. This Book, and I
>   Will tell thee so; *Sweet Saviour thou didst dye!*

The rock emblem makes possible a familiar application specifically through *Silex Scintillans*, as well as through the neotypological lyric line.

It forms the author's emblem which inaugurates the first edition, thereby stimulating expectations of a set of neotypological lyrics to follow. For it recalls conventions set by such earlier emblems as Thomas Jenner's "The meanes to get a *soft heart*," number four in *The Soules Solace.* Jenner's emblem shows God's hand striking with a hammer (labeled the law) a heart of stone lying on a cushion (the Gospel) displayed on an altar. His verse first explains a natural comparison: to break a flint, place it on a cushion. It then clarifies historical and typological relationships: in order to force David to repent and seek mercy, God placed Nathan underneath David's hard heart. It finally culminates with antitypical and neotypical applications: to be saved humans must repent by softening recalcitrance, obeying God, and recognizing Christ's mercy. Vaughan adds to this hard core another crust that includes the speaker enumerating his shortcomings and revealing his melancholy after failure; then Vaughan extends his own self-reading to include his utter dependence on God's action and his resulting affirmation. He confesses his need for God to shatter his stony heart and make a new one of flesh, thereby expressing again a Christian's transcendence of Mosaic prohibitions. The message is especially forceful when, during his celebration of the reunion of God and man through Christ, he recalls the waters of Meribah.

The expectation of neotypological lyrics is briefly fulfilled early on by a series of typological references and a few neotypological poems beginning with "Religion," the seventh of *Silex Scintillans.* But after this set, typological allusions appear only sporadically in the first edition, though several appear from "The Pilgrimage" through "The Mutinie." Another group, if one includes the Ishmael references, appears in the augmented edition beginning with "The Timber" and concluding in "Jacobs Pillow, and Pillar," though not all of these make typological references. So, just as Vaughan was falling away from Herbert's example toward reworking conventional pietistic subjects and biblical texts in his augmented edition, he was also tending toward less use of types.[8] He was, however, using the neotypological lyric most distinctively then.

The difference between the two editions is perhaps most easily illustrated in the contrast between the author's emblem and "The Stone" found in the typological cluster of the second edition. For "The Stone" Vaughan cites Joshua 24:27, wherein this named type of Christ sets up a stone to commemorate the covenant which the chosen people made with God at Schechem ("it shall be therefore a witness unto you, lest ye deny your God"). In doing so he is raising expectations of the movement from the stone to the flesh heart that is familiar from early in the neotypological tradition through the author's emblem. But this he does not emplace until the end of the next poem, "The dwelling-place," which concludes with God lodged in the persona's sinful heart. In "The Stone" itself Vaughan describes how all dumb nature keeps its covenant with God while man breaks his. Then he describes how all seemingly insensate nature is witness to accuse man of his secret sinful violations. Finally he becomes explicitly didactic, rather than imitative, in a neotypological application:

> The *Law* delivered to the *Jews*,
> Who promis'd much, but did refuse
> Performance, will for that same deed
> Against them by a *stone* proceed;
> Whose substance, though 'tis hard enough,
> Will prove their hearts more stiff and tuff.
> But now, since God on himself took
> What all mankinde could never brook,
> If any (for he all invites)
> His easie yoke rejects or slights,
> The *Gospel* then (for 'tis his word
> And not himself shall judge the world)
> Will by loose *Dust* that man arraign,
> As one then dust more vile and vain.

What Vaughan does here is preach a homily based on the potential conversion of the stone decalogue of the legalistic Old Testament into a heart of flesh through New Covenant mercy. But Vaughan's persona here, as usual, does not ever truly associate with the type, much less become identified with it. Instead, recognizing the possibility, he turns away. He also turns away from the promise and hope of the neotypological lyric in several other related and most significant ways—in seeing nature instead of man communing with God, in stopping short of conversion, and in accusing mankind of failure. He dissociates himself from people who fail and casts them among the hard-hearted who will end in legal prosecution and conviction instead of comforting them with the promise of grace after condemnation.

It is apparent that Vaughan's use of the neotypological lyric, while it is important, is limited. As critics throughout the twentieth century have noted, Vaughan uses nature and its emblems to corroborate the Bible much more often, and with more cumulative effect, than he does types.[9] He most often contrasts nature's closeness with God to man's distance from God, as in "The Stone," or presents nature as a retreat from man's failings. When Vaughan describes nature's general successes or man's rare ones, his image clusters grow out of the seeds of mysticism or the hermeticists' world soul and the alchemists' transformations.[10] Even these traditions represent only the less frequently recurring aspect of Vaughan's verse.

What is heard most often in Vaughan is the sound of *memento mori* dialogues between the soul and body, of nostalgia for the defeated monarchy and the demise of the Anglican way as in *Olor Iscanus* or some sacred pastorals, of satire and invective against the Interregnum and the Puritans, of apocalyptic invocation and imagery.[11] A fundamental part of Vaughan's sacred verse is satire against what he sees as hellish perversion of true religion which he expresses through apocalyptic perspectives. This inverts the tone of earlier neotypological lyrics. Simmonds is generally instructive when he describes "The Proffer," one of Vaughan's fiercest attacks: "as is characteristic of his sacred verse, Vaughan perceives and interprets historical circumstances (which include his personal circumstances) in terms of the archetypal patterns of Christian myth. He conceives of his own times and of his personal experiences in them typologically—that is, he sees history as the recurrent fulfillment of Biblical prophecy, the exfoliation through time of a timeless myth."[12] Granted substitution for "typologically" of "in terms of scriptural precedents (or parallels or contexts)," this perception seems accurate. And it reflects an address to God in the previous poem, "White Sunday":

> Besides, thy method with thy own,
> Thy own dear people pens our times,
> Our stories are in theirs set down
> And penalties spread to our Crimes.
>
> (29–32)

Although suggestive, neither the critic's definition nor the poet's principle is necessarily typological. Applying various biblical texts to his time and life is not the same thing as using types; when Vaughan uses types he is working within the neotypological lyric heritage much more specifically and toward different, though related, ends.

The final reckoning, therefore, is perhaps surprising. Even though he clearly understands typological prediction and antitypical good news, even though he is extraordinarily versed in the neotypological lyric heritage and at times uses it to good effect, Vaughan does not employ that tradition predominantly or extensively. Furthermore, his characteristic modification of it reveals nostalgia, regret, perhaps despair over the failure of mankind, and often bitterness over the rejection by humanity of types as part of Christ's mediation between God and man. For although typology had seemed to be at the center of human history and although God's emblems still filled nature's cosmos, Vaughan felt that types had come to be not merely ignored, but worse, abused by his contemporaries. Thus he rarely wrote neotypological lyrics like his predecessors, those in which a persona is projected into a typological scene in order to be saved so that the reader could be comforted or surprised to discover God. Vaughan was more likely to first apply scriptural and typological references quite explicitly and far beyond himself to his failing fellows. Then he portrayed their neglect of Christ's neotypical mediation and their rejection of potential salvation and reassurance. Understanding and often explicating the promise of neotypology, he lamented that, in contrast to nature and to types, man has severed himself from God. His laments blackened into tragic and satiric inversion when he despaired that the problems of recovering God's mercy have, in his own time since New Testament redemption of the faithful man's failings, been compounded. And because humankind condemned themselves by denying Christ, Vaughan turned witness against them—to warn, and failing that, to accuse and bring them to judgment. Those few neotypological lyrics he did write, those uses he made of the tradition, and those radical modifications he originated provide insights both into Vaughan's own vision and into the evolution of the neotypological lyric.

Vaughan uses the word *type* somewhat loosely. For him it can mean a copy: virtuous manners become types of divine goodness in "Of Temperance and Patience," a prose translation in the *Flores Solitudinis* (1654).[13] More importantly, it can be a symbol: cycles of vegetation, light appearing from dark, and waking out of sleep are types of resurrection in *The Mount of Olives: or, Solitary Devotions* (1652).[14] Vaughan implies that *type* can also mean prototype when he uses *antitype* for copy or sign in "Trinity-Sunday" from the augmented *Silex Scintillans*. In the last triplet he prays that his antitypical trinity of spirit, water, and blood be acknowledged, saved, and sainted. Or his *type* can mean the original as in his translation of Grotius' "*mentis Imago tuæ*," in Thomas Powell's *Humane Industry* (1661): "As your minde (then) was Heavens type first, so this / But the taught *Anti-type* of your mind is."[15] Similarly in his "The

Nativity," avowedly written in 1656 but not appearing in print until *Thalia Rediviva* (1678), Vaughan calls Christ "Great *Type* of passions! come what will, / Thy grief exceeds all *copies* still" (15–16).

Although his characterizations of *type* attest to a multitude of potential meanings, Vaughan usually approximates a Reformed definition of *type*. A secular reference appears in "The King Disguis'd," his comparison of the fleeing Charles I to Samuel. Although the poem was not printed until *Thalia Rediviva*, it presumably predicts the failure of the revolution: "Thy robes forc'd off, like *Samuel*'s when rent, / Do figure out anothers Punishment" (17–18). His precise exegetical use of *figured* for *prefigured* is in "Faith": "Then did [Christ] shine forth, whose sad fall, / and bitter fights / Were figur'd in those mystical, / And Cloudie [Old Testament] Rites" (29–32). The conclusion of "Jacobs Pillow, and Pillar," Vaughan's most straightforward neotypological lyric, provides the clearest example: "Thy pillow was but type and shade at best, / But we the substance have, and on him rest."

Vaughan's poetic employment of typology is also fairly consistent in definition. The whole of "Jacobs Pillow, and Pillar," which follows the neotypological lyric tradition, provides an illustration. The text for Vaughan's poem, one the poet also applied as an exemplum in "Rules *and* Lessons" (19–24) and as a contrast in "The Pilgrimage" (5–8), comes from a dream vision Jacob had one night during travels which served him both to flee from Esau's wrath and to search for a wife (Gen. 28:11–22). He dreamed about a ladder to heaven upon which angels were ascending and descending. At the top was God who promised the spread of the Children of Jacob (Israel), that is, the increase in spirit, influence, and size of the promised seed. When Jacob woke he raised the stone he had used for a pillow to make a pillar; he then christened it with oil, named the place Bethel (house of God), and vowed a covenant of faith and tithes.

Interpreters as strict as the Geneva annotators affirm that the ladder in Jacob's vision is an occasional type of Christ. Diodati explains that it "signifieth the communication which the Elect have with God, through the mediation of Jesus Christ, and the covenant of grace founded upon him. . . ." Others add more details: the ladder's foot is Christ's humanity and its head his divinity; the ladder marks the way to heaven and makes angelic aid possible; God's message confirms his original promise to Abraham.[16] According to Ainsworth the type is sanctioned by the end of John's first chapter when Christ declares: "Verily, verily, I say unto you, Hereafter ye shall see heaven open, and the angels of God ascending and descending upon the Son of man." The disparity between Jacob's vision and antitypical fulfillment in Christ incarnate on earth is less than the disparity which Christ is here discussing between his fulfillment on earth and final revelation at the universal resurrection. This latter discrepancy is pointed out by Guild and Mather who contrast dim reflection to direct sight of God.

Although this discrepancy is implied, Vaughan's poem opens with still, a different disparity, one between the dreadful glory of God viewed by Jacob's sin-blind children and the insightful vision of Jacob. Though his sins are lesser and he is purer, Jacob is still awed by his unique vision: "In milde, clear visions, without a frown, / Unto thy solitary self is shown" (3–4).

The opening circumstances in the poem also suggest a further, related text: Jacob wrestling all night with an angel (Gen. 32:24–30). This conflation, which the poet also applies as an exemplum in "Rules *and* Lessons" (19–24), is explained by Diodati. Following a host of Jewish commentators on the Messiah, Diodati identifies the visitor as Christ in human form. This suggestion implies that Jacob is one of God's spiritual warriors. Later in "Jacobs Pillow, and Pillar," however, is an ever-darkening rendition; according to Vaughan, the children of Israel (Jacob) are becoming the schismatic multitude who will finally crucify Christ. Because they are failing God they murmur against him even while they see Christ in another pillar that forms a type, this one the pillar of "clouds, and fire and smoke" (7). In forgiving their spiritual failings, Christ grants his aid and continues his mediation, creating a vision, however dim, of himself, his benefits, and his ordinances.[17]

Through this further, related, typological implication, "Jacobs Pillow, and Pillar" is ultimately a poem about God's congregation. For the children of Israel are, according to Paul's epistle to the Romans, not just Jews but all those who inherit belief in God. The rock pillow/pillar signifies the body of the church by the consecrating oil of the Holy Ghost; so Ainsworth extends Judaic interpretations of the pillar to the temple to the church.

Vaughan continues to chronicle and interpret Ainsworth's extension. As the church grew from a private elect to a universal institution it became corrupt, "For this rich Pearl, like some more common stone, / When once made publique, is esteem'd by none" (17–18). When it finally perpetrated the crucifixion, destruction had fully supplanted nurture.

Vaughan still has considerable church history to trace. In the Gospel, Christ's revelation establishes a different type of the temple, the human heart:

This God foresaw: And when slain by the crowd
(Under that stately and mysterious cloud
Which his death scatter'd) he foretold the place,
And form to serve him in, should be true grace
And the meek heart, not in a Mount, nor at
Jerusalem, with blood of beasts, and fat.

(21–26)

This secondary image, replacing dead rituals by sacrificing a live human heart, reinforces a familiar type. Here is the reconsecrated, anointed, christened, secret ark, Goshen, vision, Bethel, place of God.

Still another historical force twists the poem. After Christ reestablished his mystical church of believing hearts, the pillow/pillar sank beneath the physical church:

Thus is the solemn temple sunk agen
Into a Pillar, and conceal'd from men.
And glory be to his eternal Name!
Who is contented, that this holy flame
Shall lodge in such a narrow pit, till he
With his strong arm turns our captivity.

(35–40)

At this transition to the final stanza Vaughan continues to recount and lament the children of God's, and, by application his fellow Englishmen's, failures to abide by the covenant and so receive the promise God granted in his sanctuary of vision.

In the final stanza, however, Vaughan reaffirms his opening line by invoking the antitype. He had initially claimed that like Jacob, but unlike Jacob's children and Old Testament physical offspring, "I See the Temple in thy Pillar rear'd." Now he affirms Gospel abrogation and fulfillment of another type:

Thou from the Day-star a long way didst stand
And all that distance was Law and command.
But we a healing Sun by day and night,
Have our sure Guardian, and our leading light.

(47–50)

Once he has established the primary pun of Jacob's limiting, and legal, historical distance from the sun/Son's grace, Vaughan alludes to the sun of righteousness rising up with healing in its wings. He thereby returns to Herbert's Christ, the friend as well as opponent, in both Jacob's dream and "Rules *and* Lessons" (19–24): "What thou didst hope for and believe, we finde / And feel a friend most ready, sure and kinde" (51–52). The speaker confesses grace in Christ, the antitypical mediator; and by doing so he reaffirms the value of the type defined along Reformed lines. Furthermore, he applies that definition to himself and significantly extends it beyond the congregation he represents to another group he opposes, indeed condemns: the apostate who have failed to avail themselves of God's mercy and to join his communion. By recalling both the type and the antitype upon which the whole of "Jacobs Pillow, and Pillar" stands, he rightfully concludes: "Thy pillow was but type and shade at best, / But we the substance have, and on him rest."

Vaughan here demonstrates his knowledge of and abililty to create neotypological lyrics in the customary way. But he has also extended them somewhat in performance and considerably more in prospect. His somewhat transformed neotypical persona represents the whole spiritual Christian congregation in a new way both personal and universal. And he has applied the implications of typology and final judgment to the damned goats and wolves of his world in contrast to the saved sheep of his congregation.

A Vaughan neotypological lyric that follows the general tradition presents a standard of belief and vision, then applies it to his congregation. Occasionally one of these appears in the first *Silex Scintillans*. The vantage of "Faith," for example, provides the perspective of "H. Scriptures" that is essential to Christian life and salvation. Here the persona stresses the good news of Christ's abrogation of the law. Whereas "The Law, and Ceremonies made / A glorious night" (13–14), the *sol justitiae* enlightens:

> So when the Sun of righteousness
> >   Did once appear,
> That Scene was chang'd, and a new dresse
> >   Left for us here;
> Veiles became useles, Altars fel,
> >   Fires smoking die;
> And all that sacred pomp, and shel
> >   Of things did flie;
> Then did he shine forth, whose sad fall,
> >   And bitter fights
> Were figur'd in those mystical,
> >   And Cloudie Rites.
>
> >   (21–32)

The passage adapts the seventh through the tenth chapters of Hebrews: "For the law having a shadow of good things to come, *and* not the very image of the things, can never with those sacrifices which they offered year by year continually make the comers thereunto perfect" (10:1); Christ does. Success follows when the perspective of the speaker and his congregation becomes that of the poem's title, "Faith brings us home" (40). After he says "*I do believe*," he is fulfilled through Christ's riming, and resolving, echo: "And my most loving Lord straitway / Doth answer, *Live*."

A somewhat different sort of lyric, closer yet to the tradition, is "Mans fall, and Recovery." In it the persona, meditating on Old Testament history and applying it to himself, follows the failures of God's chosen people before and under the law as they first imply and then give way to grace:

> Two thousand yeares
> I sojourn'd thus; at last *Jeshuruns* king
> Those famous tables did from *Sinai* bring;
> These swell'd my feares,
> Guilts, trespasses, and all this Inward Awe,
> For sinne tooke strength, and vigour from the Law.
> Yet have I found
> A plenteous way, (thanks to that holy one!)
> To cancell all that e're was writ in stone,
> His saving wound
> Wept bloud, that broke this Adamant, and gave
> To sinners Confidence, life to the grave.
>
> (15–26)

First he precisely explicates the movement of typology, recalling the old legal condemnation in order to understand himself and also to praise Christ for mercifully abrogating it by his sacrificial blood. He then approaches the status of believer by recalling two types—the trek across the Red Sea, beyond which he has made his pilgrimage, and the living well, which purifies him:

> For God (made man,)
> Reduc'd th'Extent of works of faith; so made
> Of their *Red Sea*, a *Spring*; I wash, they wade.

The persona's progress here is characteristic of earlier neotypological lyrics. Not so characteristic is Vaughan's persona who watches others wade instead of being washed.

Vaughan's less traditional neotypological lyrics also work by presenting the kind of structure displayed in "Jacobs Pillow, and Pillar." But instead of recovery in these he applies past failures from the Scripture to present failures of his fellows he would condemn, or who condemn themselves, as is traditional in satire. These obverse standards of worldliness and sin make stark contrasts to the exaltation and vision of his neotypologically comforted and saved readership.

In "The Law, and the Gospel" Vaughan straightforwardly presents the typological movement from the Old to the New Testament, ultimately begging for a neotype. In the first stanza the persona recalls the terror and the subsequent conviction of sin that was roused when Moses brought the Ten Commandments down from Mount Sinai; here was compelled obedience. Then he recalls the grace and mercy of Christ's revelatory sacrifice: "But now since we to *Sion* came, / And through thy bloud thy glory see, / With filial Confidence we touch ev'n thee" (11–13). The passage implies a recollected contract: under the old law, to even touch the ark led to death (2 Sam. 6:3–7). Before he returns to pray for Christ's acceptance of him in the eucharist and for his own obedience to Christ's mild commandments, in the third stanza, a crucial one, he sets up two opposing groups. One is the rejecting and thereby self-condemning crowd the speaker opposes; the other is the true congregation he represents:

> Yet since man is a very brute
> And after all thy Acts of grace doth kick,
> Slighting that health thou gav'st, when he was sick,
> Be not displeas'd, If I, who have a sute
>   To thee each houre, beg at thy door
>   For this one more;
> O plant in me thy *Gospel*, and thy *Law*,
>   Both *Faith*, and *Awe*;
> So twist them in my heart, that ever there
> I may as wel as *Love*, find too thy *fear*!
>
> (21–30)

The persona sees the crowd turn away and he condemns them for it. At the same time he realizes that he must himself be convicted of sin and grow contrite in order to be saved by his faith. Thus he begs for his own prosecution under law so that it can be supplanted by mercy. But also in this poem, as frequently in Vaughan, there is a tone of melancholy irony.

That the gospel, faith, and love precede the law, awe, and fear seems to reverse both the historical order and the customary and climactic exaltation of Christianity's abundant mercy.[18] This modulation in turn leads to Vaughan's more distinctive transformation of the neotypological lyric he inherited.

Though Vaughan reaches resolution in the ultimate affirmation of "Jacobs Pillow, and Pillar," "Faith," "Mans fall, and Recovery," or "The Law, and the Gospel," consolation is not generally his theme. His harmonies derive at least as much from dissonance caused by and invective against those who lose sight of or turn away from the hopeful potential of Christianity. Often he juxtaposes a type's power for communion with God in contrast to what he sees as men's impotence and severance from God since the Gospel. Tragically for him, types seem to have provided a more effective mediation under law than Christ's directly revealed mediation. This is because men, who ought to be neotypes, spurn the antitype. Therefore, oftentimes Vaughan yearns and expresses nostalgia and melancholy for an ancient communion. Unlike Herbert, he does not often strive to become a type so that he can be absorbed into the antitype. More often he mourns for the passing of a union lost by his contemporaries and perhaps, fearfully, by himself.

In "*Isaacs* Marriage" Vaughan modifies the dual tone of the neotypological lyric to nostalgic and melancholy lament.[19] By focusing on faithless man's displacement from types, the persona forgoes any sense of exaltation. His dejection results from his loss. From the opening, types represent ancient, pure mediation, in contrast to contemporary defilement:

> Praying! and to be married? It was rare,
> But now 'tis monstrous; and that pious care
> Though of our selves, is so much out of date,
> That to renew't were to degenerate.

Vaughan develops his initial irony through an open-ended catalogue. Ancient revelation was brilliant; then customs were pristine and pious and innocent, not excessive and contrived and seducing; then angels aided man; then women were chaste, modest, and truthful, not mincing and fraudulently painted; then spiritual and human marriages were auspicious, not miserable, compacts; then souls soared. . . .

"Religion" develops so bitter a tone that finally the speaker feels compelled to turn towards the apocalypse and to pray that he and the true congregation may be parted from the ruling majority, the corrupters, of his day. He begins a comparison by identifying trees with turning over the leaves of the Bible with intent to discover God's direct communication:

> My God, when I walke in those groves,
> And leaves thy spirit doth still fan,
> I see in each shade that there growes
> An Angell talking with a man.

In progression, juniper, myrtle, and oak foliage become fountains; and types, such as Jacob dreaming and wrestling (9) and the pillar of cloud and fire (17–18), appear with such nontypological Old Testament events as angels visiting Abraham. At this point he interrupts, first in dismay over the lack of communication, then in despair to ask why, if such mediations were straightforward and prevalent in the Old Testament, there has been no direct mediation after Christ's revelation:

> Is the truce broke? or 'cause we have
> A mediatour now with thee,
> Doest thou therefore old Treaties wave
> And by appeales from him decree?
>
> Or is't so, as some green heads say
> That now all miracles must cease?
>
> (21–26)

He follows with a new metaphor to help him analyze religion: a spring of water (recalling the fountain) brings cordials (with a pun on heart) and wine from a hidden source. From their pristine source the water and wine flow underground, disastrously absorbing the world's pollution, until their purifying and curative powers become poisoned:

> Just such a tainted sink we have
> Like that *Samaritans* dead *Well*,
> Nor must we for the Kernell crave
> Because most voices like the *shell*.
>
> (45–48)

Two streams flow into the last stanza. The first, a tributary, rises from the second stanza and widens the metaphor; this is a type, the well or spring that traditionally can flow from the rock/spring of Horeb, the Johannine living well, the miracle at Cana (John 2:1–11), and the blood and water at Christ's crucifixion. But the main stream carries melancholia and near despair; this well rises from a human perspective:

So poison'd, [it] breaks forth in some Clime,
And at first sight doth many please,
But drunk, is puddle, or meere slime
And 'stead of Phisick, a disease.

(41–44)[20]

Only as if finally driven to it by despair over the immediate circumstances and their outpouring of pollution, the speaker abruptly rejects his surroundings, turns to the purifying typological rock-spring, and begs to be healed with the congregation of the faithful. Finally he approaches the communion of wine.

Vaughan's juxtapositions of contemporary failings with Old Testament successes are evident in incidental allusions to types. The faithful gathering manna and Jacob wrestling with the angel, both before sunrise, condemn modern malingering into the daytime in "Rules *and* Lessons" (st. 2–4); humanity since Christ's offer of salvation having lost childhood and even unfulfilled Pisgah-like visions of the "shady City of Palme trees" appear in "The Retreate" (26). His speakers sometimes yearn for a lost perspective, which is revealed when the Old Testament is read through the New—a perspective often missing in their time, though ever-present after God appeared in open revelation. This opportunity to regain the lost perspective, available but not fully availed of, elicits Vaughan's greatest distress.

"The Mutinie" offers one such account of a Vaughan persona wandering in mental search for God. He begins his journey, tired of making bricks in Egyptian bondage, "casting in my heart / The after-burthens, and griefs yet to come" (2–3); he becomes like a churning river that refuses to be channeled either by God or by outside forces. Although he asks God's guidance during his strife with the powers of Babel, he still chafes. As he crosses the Red Sea to wander the arid sands and endure the plague of serpents, he joins other disobedient children and murmurs against God. Therefore he must pray that he not evoke God's wrath nor grieve the Holy Spirit further, "but soft and mild / Both live and die thy Child."

The general form of "The Mutinie" initially appears to be the same as

Herbert's "The Collar," which judging from Vaughan's title, development, and close, inspired it. But it presents a wholly different development. Herbert presents the conflict of a persona who by using the terms of types battles against God, only to discover in the end that as he wrestles he also nestles inside those terms; he has already been saved. Vaughan, on the other hand, concludes not by surrendering to God's mercies and comfort, but rather by despairingly requesting that he might surrender and be comforted, like some have done (perhaps at one time he himself). Instead of gaining a personal resolution Vaughan's personae repeatedly remain in "The Storm," because they cannot recognize churning inside themselves the type of the Red Sea, much less its antitype.

Vaughan's essentially Reformed definition of type, his awareness and creation of neotypological lyrics in a traditional way, his distinctive juxtaposition of his congregation's neotypological comfort against self and Old Testament condemnation applied satirically to contemporaries who rejected their neotypical opportunities, his expression of nostalgia and melancholy lament over those losing sight of the promise in types—all lead toward his most radical transformation of his heritage, inversion, his antipodal neotypological lyric.

† † †

Vaughan's antipodal neotypological lyric needs to be interpreted in the context of his apparently increasing depression, a mood that can be discerned through his use of the traditional Christian pilgrimage wherein someone searches physically, mentally, spiritually, mystically through the world as well as through the Scriptures. Most critics agree that Vaughan follows his predecessors by his affirmation that the proper site to seek and interpret God's mediation is not so much the cosmos or even the Bible as it is the heart, God's true dwelling.[21] Vaughan's speakers often tell about an interior pilgrimage from Jacob's bed in "Regeneration" (st. 4) through the opening of "The Pilgrimage" into "The dwelling-place" of the sinful heart to "The Night," where the new temple of the heart, illuminated by the healing sun of righteousness, supplants the old temple with its dark ceremonies and ark.

How a physical pilgrimage, even in meditation, becomes an interior one is described by Vaughan in "The Search" for Christ. Though the poem begins after day has fully dawned, the persona recalls in a fine oxymoron the previous night's "roving Extasie" to discover the sun/ Son. He had searched in vain for God through the neighborhoods of

124

Christ's beginnings in Bethlehem, Egypt, and the temple in Jerusalem; he had returned to follow another route to other sites associated with Christ. He halts at Jacob's well, which is unrecognized by the physical children of Jacob but sought by the spiritual children of Israel. Although the well is transformed into his own tears of contrition, renewing his hopes and rousing him to seek Golgotha, his efforts are no more successful than before. Thus he prepares to seek Christ, not at the trodden stations or landscapes of biblical gathering places, but in the wilderness where Christ fasted and repelled the devil. Success seems close after the sun breaks through to guide him; but while he is contemplating attainment, a song interrupts to tell him that despite his painstaking scrutiny, the Bible and nature provide merely "The skinne, and shell of things" (81). The conclusion advises him to toss away old elements and dust, then turn to himself: "Search well another world; who studies this, / Travels in Clouds, seeks *Manna*, where none is." The type leads inward to the writings in his heart, since the verse tag that men live and move and exist in Christ (Acts 17:27–28) is for him reversible.

Vaughan's speakers are often disillusioned when trying to find Gospel revelation in an expedition through nature or an interior pilgrimage.[22] In "Vanity of Spirit," for example, the persona had been contemplating a fading type, "The Rain-bow," and the disappearing ring of light that encircles the "World," a ring that signifies marriage to the lamb: "I summon'd nature: peirc'd through all her store, / Broke up some seales, which none had touch'd before" (9–10). Still dissatisfied after anatomizing creation, he "came at last / To search my selfe" (14–15) but found only "Hyerogliphicks quite dismembred, / And broken letters scarce remembred" (23–24). These he tried to reconstruct and decipher. In contrast, however, to the persona of Herbert's "Jesu," he could not. Lacking the revelation of grace he fails and so offers to die for the sake of internal vision which would permit him to see grace, visible to those whose sight is corrected by Christ.

With such poems as "Vanity of Spirit," Vaughan's nostalgia deepens over mankind losing types, losing the ability to read the Old Testament through the lens of the New. Lacking the perspective of the antitype, Christ, mankind's vision is rendered darker than the mirror of Corinthians until sight of the Bible, nature, or even himself is itself lost. When this happens, self or societal condemnation rather than forgiveness becomes the focus of Vaughan's poems. And such occurrences demonstrate all the greater despair, because revelation since Christ ought to be clearer. At such moments when, for his neotypical pilgrim, humanity seems to lose sight of, ignore, or deny the revelation of Christ's mediation, melancholy blackens; usually Vaughan then turns either to allegorical identification and comfort or to the antipodal neotypological lyric.

It is perhaps not insignificant that both Vaughan's allegorical identifications of a speaker with the wanderer Ishmael and his fine antipodal neotypological lyric appear in the middle of the cluster of typological references in the 1655 *Silex Scintillans*. Many have noted his speakers' identification with the outcast son of Abraham by Hagar in "The Timber," the second "Begging," "Providence," and "The Seed growing secretly," as these recall Paul's authorizing allegorization of the story (Gal. 4:21–31). Lewalski has rightly emphasized two significant aspects of this identification. First, Vaughan follows Luther's Reformed interpretation of Ishmael as a type of the Gentiles who by providence were to be saved by Christ, and he rejects the interpretation of medieval figuralists who saw Ishmael as a type of those condemned. Second, Lewalski also shows that Vaughan is moving away from types into allegories when he finds the same kind of comfort in Ishmael that he often finds in Canticles.[23] But just as comfort takes the form of allegory, Vaughan's most distinctive and powerful metamorphosis of the neotypological lyric turns into nightmare. He converts it by a tragically ironic and bitterly despairing inversion. By a damning twist he reverts to using the type for legalistic condemnation.

"The Rain-bow" begins with a type of God's covenent of mercy to mankind, a promise that buoyed Alabaster. On those occasions when Reformed commentators take note of natural signs as types, such as Diodati's discussion of God's covenant with Noah (Gen. 9:13), they generally regard the rainbow as a sign of God's mercy. Mather, for instance, points out that the horns of the bow are downward, intimating that God agrees not to shoot another flood from his bow of wrath. Thus he tells his congregation of providential hope: "Here is ground of unspeakable Comfort to the Church and People of God in all their troubles."[24] But universally, and forebodingly, Reformed commentators also associate the flood with the apocalyptic destruction of evil by fire (2 Pet. 3:6–7).[25] This association Vaughan converts to terror.

Even when mired in despondency over man's loss of insight, Vaughan's speakers recognize the glorious mercy of the rainbow. Beginning his first geographic and later psychic search in "Vanity of Spirit," the speaker contrasts the rainbow to his own dejection: he "gron'd to know / Who gave the Clouds so brave a bow" (3–4). Because he recognizes the type, he waxes nostalgic over humanity's lost union with God and begs to recover from "Corruption" into madness since the New Testament. This position seems blindly to overlook fulfillment while it stares at loss:

> Thy Bow
> Looks dim too in the Cloud,
> Sin triumphs still, and man is sunk below
> The Center, and his shrowd.
>
> (33–36)

In "Distraction" he wishes that God had made him from the crumbled dust of failure so he would recognize providence:

> Hadst thou
> Made me a starre, a pearle, or a rain-bow,
> The beames I then had shot
> My light had lessend not,
> But now
> I find my selfe the lesse, the more I grow.
>
> (5–10)

Vaughan's persona initially apostrophizes "The Rain-bow" within a typological context darkened by melancholy: "Still yong and fine! but what is still in view / We slight as old and soil'd, though fresh and new." The poem's basic dichotomy appears in this opening topic sentence: God's covenant with man is forever being renewed, always a wonder; man's fallen perspective, despite the grace of the Gospel, renders it dated and dulled. When the persona considers how the rainbow ought to appear, he recalls the effect that pristine beam of light had on Abraham's father Terah, Abraham, his brothers, and his nephew Lot. To "the youthful worlds gray fathers" of the chosen seed the rainbow was glorious and awesome. This reference to those whom Vaughan usually calls "white fathers" supplies both an immediate tone of nostalgia and a further note of warning. In the opening of "Religion" or the whole of "*Isaacs* Marriage," or even the beginning of "The Jews," there is the same kind of melancholic nostalgia over God's closer communion with the patriarchs that appears in the first lines of "Righteousness":

> Fair, solitary path! Whose blessed shades
> The old, white Prophets planted first and drest:
> Leaving for us (whose goodness quickly fades,)
> A shelter all the way, and bowers to rest.

But there is also apocalyptic foreboding that associates patriarchal or seventeenth-century gray with the brilliant robes of the righteous rising to meet Christ. This is predicted by Revelation, echoed in "The day of Judgement":

> When shall those first white Pilgrims rise,
> Whose holy, happy Histories
> (Because they sleep so long) some men
> Count but the blots of a vain pen?
>
> (23–26)

At this juncture, however, such tones anticipate.

For a momentary antitypical mood of recognition and rejoicing the persona of "The Rain-bow," when considering the righteous, seems to controvert Vaughan's usual sense of their superior communion with God as well as their implied threat. He even seems to surpass them. For when he sees the rainbow, darkness becomes light, storms become music, clouds become smiles, healing sunshine, and renewing rainfall. Because his imperfections have apparently been corrected by Christ, he concludes this opening section by affirming his insight into the rainbow as a covenant and type:

> When I behold thee, though my light be dim,
> Distant and low, I can in thine see him,
> Who looks upon thee from his glorious throne
> And mindes the Covenant 'twixt *All* and *One*.
>
> (15–18)

Despite weak sight he can see the pure light of God streaming through the spectrum of the rainbow. In a Platonic image superimposed on Alabaster's Christian emblem, the One is signified by the brilliant unmediated light beam descending into the rainbow and the human many by the rainbow's display of color. Christ's union of godhead and manhood appears in the rainbow at the same time that the rainbow serves as a covenant mediating between deity and humanity, a covenant cherished and guided by God.

But then suddenly the persona turns to indict the failures of mankind. Vaughan continues to allude to man's repeated ruptures of covenants with God. After the fall and God's judgment banishing man from Paradise, Cain violated the second covenant between God and Adam by spill-

128

ing his brother Abel's blood. After the covenant that signalled an end to universal floods, Noah himself got notoriously drunk. Since the crucifixion and antitypical fulfillment, men have compounded corruption ("as if we did devise / To lose [Christ] too, as well as *Paradise*" [23–24]) by combining bloody violence and drunken madness in ever fouler storms. The speaker condemns modern reversions that violate and reject the saving covenant of the rainbow by relating another Old Testament story: after God saves them from the firestorm of Sodom, Lot and his daughters establish a bloody, drunken storm of incest. Such is Vaughan's generation.

The relationship between modern men and Old Testament adversaries of types leads to Vaughan's inversion of a type. In his concluding apostrophe the persona reads a dire message:

Then peaceful, signal bow, but in a cloud
Still lodged, where all thy unseen arrows shrowd,
I will on thee, as on a Comet look,
A Comet, the sad worlds ill-boding book.

(33–36)

The rainbow's new, assuring significance, as God's healing and sustaining covenant rain, reverts to its former meaning. It once again signifies God's wrathful, stormy "penal flames." Vaughan concludes, however, by strikingly multiplying his effect through still another allusion—to the apocalyptic firestorm that will finally destroy the world. That firestorm magnifies God's wrath in the lightning shot from the old bow until it will ostensibly destroy the new covenant: "By the word of God the heavens were of old, and the earth standing out of the water and in the water: Whereby the world that then was, being overflowed with water, perished: But the heavens and the earth, which are now, by the same word are kept in store, reserved unto fire against the day of judgment and perdition of ungodly men" (2 Pet. 3:5–7). Vaughan's final message concerns human beings failing the antitype. Though there may be a hint of refining fire purifying the metal of believers, earth's destruction follows human denial:

For though some think, thou shin'st but to restrain
Bold storms, and simply dost attend on rain,
Yet I know well, and so our sins require,
Thou dost but Court cold rain, till *Rain* turns *Fire*.

129

The thrust of Vaughan's inversion here follows from his sense of the reversals whereby man has lost his sense of the type and antitype. Worse than forgetting the prediction of mediating grace in Israel's history and the series of God's covenants with him, man blindly neglects, even spitefully denies and thwarts, the fulfilling antitype, Christ.

In his antipodal neotypological lyric Vaughan continues the tradition of exploiting the supporting structures. The most obvious neotypological lyric device in "The Rain-bow" is dramatization, and Vaughan's last reversal is as startling as his own acclaimed openings and Herbert's celebrated concluding recognitions. In the first pair of lines he establishes an antithesis by juxtaposing the eternity of God's covenant and man's failure to view that covenant piously. The first apostrophe to the rainbow continues to celebrate the type; it culminates in an affirmation of the covenant (3–18), reversing in the second movement of the poem, an apostrophe to man, to indict human failures which confute the compact (19–32). The last apostrophe returns to the rainbow but inverts its meaning. The poem reconciles the contending oppositions by dramatizing the conflict so that man's violations incur God's righteous, retributive punishment.

This dichotomy of opposition and conversion is deeply embedded in the structure of Vaughan's poetry, particularly in the connotative image complex of all his poetry, in which balanced antitheses are necessary for each other.[26] Only it is not here the alchemists' "great *Elixir* that turns gall / To wine, and sweetness; Poverty to wealth, / And brings man home, when he doth range" under provident and merciful "Affliction" (4–6). Nor is it here the hermeticists' world soul that transforms "The Tempest" into the wonder and love of world harmony. Here the patterns are reversed. The positive reverberations from *fresh, new, light,* and purifying *water* are absorbed by negations, *dark* and *foul,* which are extraordinarily intense for being in Vaughan's poetic matrix.

Increasing the impact of "The Rain-bow," Vaughan systematically orders the terms of his dichotomy to emphasize that reversal. He thus underscores humanity's severance from God, thereby marking his transforming inversion of the neotypological lyric. His main terms for the central combat are liquid; and his central metamorphosis during the elemental conflict changes water into fire. His text ultimately combines a type for baptism, the flood waters of affliction which purify the elect, with the apocalyptic imagery of the end of man.[27] But this is in conclusion.

In the beginning the light of God's covenant rainbow is associated

with rain that brings health and nourishment. Ultimately, two other liquids, blood and wine, invert the compact: "These two grand sins we joyn
and act together, / Though blood & drunkeness make but foul, foul
weather" (25–26). The second movement also recalls that rains can nour-
ish floods of purifying, contrite tears; and even further, the blood and
water of the covenant of grace, commemorated by eucharistic wine,
flowed from the side of Christ in order to blot out the legal testament.
Vaughan follows tradition in commingling all three liquids. But instead
of allowing the breach in the ultimate act of love to heal, man mutilates
Christ by breaking humanity's most insistent taboo, incest. Mankind's
violations are, for Vaughan, unendurably destructive and impious. By
spurning God's covenant of grace in Christ, man severs himself irrepara-
bly from meaning; in this state he passes beyond reformation. Therefore,
in the final twist, man's rejection of faith forces a just, loving God away
from nurturing with water to destroying by fire. If in this destruction
there is hope of refining a few, Vaughan halts at accusing the failures of
most.

Vaughan's time scheme, compounding the other devices in "The Rainbow," implies the same despair over man's loss of the antitype beyond the
type. Though "The Rain-bow" initially promises to establish eternity in
time ("Still yong and fine . . . fresh and new"), man's viewpoint renders
it old and fouled. At first there is hope of converting a brilliant, awe-
inspiring past vision of "the youthful worlds gray fathers" (6) into a momentary present compact, because "When I behold [a rainbow] . . . I can
. . . see him, / Who looks upon thee . . . / And mindes the Covenant"
(15–18); "When thou dost shine darkness looks white and fair" (9),
"Storms turn to Musick," and rain "spends his honey-drops" and "pours
Balm" (10–11). But this hope is dashed. For even though God always
keeps his promises, men continue to break theirs. Present outbreaks
join past violence and drunkenness. In the past "the first sin was in
Blood, / and *Drunkenness* quickly did succeed the flood" (21–22). In the
present mankind revive ancient destructions, doubly: "these two grand
sins we joyn and act together" (25). Therefore the present does not look
to an eternal compact in antitypical fulfillment; instead it looks toward
portentous future destruction in the conflagration of judgment day: "I
will on thee, as on a Comet look, / . . . .till *Rain* turns *Fire*" (35,42).

Vaughan wrote a few traditional neotypological lyrics that reflect the
beauty and unified vision of man joined to God. But his more characteristic forms modify the neotypological lyric, taking on a different cast.
When his persona becomes everyman fallen again or views a world that

has corrupted itself again and rejected Christ's revelation, his prevailing tone becomes that of regret over the loss of typological mediation between God and man. Since fulfillment in the antitypical gospel, man too often has lost not only visionary prophecy but also any notion of the perspective of Christ's direct revelation. As Vaughan depicts the situation, the fault resides in man's will. That will should urge man to saving faith; instead it spurns God, destroying itself in spite of type and antitype. The more common result is that a Vaughan speaker turns witness against and satirizes apostate contemporaries, calling for apocalyptic judgment on their fall in contrast to revelatory glory for his congregation. The other result is the antipodal neotypological lyric, Vaughan's most distinctive contribution—not merely his lament and warning that juxtaposes contemporary failure with past vision, but his bitter despair over and threat to contemporary humanity, expressed in his inversion of types and neotypes. Vaughan's indictments form an inversion of the neotypological lyric, and by suggesting their original source they also reflect the precarious dichotomy of his corpus of sacred poetry.

6

God's Immanence in All
and the Poet's Imitation of All Adams
Thomas Traherne's Transcendence of the Neotypological Lyric

It is not insignificant that the last two poets of the neotypological lyric tradition are both discoveries of the twentieth rather than the seventeenth or the eighteenth century.[1] The poetry of Thomas Traherne, the Anglican priest, was found and published at the turn of this century and that of Edward Taylor, the colonial Puritan preacher, during the 1930s. It is as significant that neither prepared his verse for publication. Traherne published one prose work and prepared another for the press; but he made no effort to present his verse to any public congregation, although his early death may have aborted such plans. Taylor published nothing during his lifetime; according to family tradition he forbade his writings to be published. Therefore, contemporary response to these poets, which might shed light on their neotypological lyrics, is unavailable. That there is less need for such data about Traherne and Taylor than for any of the other important neotypological lyricists is most significant: what seem to be the fullest portraits of the souls of both appear in works written for themselves—even as they created personae.

Traherne creates a biography for his speaker through his prose *Centuries*, particularly the third. Moreover, that same biographical pattern can be traced in his sacred lyrics. Because his literary biography follows then expands what he viewed as a universal pattern of Christian life and because his persona absorbs then extends times, spaces, and people historical and contemporary, Traherne seems to develop, indeed even to have, little sense of a separate poetic personality apart from being a universal member of the Christian congregation. Though this may result from not clearly addressing any audience in particular, Traherne does not distinguish between examining his private soul and presenting an exemplum to a congregation. Taylor's poetic record of *Preparatory Meditations before my Approach to the Lords Supper. Chiefly upon the Doctrin preached upon the Day of administration* is an intense private account of his soul's development during confessions to himself and to God at regular four to six week intervals over forty-four years beginning in 1682. In them he shows no awareness whatsoever of presenting himself as an exemplum for any audience other than himself. Thus, unlike previous neotypological lyricists, neither of the last two poets in the tradition seems concerned with presenting himself to any congregation as a poet, indeed as anything other than a pastor. Since Traherne's speaker transcends, his individual identity and full identification absorbing and being absorbed by all, the question of his being an exemplum cannot arise. And since Taylor intently concentrates on himself, there is no consideration of him becoming an exemplum.

Traherne and Taylor reveal the opposed poles that the neotypological lyric can tend toward. Because of his extraordinary sense of God's immanence in all, Traherne's lyrics transcend the form: God's presence in the universe and the poet, who recapitulates the new as well as the old Adam, elevates both world and humanity. Traherne's form exhausts the neotypological lyric by celebrating the extension of God's presence. Because of his Calvinistic sense of the unimaginable disparity between God and creation since the fall, Taylor's lyrics split the form: nothing mundane or mortal, including types, is valuable unless God chooses; nonetheless, all things worldly and human can hint at God's incomprehensible transcendence and might be chosen. Taylor's form exhausts the neotypological lyric by annihilating the unique God-bearing significance of the type and the neotype. In their hands, then, the neotypological lyric tradition itself dissolves along two diverging lines.

Although Traherne apparently did not think of portraying himself specifically as a Christian exemplum to an audience of his poetry, his first presenter considered it. When the Reverend Doctor George Hickes wrote to the publisher he had procured for *A Serious and Pathetical Contemplation of the Mercies of God, in several most Devout and Sublime Thanksgivings for the same* (1699) a quarter of a century after Traherne's death, he commended the publisher for printing the fine devotions of this anonymous author. And he calculated that he needed twenty copies of the volume to pass on: "as *I* have received great delight and benefit in reading of it: So *I* shall recommend it to persons of parts and pious inclinations, as *I* shall find Opportunities."[2] Hickes recognized the value of his unidentified poet and apparently realized, certainly whoever wrote the preface to *Thanksgivings* did, that Traherne did not seem to be aware of his value as a personal exemplum. Obviously, his personal identity was not central:

> To tell thee who he was, is I think, to no purpose: And therefore I will only tell thee what he was, for that may possibly recommend these following Thanksgivings, and Meditations to thy use. He was a Divine of the *Church of England*, of a very comprehensive Soul, and very acute Parts, so fully bent upon that Honourable Function in which he was engaged; and so wonderfully transported with the Love of God to Mankind, with the excellency of those Divine Laws which are prescribed to us, and with those inexpressible Felicities to which we are entitled by being created in, and redeemed to, the Divine Image, that he dwelt continually amongst these thoughts, with great delight and satisfaction, spending most of his time when at home, in digesting his notions of these things into writing, and was so full of them when abroad, that those that would converse with him, were forced to endure some discourse upon these subjects, whether they had any sense of Religion, or not. And therefore to such he might be sometimes thought troublesome, but his company was very acceptable to all such as had any inclinations to Vertue, and Religion.[3]

Whether or not this is an accurate historical portrayal of Traherne, it confirms the impression of many readers. It would seem that Traherne's soul was so full of love for all God had given him that his sense of God's plenitude in creation, particularly humanity, flowed out of his life and onto his pages. Nor would this be exemplary. For as the commender notes further, Traherne's discourse might seem tedious to others on occasion because he ignored their persuasion or lack of it. Perhaps he assumed that his feelings were fundamentally universal, so that his self-portrait rightly considered is shared by all.

Such a view is corroborated by the *Centuries*. To conclude the third meditation of the third century, Traherne's persona describes the condition of belonging and belongings that he began with as a child and to which he feels impelled to return:

> The Streets were mine, the Temple was mine, the People were mine, their Clothes and Gold and Silver was mine, as much as their Sparkling Eys Fair Skins and ruddy faces. The Skies were mine, and so were the Sun and Moon and Stars, and all the World was mine, and I the only Spectator and Enjoyer of it. I knew no Churlish Proprieties, nor Bounds nor Divisions: but all Proprieties and Divisions were mine: all Treasures and the Pos-

sessors of them. So that with much adoe I was corrupted; and made to learn the Dirty Devices of this World. Which now I unlearn, and becom as it were a little Child again, that I may enter into the Kingdom of GOD.

He repeats the message throughout, perhaps most notably near the beginning in the fifteenth meditation of the first century:

Adam and the World are both mine. And the Posterity of Adam enrich it Infinitly. Souls are Gods Jewels. Evry one of which is worth many Worlds. They are his Riches becaus his Image. and mine for that reason. So that I alone am the End of the World. Angels and Men being all mine. And if others are so, they are made to Enjoy it for my further Advancement. God only being the Giver, and I the Receiver. So that Seneca Philosophized rightly, when he said, *Deus me dedit solum toti Mundo, et totum Mundum mihi soli.* God gave me alone to all the World, and all the World to me alone.

Just as clearly the speaker is not the sole recipient of God's multitudinous gift of the whole universe, as implied when he contemplates others enjoying the gift and changes to second person for the next meditation. He talks plainly and often about others sharing. In the twenty-seventh and twenty-eighth meditations of the fourth century he is unusually succinct:

27

He conceived it his Duty and much Delighted in the Obligation; That he was to treat evry Man in the whole World as the Representativ of Mankind, And that he was to meet in him, and to Pay unto Him all the Lov of God Angels and Men.

28

He thought that he was to treat evry man in the Person of Christ. That is both as if Himself were Christ in the Greatnes of his Lov, and also as if the Man were Christ he was to use him. . . .

The important point is that he is not any more—nor any less—an exemplum for the congregation than any one else. For him all personalities fuse so that all or none are exempla for all, but primarily each proves to be an example of and for himself.

Just as he fuses all his exempla, Traherne also composed in such a way as to obliterate individual authorship. Carol L. Marks showed that the Church's Year-Book is the corporate composition of several copyist-writers working with a host of generally unacknowledged sources not distinguished from each other.[4] Stanley Stewart interpreted this information as showing an aesthetic: Traherne creates a multitude of voices which through harmony become one inseparable voice that is neither wholly personal nor completely universal.[5] This communal voice and its commonplaces belong to Traherne, to the composers, to the authors over the years, and to the voices of the congregation in unison over centuries. Traherne does not just direct such activity as he writes; he invites participation in it, turning the expansion of works over to his readers. So says the dedicatory verse of his *Centuries*, no matter whose the actual lines:

This book unto the friend of my best friend
As of the Wisest Love a Mark I send
That she may write my Makers prais therin
And make her self therby a Cherubin.

But if authorship is ultimately indistinguishable and is infinitely expandable in unacknowledged quotation, allusion, and paraphrase, in the persona or the reader or the new creation, it does not emanate from nowhere. Traherne's source as well as his end, he would say, is God. But a more readily identified literary mediator is the psalmodist David. The importance of Psalms to Traherne has been universally recognized, particularly in his third century. Moreover, it reappears in quotations, echoes, rhetorical and linguistic techniques, and themes throughout his works. Stanley Stewart's discussion of the relationship of Psalms to *Thanksgivings* is particularly helpful.[6] Through a comparison to contemporary psalmodists he shows that Traherne imitates David to become more representative in himself and to expand himself. Indeed, he requests and demonstrates both at the same time in "Thanksgivings for the Body":

O that I were as *David*, the sweet Singer of *Israel!*
  In meeter Psalms to set forth thy Praises.
Thy Raptures ravish me, and turn my soul all into melody.
Whose Kingdom is so glorious, that nothing in it shall at all be
unprofitable, mean, or idle.
  So constituted!
That every one's Glory is beneficial unto all; and every one magnified
in his place by Service.

(341–48)

There are two important points to consider here. First, as Richard D. Jordan has added to Stewart's account, though a Traherne speaker often sets out by imitating and emulating David, rarely does he stop with him.[7] While he identifies with David, he expands that identification, as he does in this poem, to include and transcend everyone. He does not become an exemplar like David, but he becomes a composite and then an extended believer. Second, though Traherne is similar to previous neotypological lyricists and their forebears in imitating the psalmodist and identifying with this type of the singer as a neotype, he does not follow the penitential Psalms with their dual motive and motif of contrition and exaltation. Instead he turns for his models to David's paeans of praise and hymns of thanksgiving.

Thus, even though other sources for Traherne's work have been postulated, it seems reasonable to agree with Stewart, Jordan, and Lewalski that Traherne is essentially working out of a typological tradition. Indeed it does not seem unreasonable to say that he worked more strictly than from biblical allegory or temporal recapitulations and progresses,[8] that he worked from the Reformed neotypological lyric heritage, and that as he inventively expanded that heritage he moved through and absorbed and so transcended other sources too, until he made them all universal, blurring the distinctions between them eclectically just as he attempted to expand the limits of time and space and person to limitlessness, fusing all the congregation in God.

In "Salutation," which opens his poetic manuscript, Traherne begins by imitating not David but Adam. He immediately starts to expand and transcend both types and the neotypological lyric. Initially the poet and world greet and pay respect to the creation of the child as the poet sets forth his program. God's grant of joys and treasures that fill both the child's body and the world inspire the poet's celebratory hymn. As the composite Traherne persona, God's "Son and Heir," receives his legacy, he exults in that man's proper end is to enjoy God's gifts. The volume of poems and the child's life grow together from this origin. The child begins enjoying God's gifts by surveying two realms, himself and the world; thus he comes to understand, appreciate, and imitate God's love and grandeur and to arrive in "this Eden so Divine and fair," a pristine, renewed Adam. By patterning himself on Adam, as well as on the singer David, he follows the personalization of the neotype. His fall, like that of the first Adam, and his recovery through the second, continue to follow the familiar story. But throughout Traherne so merges the speaker's times in transcendence that even when he fails and falls back, regresses as well as progresses, he is ecstatically aware that he is a renewed Adam being saved for eternity and infinity in conformity with the image of the second Adam. Traherne's characteristically diffuse, repetitive verse precisely reflects his fusion of personae only to expand all infinitely and joyously. And it is significant that his scheme, made up of expansive innovations to the potential in the neotypological lyric, must be inferred from his whole corpus rather than from any single poem.

† † †

Traherne understood typology. But just as he blurred individuality by fusing personalities and expanding them, so he characteristically came to overlook those disparities between type and antitype which Reformed typologists emphasized. He stressed their similarities to the degree that the type is virtually absorbed into the antitype. Ultimately he himself fuses with both.

In "Of Faith," a chapter of *Christian Ethicks* (published just after his death), he describes types that recur through the next two chapters:

> Our Reason it self assists our Belief, and our Faith is founded upon *Grounds*, that cannot be removed: Much more if the Things be agreeable to the Nature of GOD, and tend to the Perfection of Created Nature, if many Prophesies and long Expectations have preceded their Accomplishment, if the misteries revealed are attested by Miracles, and painted out many Ages before, by Types and Ceremonies, that can bear no other Explication in Nature, nor have any Rational use besides.[9]

Several points are notable. First, Traherne states that types are just one of many testimonies to God's perfecting activities in the universe and among mankind. Second, he seems to say that they are valuable not in themselves (alone they are inexplicable) but in their forecast. Third, he implies that they are more important as Old Testament rules than they are for Christians. All three points depart from the Reformed sense of typology and lead toward Traherne's contribution to the neotypological lyric. Interwoven among people, laws, judgments, prophecies, ceremonies, and disciplines central to the belief of Old Testament priests, he discusses rites, the visible paraphernalia of the church through outer and inner courts, and particularly the "Shewbread-Table" and paschal lamb, types which forecast the new covenant of Christ's sacrificial deliverance of the mystical church from a figurative Egypt.[10]

Traherne mentions types sporadically in his *Centuries*. Beyond repeating previous implications ("all Sacrifices being but Types and figures of [Christ] Himself, and Himself infinitely more Excellent then they all" [III. 83]), he emphasizes the change from the first Adam to the second (II. 5). He also mentions prominent types of Christ—the brazen serpent (I. 57), Jacob's ladder (I. 60), the cloud and pillar and Samson (I. 90), the priesthood of Aaron and of Melchizedek (II. 33), various references in Psalms (III. 69–94), and Adam, Moses, Aaron, and David (IV. 67–68).

Traherne interprets types impressively in *Thanksgivings*. "Thanksgivings for the Beauty of his Providence" (190–320) raises his previous estimate: "To me they exhibit in the best of Hieroglyphics / JESUS CHRIST" (274–75). They also shine through Malachi's sun of righteousness, the Psalms' happy giant, and Canticles' bridegroom imagery—all of which appear in the fourth of the *Meditations on the Six Days of the Creation* (1717, first assigned to Susanna Hopton).[11] Such evidence substantiating that Traherne did employ types directly corroborates that he was capable of using them indirectly in his poetry.

Although the neotypological lyric tradition occasionally appears straightforwardly in Traherne's poetry, generally it is indirect. He contributes to the form by extending the power that resides in types. That innovation is suggested by a series of poems in which typological efficacy extends further than what is considered typological, even by those who stretched Reformed definitions. Traherne opens "The Inference II" with two familiar recurring images, which he continually repeats and expands. One is his initial identification with the type David; the other his conception of the temple emblem:

> *David* a Temple in his Mind conceiv'd;
> And that Intention was so well receiv'd
> By God, that all the Sacred Palaces
> That ever were did less His Glory pleas.
> If Thoughts are such; such Valuable Things;
> .   .   .   .
> O! What are Men, who can such Things produce?

He continues to explain that God deems men greater than either material worlds or emblematic temples which are produced and reflected by pious thoughts. Like the type, David, Mary was chosen by God because of her cherishing thoughts to be the mother, the temple, of Christ, not because of some endowment to a tabernacle. From David and Mary humanity should learn that all people may become glorious tabernacles of Christ—

not by establishing sacred and charitable institutions nor by creating universes but by worshipful thoughts:

> Consider that for All our Lord hath don,
> All that He can receiv is this bare Sum
> Of God-like Holy Thoughts: These only He
> Expects from Us, our Sacrifice to be.
>
> (41–44)

Traherne himself expounds the tabernacle type in *Christian Ethicks*. He contrasts the inferiority of the outer court of the temple, "Admission to the Visible Ordinances, and exterior Rites of Religion," to its inner court or Holy of Holies, "the *Pale* of the *Invisible Church*," where Christians "are under the *Shaddow* of the Almighty, because they only dwell in the secret place of the most High."[12] He is expanding (by pun) the distinction between open, or unprotected, and roofed, or shaded; the ceremonies of the temple foreshadow Christ. In doing so, he joins Protestant British expositors revelling in Paul's explication, in the ninth and tenth chapters of Hebrews, of Exodus 25–38.[13] In *Orbis Miraculum, or the Temple of Solomon*, Samuel Lee declares with a host of concurring commentators that the Bible describes Solomon's temple as larger than its site in order to show that it primarily typifies the Christian church. Lee finally claims that Solomon's temple has three significations: Christ himself; Christ's mystical body, the church; and, citing Paul's first letter to Corinthians 6:19 as well as Hebrews 9–10, every saint, meaning also every elect Christian.[14]

While he is working from a typological heritage in "The Inference II," Traherne is also extending that tradition immensely. David's temple of the mind recalls his tower of armor in "Fullnesse" (21–22), which alludes to Solomon's Canticles 4:4 as the neck of the church, to God's aid in 2 Samuel 22:3, 51, and to many of David's Psalms. The imagery and conception of "The Inference II" reference is closer yet to the sequence that includes "Thoughts II":

> That Temple David did intend,
> Was but a Thought, and yet it did transcend
> King Solomons. A Thought we know
> Is that for which
> God doth Enrich
> With Joys even Heaven above, and Earth below.
>
> (25–30)

Traherne's persona and David begin to merge here, expanding a general principle: human thoughts that approximate God's become greater than prophetic types. Finally, the reference recalls expansion in "Churches II" from Solomon's finite, superseded temple to the infinite set of temples possible in the cosmos and among men.

Together these allusions imply even more extended meanings in "The Inference II." Lee considers in detail the importance of David's plans for Solomon's temple. First, following mainly 1 Chronicles 22, he indicates that David's accomplishments are considerable. Purchasing the grounds, receiving the plan from God, collecting the materials, appointing the orders of attendants, and granting the funds are all significant; but most significantly, David was humble during these preparations.[15] More importantly, Lee shows that Solomon's temple essentially went uncompleted for centuries. Solomon could not build the temple God designed through David and Nathan simply because Solomon and his temple only predict the ultimate architect and builder, whose blood cements individual believers.[16] Christ completes the temple.

Behind this last interpretation lie Psalms 89:29, Luke 11:31, 1 Chronicles 28 and 29, and 2 Samuel 7 which records David's proposal and Nathan's approval of a permanent tabernacle for God. But God appeared to Nathan in order to forestall their plans, describe Solomon's construction, and promise eternity for the house of David. The Geneva Bible commentary represents the most concise response: "This was begon in Solomon as a figure, but accomplished in Christ." By all accounts, God's plan, developed through David and executed through Solomon, is fulfilled solely by Christ.

Correspondingly in "The Inference II," Traherne exalts David's thoughts of the temple and salvation beyond any physical temple Solomon could have built. In doing so, he singled out one interpretation. He rejected the condemnation represented by Poole's *Annotations*: because David's plan was wrongheaded, rushed without God's instigation and impetuously approved without God's advice, it results in a reprimand. Considering, however, David's mistake arose from zeal, God also bestowed on him a new title, servant, and promised to extend the reign of David's line, literally and immediately in Solomon, ultimately and mystically in Christ. Traherne instead followed the generous interpretation repeated by Diodati who maintained God's question honored David:

> Words of admiration rather then reprehension. The meaning is, Hast thou had such a high thought, as for to build a firm and setled habitation, to the signs of my presence, which have hitherto been unsetled and wan-

dring? . . . I doe like of thine intention in itself, I *Kings* 8:18. But be thou content with those other honours which thou hast received at my hands: the putting of this thy design in execution is reserved for thy son.

Diodati glosses *forever* as a Davidic kingdom uninterrupted until the Messiah descends to change "this temporall and figurative Kingdome, into a spirituall and everlasting one," thereby pointing to his annotation of Hebrews 9:8. Thus, Traherne starts by finding typological implications in the temple plans God granted David and then extends David's spiritual thoughts of worship toward infinite expansions of physical places of worship. With such neotypical identifications and characteristic expansions, this notion leads to Traherne's conclusion: such thoughts in men, God's temples, Christ translates into infinite and eternal value.

Traherne further extends the significances discoverable in types to other biblical referents that the "*Word* confirms." Thus the opening of "The Evidence":

> Each ancient Miracle's a Seal:
> Apostles, Prophets, Martyrs, Patriarchs are
> The Witnesses; and what their Words reveal,
> Their written Records do declare.
>
> (5–8)

He found evidence of God's revelation still further afield: "Each Creature says, / God made us Thine, that we might shew His Prais" (19–20). His expansive circumference spreads infinitely from its typological and neotypological center.

Traherne expands his neotypological lyric heritage in several ways, one significantly if singly present. He follows Renaissance syncretists in attaching classical myths with types to echo predictions of Christ. In "Love" he associates Ganymede's elevation with Elijah's translation into heaven, identifying with both (31–34).[17] But he soon realizes that such extensions of a type are inadequate:

> But these (tho great) are all
> Too short and small,
> Too weak and feeble Pictures to Express
> The true Mysterious Depths of Blessedness.
>
> (35–38)

More often Traherne expands typology into the book of creation; creation becomes a type that breathes life into a natural image in "Goodnesse."[18] The poem, as H. M. Margoliouth suggests and Stanley Stewart demonstrates, concerns Traherne attaining infinite bliss by involving himself in all joys derived from God.[19] The final stanzas welcome an apotheosis of opulent vine and grape imagery:

> The Soft and Swelling Grapes that on their Vines
> > Receiv the Lively Warmth that Shines
> > Upon them, ripen there for me:
> > > Or Drink they be
> Or Meat. The Stars salute my pleased Sence
> With a Derivd and borrowed Influence
> > But better Vines do Grow
> > Far Better Wines do flow
> > > Above, and while
> > > The Sun doth Smile
> Upon the Lillies there, and all things warme
> Their pleasant Odors do my Spirit charm.
>
> Their rich Affections do like precious Seas
> > Of Nectar and Abrosia pleas.
> > Their Eys are Stars, or more Divine:
> > > And Brighter Shine
> Their Lips are soft and Swelling Grapes, their Tongues
> A Quire of Blessed and Harmonious Songs.

(st. 5, 6)

Although the connotations of "Goodnesse" are inseparable from typological references, they are effective in part because, as usual, Traherne has first half-concealed his types by expanding them into the book of creation. More than once he recalls his "Wonder" as God's Edenic "Son and Heir": "I nothing in the World did know, / But 'twas Divine" (23–24).[20]

Beyond these reverberations from the book of creation celebrated by a communion of saints praising God, A. L. Clements hears the mystical revelations of spiritual truths in these natural images. The circumference expands further with the recognition that "Bleeding Vines" and "Wines" refer to eucharistic imagery and to Christ as the vine of branches (men) fulfilled only as part of him.[21] These mystical meanings are profounder for rising from a typological tradition of uncounted literary and exegetical works which demonstrate that the true vine and bunch of grapes is Christ.

To see all God's creation as an expansion of the mediation available in types Traherne must follow Christ's admonition to "Return" to childhood. For this he extends typology into the neotypical self: "To Infancy, O Lord, again I com, / That I my Manhood may improv" (1–2). Returning from corruption to a child's visionary wonder about God in himself as well as in the world for Traherne takes more than self will. Since Adam's fall, man is incapable of envisioning God without Christ's renewal.[22] Adam saw grandeur in "The World" and so may humanity— through rebirth in the second Adam:

> Sin spoil'd them; but my Savior's precious Blood
>> Sprinkled I see
>> On them to be,
> Making them all both safe and good:
> With greater Rapture I admire
>> That I from Hell
>> Redeem'd, do dwell
> On Earth as yet; and here a Fire
> Not scorching but refreshing glows,
>> And living Water flows,
> Which *Dives* more than Silver doth request,
>> Of Crystals far the best.
>
> (13–24)

The typological fount and living waters of Christ are reemphasized in the pun, *crystals*. Only by receiving the living waters as baptism and eyewash can the persona recall the blessings of childhood vision. And this will require extensions of Traherne's personal neotypology similar to his expansions of the typological temple of thought into classical myth, the book of creation, and mystical numina.

† † †

Christ's redemption of the man into the child of "Wonder" did not come to Traherne so easily nor so naïvely as has sometimes been supposed. And it came by way of a biblical revelation and through a series of stages of Christian life that stem from, then absorb, and finally expand typology and neotypology beyond recognition. "Dissatisfaction" describes the persona's anxious search through the books of nature, society, and scholarship to discover a lack of fulfillment he has not been able to define:

> Mine Ear,
> My Ey, my Hand, my Soul, doth long
> For som fair Book fill'd with Eternal Song.

O *that*! my Soul: for *that* I burn:
That is the Thing for which my Heart did yern.

(76–80)

The quest ends with the disclosure, "I sought in ev'ry Library and Creek / Until *the Bible* me supply'd." The persona's lesson first appears in the Genesis account of creation (1:26–27) and reappears in such New Testament passages as 2 Corinthians 3:17: man is the image of God.[23] The search for *that* ascends to discovery in "The Bible":

That! That! There I was told
That I *the Son of God* was made,
His Image. O Divine! And that fine Gold,
With all the Joys that here do fade,
Are but a Toy, compared to the Bliss
Which Hev'nly, God-like, and Eternal is.

Amplifying the reference to himself as "The Image" of God, in "Ease" Traherne alludes to this same notion in suggesting that humanity can be remade from Adam's failures into the image of mankind's second father:

That all we see is ours, and evry One
Possessor of the Whole; that evry Man
Is like a God Incarnat on the Throne,
Even like the first for whom the World began.

(17–20)

Throughout the *Centuries*, Traherne celebrates man as God's image (I. 74, 76), though he sometimes expresses it in other ways such as God's temple by extending the temple of David's and his own thoughts.[24] His speaker exclaims that he is God's image from the fifty-eighth through the sixty-first meditations of the third century; in the fifty-ninth he elaborates on his statement in the opening chapter of *Christian Ethicks*, "Man was made in GODS Image, that he might live in his Similitude."[25] In the hymn of the sixty-seventh meditation of the first century the speaker rejoices:

Since GOD is the most Glorious of all Beings, and the most Blessed, couldst thou wish any more then to be His IMAGE! O my Soul, He hath made His Image. Sing O ye Angels, and Laud His Name ye Cherubims: Let all the Kingdoms of the Earth be Glad, and let all the Hosts of Heaven rejoyce. For He hath made His Image, the Likeness of himself, his own Similitude.

What Creature what Being what Thing more Glorious could there be! GOD from all Eternity was infinitly Blessed and desired to make one infinitly Blessed. He was infinit Lov, and being Lovly in being so, Would prepare for He hath made His Image, the Likeness of himself, his own Similitude. What Creature what Being what Thing more Glorious could there be! GOD from all Eternity was infinitly Blessed and desired to make one infinitly Blessed. He was infinit Lov, and being Lovly in being so, Would prepare for Himself a Most Lovly Object. having Studied from all Eternity, He saw, none more Lovly then the Image of His Lov, His own Similitude. O Dignity Unmeasurable! O Exaltation Passing Knowledge! O Joy Un-speakable! Triumph O my Soul and Rejoyce for ever! I see that I am infinit-ly Beloved. For *infinit Lov hath exprest and pleased it self in Creating an Infinit Object.* GOD is LOV, and my Soul is Lovely! God is Loving, and His Image Amiable. . . .

Granted that Christ can remake humanity in God's image as well as restore his childhood vision of God's reflection in the world, it is not surprising that Traherne makes little of God's revelation in types. For types, like ceremony in *Christian Ethicks*, are primarily important in the Old Testament under law before the new dispensation of grace. "Medita-tions on the First Day's Creation" implies the central lesson: since Christ has turned dark into light mankind should remember our fall with Adam but celebrate our restoration in Christ.[26]

Traherne rejoices that Christ has extended revelation beyond types. If in *Centuries* III. 69–94 he can imitate David by renewing praises of the world in psalmody, he can go beyond by identifying with all types, thereby repeatedly realizing and celebrating his own salvation.[27] In the climactic fifty-fifth meditation of the first century he absorbs the signifi-cance of special revelatory types into himself before Christ expands him into eternal salvation:

When my Soul is in Eden with our first Parents, I my self am there in a Blessed Maner. When I walk with Enoch, and see his Translation, I am Transported with Him. The present Age is too little to contain it. I can visit Noah in His Ark, and swim upon the Waters of the Deluge. I can see Moses with his Rod, and the children of Israel passing thorow the Sea. I can Enter into Aarons Tabernacle, and Admire the Mysteries of the Holy Place. I can Travail over the Land of Canaan, and see it overflowing with Milk and Hony; I can visit Solomon in his Glory, and go into his Temple, and view the sitting of His servants, and Admire the Magnificence and Glory of his Kingdom. No Creature but one like unto the Holy Angels can see into all Ages. Sure this Power was not given in vain. but for some

Wonderfull Purpose; worthy of itself to Enjoy and fathom. Would Men consider what GOD hath don, they would be Ravished in Spirit with the Glory of His Doings. For Heaven and Earth are full of the Majesty of His Glory. And how Happy would Men be could they see and Enjoy it! But abov all these our Saviors Cross is the Throne of Delights. That Centre of Eternity, *That Tree of Life* in the midst of the Paradise of GOD!

This concluding type of the cross provides a pinnacle to Traherne's list of ascending types.

What Traherne learned poetically about Christ's absorption of types from neotypological lyrics was how to initially identify with and personalize Adam: he could recapitulate the story of man, made like Adam, fallen in Adam, and renewed by the second Adam—as the image of God emblem indicates. Thus Stewart's statement is insufficient, that in the *Centuries*, Traherne becomes a poet-prophet who imitates not just types but Christ who completes types.[28] In the poetry he becomes Adam in David and Christ. He requests this transformation toward the end of "A Thanksgiving and Prayer for the NATION" (386–99) where he implies that he may absorb two types (candlestick and temple) which Christ fulfills and that his imitation of Christ might supersede David and Moses. His self-exaltation glorifies creation, humanity, and God.

Traherne's patterning of humanity on himself as both first and second Adam transcends all earlier neotypes. Where his predecessors' speakers halt at identifying with a type that is saved, praying to be saved, hearing God's invitations, and resigning faithfully to God's will, Traherne presses his to identify with God the Son in a way that surpasses even medieval imitations of Christ. His personal repetition of Christian history is clearest in his third century, especially in the concluding variations on David's Psalms. A bare summary appears in the forty-third meditation:

Man, as he is a Creature of GOD, capable of Celestial Blessedness, and a Subject in His Kingdom: in his fourfold Estate of Innocency, Misery, Grace and Glory. In the Estate of Innocency we are to Contemplate the Nature and Maner of His Happiness, the Laws under which He was governed, the Joys of Paradise, and the Immaculat Powers of His Immortal Soul. In the Estate of Misery we hav his Fall the Nature of Sin Original and Actual, His Manifold Punishments Calamity Sickness Death &c. In the Estate of Grace; the Tenor of the New Covenant, the maner of its Exhibition under the various Dispensations of the Old and New Testament, the Mediator of the Covenant, the Conditions of it Faith and Repentance, the Sacraments or Seals of it, the Scriptures Ministers and Sabbaths, the Nature and Government of the Church, its Histories and Successions from the Beginning to the End of the World. &c. In the State of Glory; the Nature of Seperat

Souls, their Advantages Excellencies and Privileges, the Resurrection of
the Body, the Day of Judgment and Life Everlasting.

Traherne represents himself and humanity only in the first three estates,
not in glory. Moreover, because the second estate, misery, is least important to him, his celebrations of the first and third, innocence and grace,
form the core of his poetry.

The progress of Traherne's persona epitomizes both a Christian's biography and humanity's history.[29] His imitation of both Adams begins in
childhood and with societal "Innocence": "I was an Adam there, / A little Adam in a Sphere" (51–52) enraptured at the sight of paradise; the
wonder of bliss "is that within / I felt no Stain, nor Spot of Sin" (3–4). In
"Eden" he does not need one greater man to bruise the serpent's head
(8–9, 29–30, 36–38). Nor before "The Apostacy" is he limited to male
roles (19–21). Furthermore, before "The Apostacy" into "The World,"
he is not deluded into believing man's high valuation of material pelf. But
such a vision soon fails, forcing him to try to recover "Innocence": "I
must becom a Child again."

In opening "Adam," Traherne describes man's initiation of the fall into
sin—wandering from God's plan, losing clear vision, and corrupting societal values. He further introduces his central linguistic conception of the
nature and transmission of the fall. Man's language, originally intended
for praise of primal, nearly divine vision has been corrupted by fallen
usage. Moreover, fallen usage transmits original sin, at least by analogy.

"Dumnesse" explains Traherne's distinctive version of everyman's imitation of Adam's fall:

> Sure Man was born to Meditat on Things,
> And to Contemplat the Eternal Springs
> Of God and Nature, Glory, Bliss and Pleasure;
> That Life and Love might be his Heavnly Treasure:
> And therefore Speechless made at first, that he
> Might in himself profoundly Busied be:
> And not vent out, before he hath t'ane in
> Those Antidots that guard his Soul from Sin. (1–8)

From the premise that man must contemplate God, Traherne concludes
that infancy, speechlessness, is an Edenic blessing. By hearing and seeing
only God the child learns love and joy, true acts of worship he has to
recover after corruption has come from listening to man's speech:

> Wise Nature made him Deaf too, that he might
> Not be disturbd, while he doth take Delight

In inward Things, nor be depravd with Tongues,
Nor Injurd by the Errors and the Wrongs
That *Mortal Words* convey. For Sin and Death
Are most infused by accursed Breath,
That flowing from Corrupted Intrails, bear
Those hidden Plagues that Souls alone may fear.

(9–16)

The recipients and the transmitters of the fall into mortality are in some
sense words for Traherne, not in their essential purpose but in their current effect of corrupting children. Just as God created man in the divine
image by breathing a living soul or spirit (with Latin overtones of breath
and wind) into his nostrils (Gen. 2:7), so man transmits his deformed
image and soul by breathing words to his offspring:

For while I knew not what they to me said,
Before their Souls were into mine conveyd,
Before that Living Vehicle of Wind
Could breath into me their infected Mind.

(23–26)

The child saw and heard God clearly in the temple of himself as long as
he was dumb and received only God's messages; but because he is human
he is inevitably tainted by original sin:

All things did com
With Voices and Instructions; but when I
Had gaind a Tongue, their Power began to die.
Mine Ears let other Noises in, not theirs;
A Nois Disturbing all my Songs and Prayers.
My foes puld down the Temple to the Ground.

(66–71)[30]

In continuation the child repeats "Adam" in order to transcend the first
with and through the second Adam. Thus the child enters the specifically
Christian phase of individual and communal growth. At first he wor-
ships voicelessly. But fallen human words teach him a different language:
"*I then my Bliss did, when my Silence, break*" (20). The wonder of grace is
that the child is never lost to the adult but always contained within him
just as the original breath of God is forever present. Christ can recover
both:

Yet the first Words mine Infancy did hear,
The Things which in my Dumness did appear,
Preventing all the rest, got such a root
Within my Heart, and stock so close unto't
It may be Trampld on, but still will grow.

(79–83)

Traherne's vision of the threshold of recovery is based in language as well as psychology and history. Clements has tacitly noted that Traherne's interpretation of the fall as transmitted by language in the context of the humanists' definition of mankind and their measure of its greatness compels a paradox. "Yet still more paradoxically, by language and intellect, by reading Scripture [as in "Dissatisfaction" and "The Bible"], by meditating through language on things [as the book of creation in "Wonder"], man may be lead back *toward* the Eternal Springs and, ultimately, be truly and fully civilized."[31] Traherne's paradox deepens. Communicating the fall are "Human Words" (21), not those messages from without and within when "I was in the World my Self alone" (36), those "*first Impressions* [that] *are Immortal all*" (85). Immortal messages emanate from the Word and penetrate the heart rather than the ear. According to the openings of Genesis and John, the Logos creates by breathing into humanity in the beginning and into each child at birth; by sacrifice the Logos has recreated and continues to recreate the child's language. Thus, for Traherne, without this Word who reveals and is revealed in the Bible and through the book of God's creatures, no redemption, no return to childhood, is possible. Traherne has created a linguistic type by imitating the Word: Adam's original words praise God; humanity's fallen words transmit sin; and these same words, in speaking about God's revelations, recall and return to God. All words are ultimately absorbed in the Word—without which there can be no words.

In the language of Traherne the impetus to return to lost childhood is supplied by that immortal vestige of the first Word the child heard, which is forever hauntingly present in nostalgia for the forgotten. "Desire," God's prevenient grace, motivates the adult:

For giving me Desire,
An Eager Thirst, a burning Ardent fire,
A virgin Infant Flame,
A Love with which into the World I came,
An Inward Hidden Heavenly Love,

Which in my Soul did Work and move,
    And ever ever me Enflame,
With restlesse longing Heavenly Avarice,
    That never could be satisfied,
That did incessantly a Paradice
Unknown suggest, and som thing undescried
    Discern, and bear me to it; be
    Thy Name for ever praisd by me.

                                      (1–13)

"Insatiableness," "Dissatisfaction," compels Traherne's personae to recover Christ by that very agent, Christ himself, whose emblems mark
the search for him and the thanks due him.[32] The fallen understanding
and eye of a Traherne speaker scan the world to search out Christ's sunlight. At first the speaker will probably miss hints in nature's ledger, for
"These are but Dead Material Toys, / And cannot make my Heavenly
Joys" (38–39). But finally he will realize that he is God's image at God's
right hand. Traherne's sense of recovery appears in "Christendom" and
"Thoughts III."

For Traherne's speaker the discovery of Christendom outside himself
is the result of Christ's grant of grace inside his soul; they are perceived
together. His speaker reads the Christian gospel in both his own soul and
the book of God's creatures, in both "My Spirit" and "Nature," when he
is granted "Sight" through the sun / Son.[33] He describes two kinds of sen-
sors—his two physical eyes that delight his senses and his inner eye
"*That* was of greater Worth than both the other" (11). The physical eyes
see natural reflections of God; the inner eye perceives the spiritual mysteries of God and Nature. Now when he examines his own "Spirit" he can
see a living, perfect, sphere of eternity, a temple inspired by God: "Thou
Ey, / And Temple of his Whole Infinitie! / O what a World art Thou! a
World within!" (108–10).[34] Now when he looks outside to "Nature,"
"Nature teacheth Nothing but the Truth" (3) and "The Worlds fair
Beauty set my Soul on fire" (6). All is for him and all is in him.

At the beginning of "The City," Traherne ultimately implies that the
works of humanity represent a fortunate fall that only contemporary
man, not Adam, can appreciate:

What Structures here among God's Works appear?
    Such Wonders *Adam* ne'r did see
    In Paradise among the Trees,
        No Works of Art like these,

Nor Walls, nor Pinnacles, nor Houses were.
                    All these for me,
            For me these Streets and Towers,
      These stately Temples, and these solid Bowers,
                    My father rear'd:
            For me I thought they thus appear'd.

      The City, fill'd with Peeple, near me stood;
            A Fabrick like a Court divine,
            Of many Mansions bright and fair.[35]

By adapting two types (the temples and courts of God) to a contemporary city, Traherne extends typology further than ever before. Traherne declares that mankind can appreciate human creations resulting from the fall because God has made them eternal, or at least transmitters, like nature, of eternity. Far surpassing mere transmittal, such human works foreshadow the New Jerusalem because they echo Christ's promise: "In my Father's house are many mansions: *if it were* not *so*, I would have told you. I go to prepare a place for you" (John 14:2). Traherne's recapitulation of Adam through the second Adam is thus extended as well as fulfilled.

Although Traherne used typology as such only moderately, he expanded its methods into infinity and eternity through and beyond previous neotypological lyrics. He expanded typological readings into the books of himself and all creation to an extent beyond even Vaughan. Perhaps the clearest example is his metamorphosis of David's conception of Solomon's temple into a foreshadowing of a Christian: Solomon's temple, which is less than the one God inspired in David's thought, predicts every Christian, who similarly and inevitably falls short of Christ. But Christ, the ultimate temple resurrected in three days, justifies every Christian believer, including the type, David, and the seventeenth-century neotype. By imitating David, other types, and Christ, Traherne's persona can epitomize human history in his own life. Because he has been created in God's image, God's temple, a Traherne speaker recapitulates both fathers of mankind through language. At first an Edenic infant, he silently celebrates God's wonders. Next, corrupted by original sin as denoted by fallen language, he breathes out his divine spirit in human words which transmit sin; he repeats Adam's fall by speaking. Finally, through the Word he seeks to relearn and can recover the innocent words of the second Adam, who encompasses fallen civilization by justifying and extending it eternally and infinitely.

Such an outline does not appear sequentially in Traherne's poetry; it is rather inferred from all his poetry, his thought and word collection of revelations of Christ that he gathered out of the Bible, the self, and the world. Traherne repeats the scheme in such a way that it is present at each stage and in every poem—sometimes during remembrance of innocence, sometimes unrecognized during depression and search for recovery, sometimes during jubilation at recovery. To a remarkable degree Traherne demands assiduous gathering of his message throughout all his poetry. He requires insights into each poem gained from all his perspectives. This is because all human times and eternity are reflected in each poem, though only one moment may be presented. His method is like that of typology and neotypology. For the speaker so identifies with the type and antitype simultaneously that the poet is gaining the expressive potential of both historical and transcendental referents and significances at the same instant. Furthermore, Traherne's overlapping stylistic repetition and diffusion and his widening circumference, which characterize his poetry and communicate the human grandeur that he sees God making possible, precisely imitate his thought and narrative.

Linguistic repetitions and diffusions, which expand to envelop all in a pattern of seemingly endless reiterations of straightforward statement, characterize Traherne's plain style.[36] Traherne's apology goes beyond Herbert's in the "Jordan" poems. In "The Author to the Critical Peruser" he calls for "The naked Truth in many faces shewn," a transparent diction that "lowly creeps" in order to define carefully. Furthermore, Traherne's call is not equivocal in its rhetorical concerns in the manner of Herbert. In "The Person" his declaration is literal, even anatomical, on the brilliant, sublime expression belonging to naked things:

> Their Worth they then do best reveal,
> When we all Metaphores remove,
>   For Metaphores conceal,
>   And only Vapours prove.
> They best are Blazond when we see
>   The Anatomie,
> Survey the Skin, cut up the Flesh, the Veins
>   Unfold: The Glory there remains.
> The Muscles, Fibres, Arteries and Bones
> Are better far then Crowns and precious Stones.
>
> (23–32)

His avowed transparency does not call for a poetics of image and trope and figure. His style consists of repeating patterns of thought, referents, syntax, even diction, in hopes that by incantation they will fuse stylistically with the visionary transcendent Word.[37]

Traherne's chanting of catalogues, heaping of synonyms, anaphora, and parallel phrases are designed to lift his reader to transcendence. Critics have shown that together these devices at once both characterize a child's consciousness and also suggest human inadequacy to express the limitless plenitude of God's creation and man's re-creation. Critics furthermore agree that by accumulation these devices reflectively seem to become one while at the same time suggestively seem to expand beyond mortal limits.[38] Moreover, his incantations of mystical image clusters (such as those associated with the eye, a sphere, the sun, a mirror, the king, a dwelling place, or a fountain) have been understood to indicate the transfer from a literal object to a numinous symbol.[39] Traherne celebrates the incarnate Word of the Gospel according to John by heaping unendable catalogues of Christian emblems, agrammatically and nonprogressively. Men's words become things which become thoughts which the Logos affirms. Traherne's mode is a direct extension of typology: through Christ's revelatory grace he shows that the Logos is embodied in and fulfills the words and thoughts of the pious, expanding all to infinity and eternity. In "Walking," the transformation is of things into "Thoughts," fallen dead material into resurrected living spirit, by "Right Apprehension" granted, renewed, and celebrated "On Christmas-Day."

Traherne's incantation starts with a catalogue of limited, numbered things that he multiplies into infinite, eternal transcendence. The challenge to his plain style derives from his need to signal states which he can only affirm to exist. To meet it he chose to repeat traditional, connotative images and phrases so that the very repetitions verify the abstractions to be truer than the concrete referents that connote them. This accounts for his characteristic dual catalogues, exemplified in a poem praising God for granting the "Desire" to move from dead to living nakedness and then for granting spiritual vision:

> Where are the Silent Streams,
> The Living Waters, and the Glorious Beams,
> The Sweet Reviving Bowers,
> The Shady Groves, the Sweet and Curious Flowers,
> The Springs and Trees, the Heavenly Days,
> The Flowry Meads, the Glorious Rayes,
> The Gold and Silver Towers?
> Alass, all these are poor and Empty Things,
> Trees Waters Days and Shining Beams

Fruits, Flowers, Bowers, Shady Groves and Springs,
No Joy will yeeld, no more then Silent Streams.
    These are but Dead Material Toys,
    And cannot make my Heavenly Joys.

      O Love! ye Amities,
And Friendships, that appear abov the Skies!
    Ye Feasts, and Living Pleasures!
Ye Senses, Honors, and Imperial Treasures!
    Ye Bridal Joys! Ye High Delights;
    That satisfy all Appetites!
      Ye Sweet Affections, and
Ye high Respects! What ever Joys there be
    In Triumphs, Whatsoever stand
In Amicable Sweet Societie
Whatever Pleasures are at his right Hand
    Ye must, before I am Divine,
    In full Proprietie be mine.

                                  (st. 3, 4)

In the former stanza the persona declares that the two disordered catalogues are unrealized because they list empty materials, unenlightened by
vision. They are essentially dull, poverty-stricken, and naked because
forlorn. Hence they form a series of queries answered by a catalogue-
lament, their would-be junctures and unity with creation loosely gathered by *and*, except for the compelling "Alass." But the repetitive single
catalogue in the latter stanza, though barer still, leads to abstractions in
which the speaker affirms to have gained transcendent spiritual life. For
when the abstractions are seen truly, they lift whoever views them to
understanding. Thus, because of their proper perspective the unified series of personified exclamatory apostrophes (*yes*) establish relationships
through cause and effect connectives (*that, whatever, whatsoever*). In short,
the members of this catalogue are granted to be transcendent and celebra-
tive because that is the persona's perception of them.

    Traherne's poetry fosters connecting and cohering significances
through incantatory repetitions. His open-ended catalogues heap to end-
lessness because each reader's multiplying vision can add to the accumulation.[40] To a distinguishing degree, each one of his poems depends on the
reader for death or life at that moment, since he attempts to imitate the
Word in his words so that plentiful, fulfilling vision will be granted his
reader by the Word. As in his expansion of neotypological methods into
all things, so in his style he opens bare catalogues toward God's infinity
and eternity.

Finally, Traherne's poetry far more than that of any of the other neo-typological lyricists depends on its audience for a wide-range reading and knowledge of his works. For it is up to the readers to re-collect, re-view, and reveal the infinite unity that the poet can only barely suggest. Like the bees in "Walking," readers must search from one bare poesy-poem to the next in order to gather the sweets of repetitive incantation which expand vision through words granted by the Word until the extended typology of all creation can be seen in the world, in the poet, in enlightened humanity:

> To fly abroad like activ Bees,
> Among the Hedges and the Trees,
>   To cull the Dew that lies
>   On evry Blade,
> From evry Blossom; till we lade
>   Our *Minds*, as they their *Thighs*.
>
>   (31–36)

Readers are called repeatedly to look through fallen words in order to gather things and then thoughts, until all are finally recovered by and in the Word. "Thoughts. I" extend the possibilities of the former bees, creating their own appetite for God:

> Like Bees they flie from Flower to Flower,
> Appear in Evry Closet, Temple, Bower;
>   And suck the Sweet from thence,
>   No Ey can see:
> As Tasters to the Deitie.
>
>   (73–77)

"Thoughts. III" become angels gathering the quintessence of God's holiness from everything, to the increase of their own souls. While they too are bees, more importantly they represent the origins of divinity that show the New Jerusalem:

>   The Hony and the Stings
> Of all that is, are Seated in a Thought,
> Even while it seemeth weak, and next to Nought.
> The Matter of all Pleasure, Virtue, Worth,
> Grief, Anger, Hate, Revenge, which Words set forth,
> Are Thoughts alone. Thoughts are the highest Things,
> The very Offspring of the King of Kings.
> Thoughts are a kind of Strange Celestial Creature,

That when they're Good, they're such in evry Feature,
They bear the Image of their father's face,
And Beautifie even all his Dwelling Place.

(22–32)

They basically become understandings, the bees that contain the fall and the recovery of mankind as temples and images of God. In the poem they are transmitted by words leading to the Word.

"The Circulation" makes clear that ultimately Traherne's readers are dependent on the Word regathering them as images of God. For Traherne, the Word can make human words well again, so once humanity can see well again, people will be able to speak well again:

Tis Blindness Makes us Dumb.
Had we but those Celestial Eys,
Wherby we could behold the Sum
Of all his Bounties, we should overflow
With Praises, did we but their Causes Know.

(24–28)

When the Word grants sight he reveals himself in all; recovery from the fall operates through fallen words that reflect the Word and forecast recovery in him. Traherne's linguistic equivalent to his expansion of the neotypological lyric is repetitive cataloguing that expands incantation to realization. For the visionary, all the world, all men, all language reflect the Bible and God's revelation because the Word recovers all.

Traherne expands far beyond other neotypological lyricists the Gospel's revelation of salvation, which for them all potentially resides in the type's and the neotype's dual referents. Beginning his imitation of David, though of David's hymns of praise rather than penance, he directly emulates types, including the first type, Adam, and even identifies with the antitype. So he immediately sings thanksgivings and celebrations exalting God, especially God in himself and others, in fact in everything. He moves easily through any immediate referent into the ultimate referent and passes almost as quickly through the four stages of human life into the transcendent. With Traherne, through God's immanence and man's imitation of that immanence, the channel of neotypology dissolves in a universal flow of all significants and all significance into the infinite and eternal.

Thus the neotypological lyric dissolves and suffuses through the fusion and then infinite expansion of expression in the persona, creation, and God in Traherne's way. But in an opposite way, it can explode through their fission. Edward Taylor's *Preparatory Meditations* exemplifies that reaction.

7

"One key whereof is Sacerdotall Types"

God's Severance Yet Sign in the World
and the Poet in Edward Taylor's *Preparatory Meditations*

There is no contemporary account reacting to Edward Taylor's self-presentation, as there are full ones for Donne and Herbert and a scanty one for Traherne. Nor is there any evidence that Taylor might have been creating a persona of himself or of a representative Christian for any audience of *Preparatory Meditations* apart from God and himself, such as Southwell or Vaughan provide in prefaces and even Alabaster occasionally supplies in his verse. However, unlike the help historical biography renders for readings of Southwell's or Alabaster's poetry, efforts to apply historical biography to the *Preparatory Meditations* have little effect on interpretation. When Norman S. Grabo worked out a moderately full account of Taylor's active life, except for several corroborations from theological studies, that account provided few penetrating insights into these poems; thus Grabo hypothesized Taylor's passive life as a meditative mystic in order to explain the speaker.[1] And after Karl Keller distributed that active life into student, dissenter, minister, family man, frontiersman, and doctor-scientist, he then had to turn from this pilgrim's life toward Taylor's creation of the myth of himself for himself, in order to discuss *Preparatory Meditations*.[2]

Every indication is that through the long span of his creative life Taylor did not merely avoid showing these poems to others, he effectively thwarted their presentation for more than two centuries. His case, therefore, differs from all the other neotypological lyricists; and therefore it would seem inappropriate, actually inaccurate, to refer to a speaker or persona in *Preparatory Meditations* apart from Edward Taylor. The concept of persona seems alien here, in direct contrast to its usefulness in calling to attention the self-conscious presentations of dramatic personae that are often congregational exempla as well, which is characteristic of the other neotypological lyricists. *Preparatory Meditations* presents Taylor uniquely to himself and God, without him so much as admitting that anyone else overhears.

Thus, in the final analysis, one of Taylor's *Meditations* that recalls Herbert's "Windows" is considerably different from that poem. Taylor's fifty-ninth meditation of the second series, as well as Herbert's "Windows," expresses the necessity for and capability of Christ to reveal God to man. Furthermore, both poems present Christ revealing himself to believers in terms of light passing through a medium the poet identifies with. But the believing viewers in each of the two scenes differ. It is not inaccurate to claim that the persona in the "Windows" of *The Church* is the poet who can see Christ in himself. But the poem focuses on distinguishing the function of the poetic persona as a priest who serves as Christ's visible medium for his congregation. Taylor, on the contrary, does not focus on himself as a poet or as a minister. Instead, his poem affirms that he can see Christ in himself through Christ's grace and grant of faith enabling him to identify with a type.

Taylor begins by placing himself as a neotype in a typological context. Recalling Paul's explanation of the chosen people's wanderings, he begs Christ to apply these types to his own personal spiritual insight:

> Wilt thou enoculate within mine Eye
>   Thy Image bright, My Lord, that bright doth shine
> Forth in the Cloudy-Firy Pillar high
>   Thy Tabernacles Looking-Glass Divine?
>   What glorious Rooms are then mine Eyeholes made.
>   Thine Image on my windows Glass portrai'd?[3]

First he establishes the image pattern of the window/mirror/telescope of his primarily spiritual eye in the tabernacle/church of himself. Next he turns to consider the cloudy-fiery pillar as God's visible manifestation and open type of Christ.[4] Pitch to God's foes, it illuminates and shelters his elect: "Sure't is Christ's Charret drawn by Angells high. / The Humane jacket, typ'te, of's Deity" (11–12). In his transition Taylor particularly concentrates on illumination, with puns on the Son's light and deity ("A Sun by night, to Dayify the dark" [13]), welding the two central image clusters together: "Christs Looking Glass that on his Camp gives Shine. / Whose backside's pitchy darkness to his foes" (19–20). After realizing associations with the prophetic watchtower and tabernacle, he describes the triple mediatorial mystery: Christ becomes in the pillar a king guiding and protecting, in the cloud a priest baptizing and propitiating, and especially in the fire a prophet illuminating.[5] He ends by repeating his initial request that the "shining Pillar Cloud and Fire" replace the beam in his eye and guide his pilgrimage. As the poet nears heaven he makes a vow in a triple pun on the method of typology, on the type he wants Christ to make good in him as in the new covenant, and on the protection of Christ's grace: "I shall thy praise under this Shadow sing." A conclusion could, from the implications and development thus far, easily integrate the notion of a poet-priest exemplifying himself to other members of the congregation. This is what Herbert does, and he is thereby characteristic of neotypological lyricists. But Taylor does not; he concentrates on examining himself, for himself and for God.

Taylor's choice not to present himself as an exemplum follows from his Calvinistic stance of self-deprecation. And because of that very faith his meditations show an exhaustion of the English neotypological lyric directly counter to Traherne's. Where Traherne's poems unite all creation through God's immanence in the world and in the persona as both Adams, thereby elevating all above types, Taylor's poems sever not just neotypes as here but ultimately even types themselves from their unique potential for significance. His Calvinistic sense of the unimaginable discrepancy between maker and creation, in the present as well as the past, requires that nothing human or mundane has worth except to the degree God chooses. Yet his very same sense affirms that everyone and everything hints at God. His meditations mark another kind of disjunction within the neotypological lyric; and in doing so they also mark the opposite extreme of the tradition.

Three biographical facts help explain the disjunction in Taylor. The importance in his life of the Lord's Supper is obvious, for he wrote his meditations, "Chiefly upon the Doctrin preached upon the Day of administration," preparing himself for that central act of worship. It is most significant that one of the two sermon series that he prepared carefully, with an eye toward publication, is *Edward Taylor's Treatise Concerning the Lord's Supper.*[6] In these sermons preached in 1694 he demonstrates both his reverent awe of and his exultant joy in the occasion. He argues militantly against Stoddardism, the invitation to communion for halfway covenanters whose conversions and faiths were not so confirmed as to entitle them to full membership in the congregation. And he comments repeatedly on the special preparations for communion required of the soul of each member of the elect. In celebration he describes the full, exciting emotion of the commemoration. Universally critics have agreed that in writing the meditations Taylor was performing two sacred duties: severe self-examinations for sin, contrite confessions of worthlessness, painful penances for failure, and humble petitions for grace; and praises of God's compassionate mercy and glorious grandeur. Judging by the critics' universal referral to the quotation from the one hundred and tenth meditation of the second series, none would deny Taylor that "this rich banquet makes [him] thus a Poet" (24). And nearly all critics testify that Taylor's is the most personal of verse.

Besides the saving importance of the occasion in the therefore solely personal presentation of *Preparatory Meditations*, a second biographical fact is helpful for understanding Taylor: he was a Calvinist. This fact has led to a less widely accepted hypothesis. From his doctrine and through his equation of writing poetry with worshiping, Taylor created a fairly complete and wholly radical aesthetic and poetic.[7] Indeed many discussions which, like Grabo's, begin by dealing with Taylor's historical biography or poetic personality quickly become theories of his poetics.

A third helpful biographical fact is closely related to Taylor's personal presentation in meditations of his preparation for the crucial act of worship and to the radical Calvinistic aesthetic and poetic that he developed. He had what amounts to a scholar's interest in and knowledge of typology. Taylor's reliance on typology was so habitual that typological references appear in his manuscript notes; and in fact, fresh manuscript evidence of his typological studies continues to surface. Moreover, the first thirty of his second series of meditations concentrate on and attest to his knowledgeable study of typology.[8]

Out of his doctrinal Calvinism, his exegetical scholarship in typology, and his neotypological lyric heritage, Taylor developed an aesthetic and poetic of a most personal sort. While he recognizes himself as a neotype in neotypical situations and poetic matrices with typological motives and motifs, he still strips types as well as himself of unique significance. This means principally that for him no one thing has inherent value apart from God; nothing untouched by Christ, the sole mediator, has any significance. It then follows that anything in creation, anyone among mankind can display God's handiwork and Christ's mediation, but only if it has been accepted by and fulfilled through Christ. Ultimately it indicates that Taylor is operating under a revolutionary set of aesthetic assumptions. His reformation of neotypological lyrics is radically Calvinistic, the ultimate variant of this divergent path. He splits type, neotype, and antitype apart, negating the expressive potential of the first two whenever these lack Christ's direct and immediate grace, but providing extraordinary, indeed unfathomable, power when they do. And his poetry requires a new standard for evaluating how and when Christ grants their union.

† † †

To an extreme unusual among Reformed typologists and unique among neotypological lyricists, Taylor's types seem immeasurably inferior to the antitypes they predict. His sense of disparity is repeatedly confirmed in the series of wedding garment sermons on the Lord's Supper. The "dull and dark typical way" points partly to predictive similarity but especially to "utter dissimilitude." Together these qualities delineate such types as manna of the Lord's Supper and the drink at Horeb of Christ.[9]

What characterizes Taylor's idea of types and underlies his basic transformation of the neotypological lyric is his stress on the gap separating a type from its infinitely superior antitype. His definitive emphasis on that discrepancy is marked by the *Christographia* sermon series, where he immediately poses his attitude toward typology: "Our Apostle in this Chapter layes before us the insufficiency of Legall rites, and Sacrifices for the doing away of Sin in that they were Shaddows, and not so much as the Image, of the things they imported. Hence a necessity followed of their Weakness, and of the accomplishment of them in time by the taking place of that good thing in which the Efficacy lay."[10] While they are forecasting Christ they fail, thereby exhibiting their need for the mediatorial savior. For Taylor, Christ's antitypical fulfillment, power, majesty, and beauty are as superior to types as they are to men.[11] Taylor celebrates Christ's completion of all insufficient types by embodying truth. Without his fulfillment they would be less than meaningless; they would be false:

> As he is the Object of all the Old Testament Prophesies, and Metaphoricall Descriptions of the Messiah. He was variously foretold in the Old Testament even from Adam to the latter end of Malachy. As in Prophesies, Promises, and Types, which differ one from another, onely as to the manner in which hee was shewn: as he was held out in the Prophesie, he was foretold without any express obligation upon it, yet implicitly there was an obligation upon the Author to effect the matter prophesied. As in the Promise, God doth as I may say, put in bond to do the thing Promised. And as he is foretold in the Type, God doth as it were pensill out in fair Colours [199] and [ingrave] and portray Christ and his Natures and Properties in him. . . . Hence all the Truth in these Prophesies, Promises, and

Types lodges in Christ. Christs coming made them True. Their Truth lieth in him. He is the truth of them.[12]

To conclude the series he sums up Christ's mediatorial offices of prophet, priest, and king, using representative types such as, respectively, Abraham, Moses, Samuel, and Isaiah; Melchizedek and Aaron; David, the dancing sun of righteousness, and Solomon's glory.[13]

Taylor's poetic exposition of typology begins with commonplaces.[14] He uses typology to supplement his attempts to praise Christ. Foiled by human incomprehension he reapproaches Christ through Jacob:

> I spy thyselfe, as Golden Bosses fixt
>   On Bible Covers, shine in Types out bright.
> Of Abraham, Isaac, Jacob, where's immixt
>   Their streaming Beames of Christ displaying Light.
>   Jacobs now jog my pen, whose golden rayes
>   Do of thyselfe advance an holy blaze.
>
> (II. 6. 7–12)

Having drawn a series of comparisons of Jacob to Christ, Taylor describes Christ compensating for the shortcomings of both the type which forecasts and the poet who interprets him:

> In all those Typick Lumps of Glory I
>   Spy thee the Gem made up of all their shine
> Which from them all in thickest glory fly
>   And twist themselves into this Gem of thine.
>   And as the Shine thereof doth touch my heart,
>   Joy sincks my Soule seeing how rich thou art.
>
> (31–36)

As in *Christographia*, also in his *Meditations*, Taylor usually puts severe stress on the immeasurably superior new covenant superceding the old. Two meditations on Matthew 26:26 ("As they were eating, he took bread and blessed") are explicit. In these the communion is infinitely greater than its type, the passover. Recalling that "first Edition" covenants are "Deckt up in Types and Ceremonies gay" (20), Taylor emphasizes the new dispensation in the kernel, Christ, and his sacrament:

> But when the Pay day came their kirnells Pickt.
>   The Shell is cast out hence. Cloudes flew away.

165

Now Types good night, with Ceremonies strict,
   The Glorious Sun is risen, its broad day.
Now Passover farewell, and leave thy Place.
Lords Supper seales the Covenant of Grace.

(II. 103. 31–36)

He gives to the transfer from physical to spiritual, from law to good news, its most antithetical expression.

In Taylor's application even acclaimed personal types such as Jacob (mainly early in II), ceremonial types such as passover for communion and circumcision for baptism (II. 22 and 70 especially), and occasional types such as the wanderings of Israel (II. 58) avail nothing without direct reference to Christ.[15] In the fiftieth meditation of the second series, which parallels the exposition in the ninth sermon of *Christographia*, he returns to John 1:14: Christ is "Full of Truth." He is the smaragdine box in whom all truth, types, promises, and ordinances rest and by whom all appear, are illuminated, and become divine:

Thou givst thy Truth to them, thus true they bee.
   They bring their Witness out for thee. Hereby
Their Truth appeares emboxt indeed in thee:
   And thou the true Messiah shin'st thereby.
Hence Thou, and They make One another true
And They, and Thou each others Glory shew.

Hence thou art full of Truth, and full dost stand,
   Of Promises, of Prophesies, and Types.
But that's not all: All truth is in thy hand.

(31–39)

Taylor accomplishes a variety of purposes with typology in the *Meditations*. His simplest is religious evocation. The representative twelfth meditation of the first series focuses on the red robes of Bozrah (Isaiah 63), which Stanford annotates. Meditations of this sort usually conclude with the poet's sense of insignificance and incapacity in the presence of Christ's infinite self-sacrificing love.

His next simplest poetic use of types occurs when he applies the significance of one or more to himself, usually in a supplication. In a particularly consistent meditation he gains insight through Christ identifying with manna while he is feeding thousands, John 6:51, "I am the Living Bread, that came down from Heaven" (II. 60 [A]). As his emphasis turns from the literal to the spiritual, from sustenance to insight, the poet's opening hunger and thirst for righteousness attach the manna pot inside the ark. He finally promises to praise Christ's glories in return for angelic food. In immediately following meditations, which draw on Israel's Sinai trek, he creates parallel pleas based on the rock of Horeb and the brazen serpent.[16]

One of his more complex poetic uses appears when he creates image clusters around types.[17] Ursula Brumm explicates the tree of life as Christ, the vine.[18] She reads the more significant and pervasive allusions, images, and puns emanating from the eucharistic types—*aquae vitae*, rock of Horeb, spring or *beer*, cluster of grapes, and Joseph the butler— that Taylor consistently employed.[19]

His most poetically complex exploitation follows the neotypological lyric tradition. Karl Keller has remarked that Taylor, because he employs wit in applying types to himself, stands apart from other New England typologists: "Taylor is for the most part attracted to types into which he can slip himself without any way changing the nature of the original type-antitype relationship, thereby sneaking himself into the plan of salvation by means of the vehicle of language."[20] From the perspective of Taylor's neotypological lyric heritage, placing himself in and calling attention to himself within might provide a more accurate description. But essentially Keller seems to describe precisely a poet so placing a neotype as to tap the expressive and redemptive potential of the dual referents in the relationship between type and antitype. Typical of the tradition's essential method and last poet is Taylor's fifty-ninth meditation in the second series, in which he prays to identify with the pillar of cloud and fire. A similar example of Taylor's neotypological lyric is his meditation on Colossians 2:11–12, in which he begs to identify with the antitype, baptism, as well as with the circumcision that baptism replaces, thereby providing a superior new symbol of supplanting the flesh with the spirit (II. 70). Prominent, forthright, and surprising is his meditation on Galatians 4:24 in which Taylor reverses the familiar Reformed interpretation. He asks to be not the lost servant son of Hagar but instead the true spiritual heir of Abraham, a neotypical son of Sarah and "thy blesst Promisd Seed" (II. 4).

† † †

Although types are important for his single meditations, series of meditations, imagery complexes, and neotypological lyrics, they are not the prime bearers of divine revelation. They are but a single key. In his tract on the Lord's Supper he argues that "Natural things are not unsuitable to illustrate supernaturals by"; without them "we could arrive at no knowledge of supernatural things, for we are not able to see above naturals."[21] Notably this program sanctions no particular mundane things. Further, while he points out in *Christographia* that Christ is the tenor of all Old Testament vehicles, particularly types, at the same time he tends to deny them singular metaphorical value: "Nay, all those that he instituted Whether of a Morall, or Ceremoniall Significency are abolished. For the truth of all is in Christ Col: 2. 17."[22] Since Christ, the sole mediator, has become flesh in order to reveal God, types, which gained significance by limited and predictive mediation, have depreciated. Since Christ, they merely confirm what is known. Taylor's sermon, which has already been noted for restricting typology to a Calvinistic definition, emphatically reaffirms: Christ embodies truth. Nothing apart from Christ has any inherent significance; any significance descends from Christ. In Taylor's view, then, types have special significance only because they have been chosen and fulfilled, that is, only because they have predicted accurately. Furthermore, anything at all that God chooses in Christ gains all possible revelatory significance. A system such as Taylor's moves toward a new aesthetic, exhausting one line of the neotypological lyric.

Recent discussions of Taylor's Calvinistic aesthetic have focused on the characteristic discrepancy between tenor and vehicle in his metaphors, the failures of mundane existence and human expression to approximate a gloriously transcendent God. His aesthetic correspondingly follows Calvin's singular stress on man's utter worthlessness as a means of moving people to repent and confess faith in order to be saved. In addition, these discussions have emphasized that Taylor understood the failure of symbolic language to express God; and they have concluded that because of this understanding Taylor demanded that writer and reader try to annihilate words and analogies in order to cope with reality as well as to instill faith.[23] One hypothesis yet to be extended is that Taylor tacitly assumed imperfect poetic expression could succeed and furthermore he believed any such success rests solely in Christ's grace. Paradoxically, for Taylor poetry succeeds at the very point of confessed failure, to the degree that Christ shines through to illuminate and glorify it. A poet cannot recognize its success, as Marvell says in "The Coronet," for such an acknowledgment signals the failure that derives from pride. Thus, Taylor demonstrates the most radical adherence to a fundamental tenet of all the neotypological lyricists: the criterion for judging a poem's success, determined in part by readers, as was church election by Taylor's congregation, is whether that poem is made true by Christ absorbing and saving it. This criterion is the same he describes for testing types and creation: meaning and truth cannot inhere in any unless Christ has granted value to its inescapable worthlessness. Taylor affirms that Christ chooses whatever he wants to be his poem and symbol. The poet, like the type, or anything else, can only strive—and wait.

Taylor begins by considering his personal and poetic lack of meaning and worth in comparison to God. Opening one of his clearest poetic accounts of types by considering Colossians 2:3, "In whom are hid all the Treasures of Wisdom, and Knowledge" (II. 14), he is in anguish over his corroded emptiness: "My Heart is Fistulate: I am a Shell" (5). As he looks for meaning he begs Christ not only for a medicine to cure sin but also for a sign of spiritual healing:

> Shall not that Wisdom horded up in thee
> (One key whereof is Sacerdotall Types)
> Provide a Cure for all this griefe in mee?

This second stanza sets a pattern for corresponding asymmetrical requests in the third and fourth stanzas. These add to the original type, a priest sacrificing and curing, two more, a prophet illuminating "(which / Prophetick Types enucleate)" and a king cleansing and perfecting "(Which Kingly Types do shine upon in thee)." The fourth hesitantly questions the value of types, "Pointers" toward wisdom, until the fifth reveals their inadequacy to signify the glory of Christ's truth:

> How Glorious art thou, Lord? Cloathd with the Glory
> Of Prophets, Priests, and Kings? Nay all Types come
> To lay their Glory on thee. (Brightsome Story).
>
> (31–33)

They are rays emanating from the sun/Son, dependent on their source for any wisdom they might show. Christ bestows light for dark, glory for failure, meaning for emptiness, wherever he chooses, so Taylor concludes by praying for Christ to supply wisdom to his lineaments, for Christ to preserve and crystalize the barren poem and poet:

> Draw out thy Wisdom, Lord, and make mee just.
> Draw out thy Wisdom. Wisdoms Crown give mee.
> With shining Holiness Candy my Crust.

Taylor next relates his personal and poetic failure to that of typology. To return to the meditation "Full of Truth" (II. 50) is to recognize that for him no type, no more than himself nor poetry nor anything else, possesses any revelatory power; it can show Christ only when Christ chooses. His theory implies a leveling of typological metaphor, a denial of the unique value of types. Taylor tells a parable about man's creation, fall, and redemption: God created an ancestral pearl box (suggesting the soul) filled with truth and beauty that later fell and broke and was refilled with falsehood and bitterness. To repair it, God created a second box, richer than the first, to recover the truth he promised through types during the intervening 4,000 years. Coming to the incarnation, Taylor turns from his parable to a direct prayer to Christ, in whom is "emboxt" all truth:

> Hence thou art full of Truth, and full dost stand,
> > Of Promises, of Prophesies, and Types.
> But that's not all: All truth is in thy hand,
> > Thy lips drop onely Truth, give Falshood gripes.
> > Leade through the World to glory, that ne'er ends
> > By Truth's bright Hand all such as Grace befriends.

(37–42)

Precisely at that point where types would most likely prove to be unique truth-bearers, Taylor recoils "But that's not all": Truth is Christ. However, to his own inexpressible gratitude and his sense of the gratitude owed by all fallen humanity, God's grace can grant truth to all. Hence, as an expanded neotype he can ask that his own heart become a box of truth by becoming Christ's dwelling. This Calvinistic axiom of the lack of worth of anything, even types, untouched by grace, is consistent in Taylor's meditations. It forms the foundation of his distinctive reduction of all creation (especially himself), his sense of the inexpressible glory of God, and his immense gratitude for God's grace.

A corollary of hope follows from Taylor's theory which levels typological metaphors with metaphors in the self and the world. The burden of the opening meditation of his second series is that all things, no matter how fallen, can be media for Christ's truth; they can be like types—if Christ's love grants it. That stained leather jacket, the poet, can faithfully hope, not so much because "The glory of the world [is] slickt up in types" as because Christ shines forth "In all Choise things chosen to typify" (13, 14). Human wonder about imputed truth and grace derives less from the presence of Christ's glory than from his grant to particular beings. Taylor is thus encouraged to beg that grant and to praise the inexpressible gift and giver by reducing those chosen:

> The glory of all Types doth meet in thee.
>   Thy glory doth their glory quite excell:
> More than the Sun excells in its bright glee
>   A nat, an Earewig, Weevill, Snaile, or Shell.
>   Wonders in Crowds start up; your eyes may strut
>   Viewing his Excellence, and's bleeding cut.
>
> (19–24)

The notion that Taylor intensely meditated on and maintained that Christ repairs the inadequacies of the world and the poet, as well as the type, is supported by such meditations as "Things Present" (I. 35). When considering communion, he expatiates over the multitude of contradictions in actions, things, and influences in this world. As he thinks about the contraries, hell and heaven, clashing on earth, he wonders how God can reveal providence and reconcile all:

> How Glorious then is he that doth all raise
>   Rule and Dispose and make them all Conspire
> In all their Jars, and Junctures, Good-bad wayes
>   To meliorate the self same Object higher?
>   Earth, Water, Fire, Winds, Herbs, Trees, Beasts and Men,
>   Angells, and Divells, Bliss, Blasts, advance one stem?
>
> (19–24)

That God's order, and hence he himself, can shine through the oppositions is indicated by the order of opposing sets: the elements (with one displaced) and links in the chain of being rise from bottom to top reflecting the contrary potentials, bliss-blast. But the poet seeks greater order, not so much in the universe as in himself. About to partake of communion, in both senses of the meal and the personal union it symbolizes, he recognizes that only the Lord can unite and illuminate; he breaks into a colloquy:

> Oh, that the Sweets of all these Windings, spoute
>   Might, and these Influences streight, and Cross,
> Upon my Soule, to make thy Shine breake out
>   That Grace might in get and get out my dross!

171

> My Soule up lockt then in this Clod of Dust
> Would lock up in't all Heavenly Joyes most just.

(31–36)

Christ's grace, which illuminates the poet, allows his spiritual insight, and can fill all lowly temples, could enable him to see more clearly how love fills him.[24]

His self-characterized poetic failure is one essential element of Taylor's poetry. Another is the failure of language to approximate and accommodate God's incomprehensible, beyond inexpressible, truth. And contemporary critics have corroborated the roughness of the *Meditations*— elisions of terminal g's, riming of nasals, slant rimes, irregularity of unaccented syllables, coinages, repetitions of words and roots, inversions, internal interjections, and compressions.[25] In his prologue Taylor prays, "Lord, Can a Crumb of Dust the Earth outweigh, / Outmatch all mountains, nay the Chrystall Sky?" and the constituents of his polarized verse plead, how can he express the glory of Christ in the pun. Granted celestial implements and medium, he would still "but blot and blur yea jag, and jar / Unless thou mak'st the Pen, and Scribener." He laments his failure, begging God that his poetry not be self-destructive or ridiculous; and he requests a spiritual influx to prove God's presence. Taylor's poetry seems little concerned with expression but preoccupied with Christ's illumination of the words and the poet. It oscillates between petitions for Christ's truth and confessions of men's failures in discourse.

Because of the pervasive and inevitable failures of his words, Taylor is always explicitly and implicitly praying for Christ's grace to justify his poetry. His meditation on Revelation 19:16 is characteristic of the way he seeks aid for his words. In "King of Kings" the poet is reduced to repeating the word, *king*, and transforming the declaration, "Thou art my 'King of Kings'" (I. 17).[26] But were words somehow to become adequate, Taylor would still consider the poet inadequate. In rapture over the promise in John 10:10, "I am come that they might have Life" (II. 87), he has to acknowledge his inability to describe life. His faulty comparisons reflect both man's original sin against life ("But oh! Sin fould this Glory: Man hath lost it: / Death by a Sinfull Morsell killd and crost it" [29–30]) and Christ's sacrifice to renew life which increased the inestimable gap between man's inadequacy and God's perfection.

Ultimately, the failure of words results from a failure of thought.[27] Taylor painfully pursues those thoughts from which his words might flow:

My Only Dear, Dear Lord, I search to finde
　　My golden Arck of Thought, thoughts fit and store:
And search each Till and Drawer of my minde
　　For thoughts full fit to Deck thy kindness o're,
　　　But find my foreheade Empty of such thoughts
　　　And so my words are simply ragged, nought.

(II. 141)

What he prepares to adorn Christ with comes out empty wind that darkens brilliance, a homely style that thatches a golden palace. His condition seems hopelessly bathetic before sublimity; he affirms, however, that flaws in poet, language, and thought can be repaired but only inasmuch as Christ shows through them.

Thus, Christ's restoration of the fallen poet and poetry forms a double motion in Taylor. Christ creates poetry by granting visionary thought that makes words good in spite of themselves. In addition, Christ redeems the failure of the poet who, if Christ shows through him and his meditation, displays worthy thought not merely in the words of a poem but even more in the controlling voice of the *Meditations*. Together these form Taylor's central addition to and his mode of exhausting the potential in the neotypological lyric.

The final test for Taylor of his success or failure rests on whether or not the audience (in the case of the *Meditations*, Taylor himself), the poet, and his God see the poet as a vision Christ shines through. This test explains Taylor's reliance on types; because types' prophecies and promises have already been fulfilled by Christ, they make compelling models for the neotype, who may become their equivalent. In a striking poem (II. 9) where types give way, Taylor recalls the prophecy of Moses, "Deut. 18 [15] The Lord thy God will raise up unto thee a Prophet—like unto mee"). He begins by considering how Moses reflected Christ beforehand, antitypical fulfillment rendering his own typological reading somewhat clearer than the dark image of Corinthians:

Lord, let thy Dazzling Shine refracted fan'de
　　In this bright Looking Glass, its favour lay
Upon mine Eyes that oculated stand
　　And peep thereat, in button moulds of clay.

The brilliant beams gain illumination precisely because Christ has verified them by fulfilling a long list of typological parallels in the foreshadowing mirror of Moses, "All which shine gloriously in thee that wee / Do Moses finde a Well drawn Map of thee" (47–48). Echoing Revelation, the poet next begs that the tears be wiped from his eyes and that he sing with the blest choir. Taylor would himself be a looking glass or a musical instrument, like Herbert, a medium through which Christ communicates:

> I long to see thy Sun upon mee shine,
>   But feare I'st finde myselfe thereby shown worse.
> Yet let his burning beams melt, and refine
>   Me from my dross, yet not to singe my purse.
>   Then of my metall make thy Warbling harp:
>   That shall thy Praise deck't in sweet tunes out warp.
>
> (55–60)

Returning to the commercial-coinage imagery of his earliest *Meditations* and following the tradition of the "Burning Babe" through his own *Meditation* II. 105, he asks to be purified in the Isaiahan furnace of Christ's mercy.

Taylor's affirmation that Christ can shine through poetry and poet rests on his belief in Christ the Logos verifying visionary thought. As in the *Christographia* sermons' absolute definition, truth is Christ. A pair of remarkable poems establish this point. In the forty-third meditation of the second series Taylor opens characteristically by deprecating his cramped tongue's inaptitude to glorify God. Speech forms too coarse a medium for deity because, in a trinity echoing Father, Spirit, and Son,

> Words Mentall are syllabicated thoughts:
>   Words Orall but thoughts Whiffld in the Winde.
> Words Writ, are incky, Goose quill-slabbred draughts,
>   Although the fairest blossoms of the mind.
>
> (13–16)

These lines describe not one but a series of removals from truth; and at each interval between removals there is a gap of inadequacy between the referent and the potential to signify it. Even before the series begins, God transcends the ideal of thought. Then, conscious thought in mental words or images is broken into fragmentary hieroglyphs; next, oral language is ironically lost in the spiritless breath of spoken words which should transport it; last, whatever life rests in oral words is befouled and blackened by pitch in the fallen medium of writing, the records of humanity.[28] Yet words in poems, even after the series of disastrous dislocations, somehow have to reflect God, however darkly. Frustrated, the poet despairs: "Then can such glasses cleare enough descry / My Love to thee, or thy rich Deity?" (17–18). His answer is—of course not, for words are smoke fumes, smut, "Will-a-Wisps," bogs of frogs, mud from a clod, clouds. But his answer must also be—yes of course, if only because words are all the poet has, though finally only because Christ the Word has justified them:

> Yet spare mee, Lord, to use this hurden ware.
> I have no finer Stuff to use, and I
> Will use it now my Creed but to declare
> And not thy Glorious Selfe to beautify.
> Thou art all-God: all Godhead then is thine
> Although the manhood there unto doth joyne.
>
> (25–30)

For Taylor the poem can be made good, first because it confesses faith in Christ, and second because the Word of God took on the form of man. At the same time that the poet is balked from understanding and expressing paradoxical mystery, precisely his act of faithfully displaying failure permits Christ's grace to justify him and his poem. If Christ is inapprehensibly transcendent, he is also inexplicably finite and graspable for the poet: "Thou art Almighty, though thy Humane tent / Of Humane frailty upon earth did sent" (35–36). Confounded by the mystery, the poet's wondering thanks are as inexpressible as Christ's grace and essence. And therefore in his failure, indeed through his credent confession of failure and request of Christ's grace, he concludes that his words can be made good by the Word: "Be thou my God, and make mee thine Elect / . . . .I'le bring thee praise, buskt up in Songs perfum'de, / When thou with grace my Soule hast sweetly tun'de."

In the immediately following meditation, on John 1:14 "The word was made Flesh," Taylor expands from words to rhetoric, the art of the speaker. Confounded in his attempts to understand the paradoxical mystery of the union of God beyond estimate with mankind beneath it, he turns immediately to a type, Jacob's ladder (which also inadequately signifies Christ's dual nature), then directly to fulfillment.[29] Again he reiterates that whatever has value has gained it through Christ:

> Things styld Transcendent, do transcende the Stile
> Of Reason, reason's stares neere reach so high.

But Jacob's golden Ladder rounds do foile
    All reasons Strides, wrought of THEANTHROPIE.

(7–10)

Faithful confession of the Word-made-flesh signifies fallen human and typological inadequacy; both become good only through being justified by the grace of the inexpressible truth, Christ. Taylor, as ever, concludes with a prayer asking that the Word complete his poem and himself: "Unite my Soule, Lord, to thyselfe, and stamp / Thy holy print on my unholy heart. / . . . If thou wilt blow this Oaten Straw of mine, / The sweetest piped praises shall be thine." Taylor envisions when the Word inspires or shines through to justify words, no matter at what degree removed, then the piles of fallen and discarded images from the world, the tatters of repeated interjection and repetition and parallel, the strings of sacred polyptoton and pun, are converted into the whole cloth of Christ's glory. And the success of the poet and poem appear at that instant when his contrite recognition of failure allows his request for forgiveness and his affirmation of faith.

Types are important in Taylor's *Preparatory Meditations* for references, definitions, explications, applications, image clusters, and neotypical self-portrayals. But because Christ has already fulfilled their promise, types for Taylor possess no more inherent value in signifying God than anything else does; they are deposed as unique bearers of divine revelation. Paramount is his Calvinistic sense of the abyss between God's all and creation's null, a principle that denies independent significance for any, apart from God's grace through Christ's mediation. His wonder is that justification can come through Christ's mercy on contrite confession of failure, affirmation of faith, and thankful praise. The world, humanity, thoughts, words, the poet himself, bear significance equivalent to that of types if Christ shines through them. The Word, Truth, can abrogate their independence and grant importance, sanctification, and glorification. Taylor has created a new Calvinistic poetic expectation—paradoxical success out of confessing failure, potential union and worth out of recognizing severance and insignificance.

For his innovative exhaustion of the neotypological lyric and sacred aesthetic, Taylor created a style of ragged and patched imperfection through which Christ can display perfect robes of glory. The central device of his failed style perfected is repetition of a root, a word, a phrase, as if the repetitions corroborate the thought behind the language. The poet repeats himself until he finally confesses the failure of words and

176

referents to express transcendence. In essence, he prays for an infusion of grace to weave the repetitious language and thought around Christ, who can transform the fragments and rags of words and ideas into magnificent whole cloth. The patterned movement from bathos to transcendence often rises from puns and pun clusters. For example, Brumm has shown that *beer*, the Germanic beverage, becomes the Hebraic spring or well that baptizes, and Keller has noted several wine/vine and cordial/heart series.[30] The related neotypological device of repetition is clear in the meditation on John 3:14, "As Moses lift up the Serpent in the Wilderness so must the Son of man be lift up" (II. 61). Repetitions of *serpentine*, *serpents*, *poison*, *stinging*, *burning*, and *brazen*, all associated with the plague of serpents in the wilderness and thereby signifying original and continuing epidemics of sin, are verbally transmuted through homeopathic antidote into *gold*, *health*, *virtue*, the *sovereign* or *salve* of Christ on the cross. Through the poem Christ perfects a type that shows sin and to a degree moderates plague. He could also choose to perfect the poet: "I by the fiery Serpent bitt be here. / Be thou my brazen Serpent me to Cure" (37–38). In Taylor's leveling, reversals through puns and renewed significations are not limited to types, for Christ can lift his bathos to transcendence in the world: tobacco can be as much a panacea as the serpent, and transforming image clusters from mining, metallurgy, minting, and distilling can be as emblematic as tabernacles.[31]

The assumption behind Taylor's style requires that even mere similarities between word sounds can display Christ through imputed grace. In the forty-eighth meditation of the second series, on Revelation 1:8, the poet expatiates on "The Almighty." He begins with a riming saw, "O! What a thing is Might right mannag'd?" After a series of exchanges he decides that might and right are inseparable. The poet becomes more and more frustrated in expounding gradations from *might* to *mighty* until all humanity is confuted outright by the concept of *almightiness*. Then he achieves his central pun wherein rags of riming, punning, and repeating demand the interweaving of poem and poet:

> But what am I, poor Mite, all mightless thing!
>   That cannot rive a rush, that I should e're
> Adventure t'dress Almighty up, or bring
>   Almightiness deckt in its mighty geere?
>   Then spare my Stutting Stamring, inky Quill,
>   If it its bowells on thy Power distill.

(13–18)

The poet confesses failure, begs to be made good; yet as his poem stammers and stutters he becomes increasingly aware of his poetic failure and smallness, a mite who dares to address and dress the Almighty. He is thereby reduced to pointing repetitively to the unfathomable distance between God and nature, Christ and man, all and nothing. But as the poet and world are diminished, so are the powers of evil and darkness: "Their Might's a little mite, Powers powerless fall" (27). The poet takes comfort in the faith of his confession that Christ's imputed grace can justify and sanctify, and also in the faith that almighty love, grace, truth, justice, wisdom, holiness can shine through the poem and the poet. Christ can reweave fragments and rags of repetition, or nothing, into the whole, holy cloth of all, transform them from less than a mite to identification with the Almighty:

> If thy Almightiness, and all my Mite
>   United be in sacred Marriage knot,
> My Mite is thine: Mine thine Almighty Might.
>   Then thine Almightiness my Mite hath got.
>   My Quill makes thine Almightiness a String
> Of Pearls to grace the tune my Mite doth sing.
>
> (37–42)

What makes the poem good is the Word fusing with repeated words, Christ with Edward Taylor. For Taylor the marriage is no mere fusion of puns. Puns only represent ink on the page, behind which are words whiffled in the wind, behind which are fragmentary mental words, behind which are inexpressible mental ideas, behind which is God. And when God shows through, the nothing, poet, poem, and words become good, but not with inherent powerlessness. Rather, they are saved in their self-acknowledged failure and reliance on Christ's grace. From Taylor's radically unique perspective, it is possible for the most-failed poem to be the greatest. His new style creates a different and paradoxical value, union out of severance. And it derives from his exegesis of types.

† † †

As he worshipped God through his *Preparatory Meditations before my Approach to the Lords Supper*, Taylor created a radical aesthetic and style out of his Calvinistic beliefs. As these evolved, the aesthetic with its concomitant style required that Taylor's neotype split apart the type and the neotype in the referential interaction that had released to his neotypological forebears an immense potential for affirming salvation. But for Taylor the mundane world was so infinitesimally and insignificantly bathetic in contrast to the unimaginably transcendent godhead in Christ that the chasm between the dual referents in the motifs of the type and the extreme oscillation between the dual motives of the neotypological lyric made their earlier form of expression virtually impossible. The signs could no longer express both type and antitype, but in opposition had to refer to either the one or to the other, either world or God. When Taylor centered himself between the two, they flew apart. His successful release of potential in their interacting, expressive explosion amounts not to an incomplete conversion but to a total transformation that exhausts their energy.

Taylor's recurring metaphor for his radically Calvinistic poetic and style is Christ's transfiguration of tatters into robes of glory.[32] Whereas in the twenty-sixth meditation of the first series the poet laments that his "Linsy-Wolsy Loom deserves thy blame. / Its all defild, unbiasst too by Sin" (10–11), in the previous meditation he begs for himself Christ's merciful endowment to believers: "But, my sweet Lord, what glorious robes are those? / . . . Dost thou adorn some thus, and why not mee?" (19, 25). The robe or wedding garment emblem is most prominent in the last meditations of the first series.[33] The forty-first sets the metaphor's potential by expressing awe over Christ's robe of flesh, the mystery of God incarnate:

> The Magnet of all Admiration's here.
>   Your tumbling thoughts turn here. Here is Gods Son,
> Wove in a Web of Flesh, and Bloode rich geere.
>   Eternall Wisdoms Huswifry well spun.
>   Which through the Laws pure Fulling mills did pass.
>   And so went home the Wealthy'st Web that was.
>
>   (7–12)

His next meditation suggests that the metaphor's power can spread to the believer's worship and the poet's celebration: "Unkey my Heart; unlock thy Wardrobe: bring / Out royall Robes: adorne my Soule, Lord. . . . Adorn me, Lord, with Holy Huswifry. / All blanch my Robes with Clusters of thy Graces" (19–20, 37–38).

The robe metaphor demonstrates how Taylor radically expended the force of typology and the neotypological lyric while he was using up the tradition by pushing it to Calvinistic limits. What is critical is that he acknowledges the typology of the robe only momentarily and suggestively while he emphasizes the robe of Revelation that transcends, even envelops the Old Testament foreshadowing in its folds. Christ's appearance in the robe abrogates for Taylor any inherent value in robes as types or neotypes and thus annihilates their independent worth in lyrics.

Two major typological robes were available to Taylor. Aaron's robe as a type of Christ's priestly garment, even his flesh, is commonly acknowledged by Calvinistic exegetes. Mather supports the basic texts found in the twenty-eighth and thirty-ninth chapters of Exodus with references from Zechariah 3:4, Psalms 132:9, 16, and Job 29:14, in order to elaborately demonstrate that Aaron's priestly garments are a "shadow of an higher Spiritual Clothing," Christ's clothing when he absolves the sins of the elect and imputes righteousness to them.[34] The spiritual significance of the colors of the priest's robe heighten the sense of that justification and the sanctification that Christ grants believers. "The mystical signification of this Garment is the Righteousness of Christ, not only in regard of his own person, but also wherewith he clothes Believers."[35] Commentators such as Guild and Thomas Taylor extend Mather's texts to Hebrews 5 and especially to Revelation 1.[36]

Often in his meditations (especially in I. 12–15) Taylor combines Aaron's robes with the robes of Bozrah. He uses them significantly in the twenty-third meditation of the second series. Aaron projects Christ's atonement, but fulfillment is so glorious that "His Type is all unmeet / To typify him till aton'd and sweet" (23–24). Before he presents the details of Aaronic typology Taylor denigrates its independent value; any value it has derives solely from Christ. Only afterwards does he introduce an elaborate series of parallel sacrifices including two goats which signify Christ's human and divine natures:

> A'ron as he atonement made did ware
>   His milke white linen Robes, to typify
> Christ cloath'd in human flesh pure White, all fair,
>   And undefild, atoneing God most High.
>
> (25–28)

In conclusion Aaron appears in a new, transcending robe made by Christ, a robe merely foreshadowed by Aaron's original:

> Thus done with God Aaron aside did lay
>   His Linen Robes, and put on's Golden Ray.

And in this Rich attire he doth apply
  Himselfe before the peoples very eyes,
Unto the other Service, richly high
    To typify the gracious properties
    Wherewith Christs human nature was bedight
    In which he mediates within Gods Sight.

                                          (53–60)

Any value in the Taylor type derives solely from displaying the mediation of the antitype, which justifies, sanctifies, and glorifies it. Taylor here, as in II. 59, comes to a different end from Herbert's use of the same materials. For Taylor does not emphasize that Christ is seen through someone, but rather that Christ is seen at all.

Taylor's feeling about the utter lack of inherent value in a type is even more evident in that he ignores the second kind of typological robe available to him. The robes and clothing of Christ's righteousness and grace foretold by Isaiah 61:10 and Ezekiel 16:8 are acknowledged by Diodati and the Westminster Assembly annotators. But when Taylor creates opportunities to follow this type, he shuns it, choosing in its place the direct impact of the robes worn by Christ and the elect in Revelation (II. 94) or those which mystical tradition derived from the Song of Songs (II. 143 and 147).[37]

As Taylor disposes, whatever value Christ bestows on types is wholly dependent on himself as the antitype; furthermore that value lasts only until he envelops all. In the tenth meditation of the second series Taylor describes an Old Testament continuum wherein each type predicting Christ seems to absorb the value of the earlier members of the series. He opens bluntly by ousting Mosaic for Joshuan typology: "Moses farewell." After briefly honoring Moses, he leaves "To follow Josuah to Jordan where / He weares a Type, of Jesus Christ, divine." As he crosses the Jordan into the Promised Land he leaves behind the rock of Horeb, manna, the cloud and pillar, "My Old-New Cloaths my Wildernesses Ware" (21), since with the new circumcision he gains types closer to Christ: "I drink the Drink of Life and weare Christs Web / And by the Sun of Righteousness am led" (29–30). In conclusion the poet recognizes that as the approach nears Christ previous types dissolve:

That blazing Star in Joshua's but a Beam
  Of thy bright Sun, my Lord, fix such in mee.
My Dish clout Soul Rence Wring, and make it clean.
  Then die it in that blood that fell from thee.

Ultimately he recognizes that the robes of the neotype are dishrags that must be washed in the grace-granting, antitypical blood of the lamb before they can become robes of any significance. Behind this series of absorbing transcendences is Taylor's notion that types have already been fulfilled and thus receive only whatever value Christ grants to them. At best types are ancillary, minimal reduced signs of God, in a nontransubstantiating metaphor. They are like the signs and seals of the lord's supper:

> What Royall Feast Magnificent is this,
>   I am invited to, where all the fare
> Is spic'd with Adjuncts, (ornamentall bliss)
>   Which are its robes it ever more doth ware?
>   These Robes of Adjuncts shining round about
>   Christs golden Sheers did cut exactly out.
>
> (II. 108. 1–6)[38]

With the logical term, *adjunct*, so important to Ramistic Puritans, Taylor severs accompanying attributes from the essence they cling to.[39] Once the essence, the sole meaning, has appeared in the flesh, types and neotypes are recalled only to discover whether or not they have been vessels or robes that Christ appears in and transforms. Finally, their value follows after imputed grace.

Taylor breaks the typological exegesis tradition by moving directly through the robes of justification and righteousness, priesthood and glorification, to Christ's robed appearance in Revelation. And he can split the neotypological lyric heritage by moving directly through self-examination to discover if he is one of Christ's elect, robed in Revelation. In the forty-sixth meditation of the first series Taylor skirts, as having no greater significance than anything else mundane, potential typological references to the robes of righteousness in Isaiah and Ezekiel and to Aaron's priestly robes, even while he hints of dyed, sacrificial robes (21–22). Nothing has significance apart from the justification, sanctification, and glorification of Christ's grace: "Rev. 3.5. The same shall be cloathed in White Raiment."

He opens the forty-sixth meditation characteristically, minimizing human significance and magnifying human wonder at Christ's saving grace: "Nay, may I, Lord, believe it? Shall my Skeg / Be ray'd in thy White Robes?" The poet is reduced in terms familiar from the many meditations that echo the "Prologue": a dingy, dark, "Dirt ball," "Ball of dirt," "bit of Dirt," "Lump of Clay." He becomes a decaying dung cart. But he realizes though he be a dung cart, he can also be a purse filled by whatever God provides, as in still other meditations (I. 2, 6, 7, 45). God's preacher and poet, he can become a vessel of light, like Herbert, in I. 28. So, while the poor mortal is reduced from valueless vessel to purse to chaotic dirt ball to snail's horn to dung cart, he is alternately raised by God's grace through the central imagery of the poem: his skeg (torn garment) is covered by the gleaming white raiment of Revelation, his makeshift frame thatched in heavenly light, his dull jumble enlightened beyond the stars and the garb of angels. His mortality is transformed into immortality. Finally, following the variations on David and psalmody of many neo-typological lyrics, as God's instrument his strings are tuned.

Taylor requests that Christ weave whole cloth out of shreds of word repetition, rags of punning, bits of asymmetrically parallel and convoluted syntax, and threads of repeated sounds. He believes that in order for the tatters of fallen language to become a poem, a miracle of grace must clothe in brilliant righteousness a worse than insignificant dirt ball; Christ the Word is necessary to make a Christian and his words worthwhile.

Taylor founds his poem on the prayer that Christ join the mortal nothing to the immortal all by clothing the dark, sinful "jumble of gross Elements" in pure white robes; hence Christ is recurrently envisioned as covering the dirt ball with *white robes, tissue, webs of glory, silk, taffity, twine,* and other words based on the same roots. The glory of the clothing of righteousness is underscored by reinforcing puns. In the first stanza *arrayed* puns on rays of light from the raiment (2, 4); and the poet places his sin "where an Evill Spirit tents" (6), thereby hinting at glorification. Punning continues in the second stanza: *lawn* is a doubly appropriate covering for dirt; the stars' *fret* over human brilliance from Christ also refers to cloth being rubbed. Wordplay continues. "This Saye's no flurr of Wit" (19) covertly puns on the failed test for human fitness while it overtly puns on a saying and the material, serge. In another instance, his garment has been "Fulld in thy mill by hand" (29): that is, the cloth has been beaten so it is cleansed and thickened; the act is baptism.

Similarly, what seems at first to be a multitude of syntactic disruptions are actually repetitions of invocations in hopes of the poet being granted salvation. "Nay, may I, Lord, believe it?" is the first of many instances where the poet interrupts himself by addressing the Lord out of astonishment or to make a request. Other interruptions include "But yet my Lord" (11), the cloth "Is only worn, my Lord, by thee and thine" (18), "Wilt thou, my Lord" (37), "Then Lord, my tumberill" (43). But these seeming interjections form the necessary requests that, if granted, finally weave the poem into a whole garment. Syntactic disruptions carry from the poem's opening, which is interrupted by an interjection, through its middle of inadequate comparisons, which is smoother yet still full of strong, internal, multiple pauses, to its conclusion, which is inverted: "And when my Clay ball's in thy White robes dresst / My tune perfume thy praise shall with the best." After an initial dependent clause with its single unexceptional inversion, the final independent clause is radically inverted. The direct object (which except for context could be the subject) precedes the verb; the subject is then centered between the preceding main and succeeding auxiliary verbs; meanwhile an adverbial (or adjectival) phrase trails off, concluding with *best*. The inversion is most effective, for in it the poet is syntactically married to Christ in a single white raiment based on the central unifying *praise* of Christ. What Taylor renders God is returned by grace through Christ to render again, for it is of Christ in both senses. Syntactic disruptions are justified, sanctified, and glorified.

Sound patterns through the meditation further support the notion that Christ knits a robe out of the poem and poet. The early, false end rimes, *Cribb/rig* (2, 4) and *deckt/fret* (7, 9) are resolved in the concluding *dresst/best* when Christ becomes the agent as well as the object of Taylor's praise. But the truest tones in the meditation are the sounds of the assonantal *adorn, glory, morn, glory, ore, worn, lord* of the third stanza and the repeated alliterative *w* of stanza five lead to the assonantal coupling, *tune/perfume*, and the alliterative coupling, *perfume/praise*. The linking *perfume* is both supplied by and rendered to Christ.

For Taylor types fail, just as sounds, words, language, poems, ideas, and all mundane things fail; without Christ they are nothing. What justifies them across the infinite Calvinistic abyss is contrite confession of failure coupled with faithful requests and grateful thanks for the righteous, sanctified, glorified robes woven by Christ, the Man and the Word, for the poet and the poem. Although Taylor has severed meaning from all things, even types, when they are apart from God, he has faithfully left it to Christ to weave out of fallen, tattered repetitions of image, word, pun, broken syntax, and sounds the whole brilliant white raiment which covers poets and poems incapable of expressing transcendence. His wonder is that they can become true hymns when Christ shines through them so blindingly that they are absorbed into his glory.

Together Traherne and Taylor exhausted the English neotypological lyric as each moved toward opposite directions from the center of the expressive potential in types. They finished what a gifted series of English sacred lyricists had begun, a poetic expression in response to demands the Reformation and Counter-Reformation had placed on them—to care for their souls and to rely on and rigorously study the Bible. Reformed incorporation of strictly defined types into the literal interpretation of the Bible and Reformed direct application of the Bible to contemporary lives promoted the powerful expressive potential of a neotype identifying with a type. For a type's dual reference to human failures in history coupled with the antitype's redemption and exaltation of the type permitted, indeed encouraged, the contemporary neotypological lyricist to imitate and identify with the type David. Such lyricists could humbly mourn their failings and confess their contrition and at the same time, without self-condemning presumption, celebrate their transcendence in God by Christ's grace. The line of neotypological lyricists added to these central characteristics in many ways, experimenting not only with the governing motifs and expressive complexes of typology and the motives and rhetoric of psalmody but also with elements of sacred forms such as meditation, of secular such as Petrarchism, and of both sacred and secular such as emblems. Through tending their own souls they sang to comfort and to present in their personae dramatic exempla for their congregations. These characteristics the lyricists, even minor innovators like the emblematists and followers like Washbourne and Harvey, held in common through tapping the redemptive and expressive potential of the neotypological lyric.

But beyond what they all shared, each of the successive masters of the form, Southwell, Alabaster, Donne, Herbert, and Vaughan, made essential contributions to it, made it particularly his own. The final craftsmen, Traherne and Taylor, expended its expressive potential. For like any other resource, expression can be exhausted in one realm; and for these poets that realm was the sacred. In one direction from the releasing reaction, Traherne expanded God's revelation in the type and the neotype into his own celebration of God's immanence in the world and the poet's imitation of both Adams. In the other, Taylor annihilated the inherent deity-bearing significance of the type and the neotype by exploiting the severance of world, mankind, word, and poet from God, in order to convert all into confessions of failure and avowals of faith through which God's grace can reunite them with the Word.

The neotypological lyric was finished. As others have studied it, the story of typological extensions into sacred and philosophical allegory and expansions into moral, social, political, and other domains of poetry is yet to be fully told. But the potential of neotypology for powering and forming specifically Christian lyrics, for founding a literary aesthetic, had been exhausted.

Notes

Preface

1. This is still perhaps the most helpful short account of typological exegesis for literature students.
2. Clark, pp. 560–84.
3. See Roston, particularly pp. 69–78; Zwicker, especially pp. 3–27; see also Lewalski's *Milton's Brief Epic* and *Donne's 'Anniversaries' and the Poetry of Praise.*
4. See Grant, particularly pp. 1–17 and 213. It is not negligible that a number of the poets here have been approached from a consciously Augustinian premise; see notes in my respective chapters, Mark Taylor and Stanley E. Fish on Herbert, Ross Garner on Vaughan, Elisabeth Jefferis Bartlett on Traherne, and William J. Scheick on Edward Taylor.

Chapter 1

1. Taylor, *Christ Revealed*, pp. 6–10.
2. I use the first volume, *Miscellanies of Fuller Worthies' Library*, ed. Alexander B. Grosart. Washbourne's full awareness of what he was doing with types is evident throughout the volume, mainly because his uses are precise. For example, in "A Colloquy upon the Ascension, Commonly Called Holy Thursday," Washbourne's angels ask who is coming clothed in the dyed garments of Bozrah and riding in Ezekiel's chariot; and his "Fountain" of Zechariah 13 flows into the *aqua vitae* of Christ's side. But he is also capable of extending typological associations. In "The Vine Wasted," for instance, he conflates the grape vine of the eightieth Psalm with the bunch of grapes that typifies Christ's mystical body; then he has God's right hand plant the vine.
3. See Woollcombe's essay in the collection, ed. with Lampe, pp. 60–65.
4. Two of the best lists, which also help define, are Patrick Fairbairn, *The Typology of Scripture*, 1:22; and Robert E. Reiter, *In Adam's Room*, pp. 17–19.
5. See Woollcombe and Lampe, p. 40ff.
6. The openings of R. P. C. Hanson, *Allegory and Event*, Auerbach, "Figura," and Madsen, *Shadowy Types*, are useful.

7. A very useful discussion, with a catalogue of twentieth-century scholarly testimonials, appears in Joseph A. Galdon's *Typology and Seventeenth-Century Literature*, pp. 38–111.

8. Madsen, p. 38.

9. Besides those already cited, other helpful theological studies include: for early development Jean Danielou's *From Shadows to Reality*; for the period from Augustine to Luther, James Samuel Preus' *From Shadow to Promise*; and for general surveys Henri de Lubac's *Exégèse médiévale*, and Beryl Smalley's *The Study of the Bible in the Middle Ages*.

10. See Preus' argument, pp. 153–212. For broad formulation of Luther's exegesis see Jaroslav Pelikan's *Luther the Expositor*.

11. Calvin, *Institutes*, trans. Battles, ed. McNeill.

12. For Tyndale, I quote *Doctrinal Treatises and Introductions to Different Portions of the Holy Scriptures by William Tyndale, Martyr, 1536*, ed. H. Walter; this quotation is from p. 303.

13. See Blench, especially his most helpful chapter on scriptural interpretation, pp. 1–70.

14. Ibid., p. 42.

15. Ibid., pp. 62–64.

16. I quote and cite the Cambridge, 1609 edition of Perkins' *Works*; these quotations are from 2:730–62.

17. See especially pp. 740–42, 745–46, ibid.

18. See especially Book 4, chapter 2, and the introduction to chapter 3, ibid. In a later edition (London, 1621) the columns of parallels run through pp. 193–200.

19. See Perkins, 2:19, 39–40.

20. See Blench, pp. 50–52, 62.

21. Davies, *1534–1603*, pp. 234–36.

22. Charles K. Cannon called attention to and provides an enlightening discussion of "William Whitaker's *Disputatio de Sacra Scriptura*: A Sixteenth-Century Theory of Allegory."

23. For Whitaker, I quote *A Disputation on Holy Scripture against the Papists*, ed. and trans. by William Fitzgerald; this quotation is from p. 404.

24. Ibid., p. 406.

25. Ibid., p. 407.

26. Ibid., p. 409.

27. Ibid., p. 410.

28. Ibid., pp. 466–73.

29. See Blench, pp. 2, 28–30; and Davies, *1534–1603*, p. 303.

30. Williams, p. 255.

31. See prefaces and introductions to William Guild, *Moses Vnuailed*; Henry Ainsworth, *Annotations upon the Five Bookes of Moses*; Francis Roberts, *Clavis Bibliorum*; R.G., translator of John Diodati, *Pious and Learned Annotations upon the Holy Bible*; John Everard, *The Gospel-Treasury Opened*, particularly the 190's and "The Mysterie, or the Life and Marrow of the Scriptures," pp. 231–317; and Samuel Lee, *Orbis Miraculum, or the Temple of Solomon*, pp. 166–80.

32. Mather, *The Figures or Types*. These were posthumously printed in Dublin, 1685.

33. Ibid., p. 56; his discussion extends through p. 61.

34. Ibid., pp. 676–77.

35. Lee, p. 168.

36. Ferguson, pp. 312–13; see also pp. 275–420.

37. Ibid., pp. 178–79.

38. Mather, p. 69; see pp. 67–73.

39. Smith, pp. [A6r], 64–66. See the intelligent appraisal by Christine W. Sizemore, "The Authorship of *The Mystery of Rhetoric Unveiled*."

40. Mather, p. 73; Mather shows on p. 74 that not just David but even Moses had specific shortcomings.

41. Mather, particularly pp. 50–51, 85, 148–49.

42. Mather, see sermon and chapter divisions as well as definitions, especially those on pp. 209–14.

43. Weemes, pp. 30–32.

44. In addition to using tracts already cited, I will document corroborating typological interpretations from a variety of popular as well as specialized analogue sources in order to display how widespread the knowledge of typology continued to be throughout the period. Several particularly useful ones deserve special mention. For early Protestant thought the sidenotes of the Geneva Bible are helpful; I quote these from *The Geneva Bible; A facsimile of the 1560 edition*. Further help with Protestant annotators besides the valuable Diodati is the Westminster Assembly's judicious summary *Annotations upon All the Books of the Old and New Testament*; and two great compilations from annotators of the previous century and a half gathered in the mid and latter seventeenth century by Matthew Poole and John Pearson. I follow Poole's *Synopsis Criticorum* and Pearson's *Critici Sacri*. The finest epitome of the previous century as well as older Catholic thought on biblical interpretations is the compendium of *Commentaria* gathered in the early seventeenth century by Cornelius à Lapide; I quote the eighteenth century edition. In general I cite Catholic parallels for Catholic poets, Puritan for Puritans, and often Anglican for Anglicans; and I usually cite parallels that derive from sources preceding the poems they annotate.

45. I quote Arthur Golding's translation of *The psalmes of David and others. With J. Caluins commentaries*, pp. xv [2]v.

46. For Calvin's commentary I use the translation by Christopher Rosdell, *Epistle of Saint Paul*, pp. 46–47.

47. See also Davies, *1534–1603*, p. 302, and *1603–1690*, pp. 124–25.

48. Perkins, 2:2, 762.

49. Davies, *1534–1603*, p. 431.

50. Ibid., pp. 415–32; this close relationship is an ever-present theme in White.

51. The best guide for Latin hymnology up to the Reformation is Ruth Ellis Messenger's *The Medieval Latin Hymn*; the most stimulating is Louise A. Armstrong's *The Medieval Latin Hymn; A Study of a Literary Genre As It Developed in a Dying Language*; additional information can be found in F. J. E. Raby's *A History of Christian-Latin Poetry from the Beginnings to the Close of the Middle Ages*. Of general collections I found most helpful A. S. Walpole and A. J. Mason's carefully introduced and heavily annotated *Early Latin Hymns*. For literary analysis, see Erich Auerbach's discussion of the development in "Dante's Prayer to the Virgin (Paradiso, XXXIII) and Earlier Eulogies"; identifications of sources for recurring *figurae* usually derive from editions of Adam of St. Victor, *Ouvres Poétiques* by León Gautier; *The Liturgical Poetry*, trans. Digby S. Wrangham; and *Le Proses* by Pierre Aubry and E. Misset. See also Walter J. Ong's "Wit and Mystery: A Revaluation in Mediaeval Latin Hymnody."

52. See Peter Dronke's *The Medieval Lyric*, especially p. 85.

53. See Leo Spitzer's seminal "*Explication de Texte* Applied to Three Great Middle English Poems," reprinted in *Essays on English and American Literature*. For other examples see Stephen Manning's *Wisdom and Number*, particularly pp. 85–88 and 153–54; Sarah Appleton Weber's *Theology and Poetry in the Middle English Lyric*, pp. 48–50; Douglas Gray's *Themes and Images in the Medieval English Religious Lyric*, especially pp. 12–17 and 84–86; and Edmund Reiss' *The Art of the Middle English Lyric*, pp. 108–14 and 144–64.

54. Fletcher, pp. 20, 41.

55. For Drummond, I quote *Poems*, ed. William C. Ward.

56. Richards, pp. 118 and 85.

57. Lever, E2r, v.

58. Fitz-Geffry, pp. 16 and 4–5; 13, 11, and 43.

59. *Apollo Christian*, p. 16; types appear frequently throughout the work.

60. For Wither, I cite the Spenser Society reprints.

61. Ibid., pp. 239–40.
62. Ibid., p. 1.
63. Ibid., p. 36.
64. For Harvey, I quote the Fuller Worthies' Library edition of *The Complete Poems*.
65. For a discussion of related Petrarchan traditions and some Renaissance uses, see George C. Hudson Jr.'s *The Heart of Stone: An Image of the Spiritual Condition of Man in Seventeenth-Century Poetry*.
66. See Richard Day's *A Booke of Christian Prayers*, p. 16.

Chapter 2

1. *The Whole Booke of Davids Psalmes*, p. Ay, v.
2. Lewalski, "Typological Symbolism," pp. 109–10; Lewalski also emphasizes the additional motivation in identifying with David the psalmist.
3. For accounts of English Renaissance psalmody see Hallett Smith, "English Metrical Psalms in the Sixteenth Century and their Literary Significance"; Lily Bess Campbell, *Divine Poetry and Drama in Sixteenth-Century England*, pp. 34–54; and especially Coburn Freer, *Music for a King*, pp. 14–49.
4. Freer, p. 35.
5. Ibid., pp. 36–40; for interior drama see H. A. Mason, *Humanism and Poetry in the Early Tudor Period*, pp. 203–21.
6. For Wyatt, I quote *The Collected Poems of Sir Thomas Wyatt*, ed. Kenneth Muir and Patricia Thomson; this quotation is from p. 98.
7. For expansion see Mason, pp. 240–48, and Robert G. Twombley, "Thomas Wyatt's Paraphrases of the Penitential Psalms of David," especially pp. 345–47.
8. *Wyatt*, p. 98.
9. For Hunnis I quote the London, 1600 edition of *Seven Sobs*.
10. I quote Heywood in Guiney, *Recusant Poets*, p. 166; the poem also appears as number 127 of Rollins, *The Paradise of Dainty Devices*.
11. For Hall, I quote the edition by Russell A. Fraser.
12. *Miscellanies of the Fuller Worthies' Library*, 2:147–48.
13. Barnes, A3v. See as well the Scot, Alexander Hume's "Epistle to the Reader," *Hymnes, or sacred songs . . . and certaine precepts*.
14. See the discussion by McDonald in *The Poems of Robert Southwell, S.J.*, ed. James H. McDonald and Nancy Pollard Brown, pp. 109–10, with additional discussions on pp. lxxxv, 175.
15. Hogarde in Guiney, p. 134.
16. Barnes, [A2r].
17. See Barnes' sonnets 21 for Moses, 68 for the Marian "Iesses precious braunch."
18. For the less interesting Sinai desert see Lok's sonnet 2:80, for the second Adam, 2:98, for the Marian Gideon's fleece 1:65.
19. For an extensive account of Jesuit determination of Southwell's poetry see Pierre Janelle's *Robert Southwell, the Writer*, particularly pp. 93–141.
20. Southwell, *Spiritual Exercises and Devotions*, p. 36.
21. Ibid. Also see particularly the twelfth and sixteenth exercises.
22. Ibid., p. 61.
23. Ibid. For an unusually clear example see the fifty-sixth exercise.
24. Ibid., p. 105.
25. Southwell, *Epistle of Comfort*, and *Two Letters and Short Rules*.

Notes

26. Vincent B. Leitch's helpful unpublished essays on religious despair pay considerable attention to Southwell.
27. Southwell, *Poems*. Brown notes that this may not be Peter's soliloquy, but the mode is identical.
28. Ibid. See Brown's helpful commentary.
29. Cf. Southwell's "A holy Hymme," lines 19–30.
30. There are the "Orient starre, / That shal bring forth the Sunne that lent her light" (1–2) from the *stella maris* tradition, "this little cloud the showers" (9) which recalls the dew of manna (Exod. 16) often read as Mary, and, of course, "the *Jesse* rod" (17).
31. For a beginning catalogue of types see Carolyn A. Schten's "Southwell's 'Christs Bloody Sweat': A Meditation on the Mass."
32. For the opening discussion see Janelle, pp. 254–67; for critical development, see Martz's *Poetry of Meditation*, pp. 184–93; for continental contexts, see Bruce W. Wardropper's "The Religious Conversion of Profane Poetry," *Studies in the Continental Background of Renaissance English Literature*; for examples, see Brown's notes in Southwell, *Poems*. But also note the caveat by Rosemond Tuve, "Sacred 'Parody' of Love Poetry, and Herbert."
33. See Martz, *Poetry of Meditation*, pp. 102–07; see also Brown and McDonald, pp. xciii–xcv; and finally, see John R. Roberts, "The Influence of *The Spiritual Exercises* of St. Ignatius on the Nativity Poems of Robert Southwell." Despite her convincing case that "Christs bloody sweat" is essentially involved with eucharistic symbolism, Schten does not compel assent in substituting the passion for Gethsemane.
34. Martz, *Poetry of Meditation*, p. 42.
35. Lapide, *Commentaria*; all Lapide's relevant annotations, unless cited otherwise, are to Matt. 26:40–41.
36. Southwell, *Epistle of Comfort*, p. 26.
37. See R. H. Bowers' informative *The Legend of Jonah*, p. 31.
38. See Lapide on Heb. 11:7 and Gen. 6–8, where Noah is usually Christ and the ark either the church or the human soul.
39. See, for example, the popular account in Book 17, chapter 148, of the enlarged and amended edition of Stephen Bateman's translation of Bartholomaeus, *Batman vppon Bartholome*, pp. 319v–320r.
40. For biography I rely on the prefatory matter of G. M. Story and Helen Gardner's *Sonnets of William Alabaster*, pp. xi–xxiii and xxxvi–xxxviii, and often rely as well on their commentary. Some other helpful biographical material is available in Robert V. Caro's *Rhetoric and Meditation in the Sonnets of William Alabaster*, pp. 13–38.
41. Alabaster, *Sonnets*, p. xxv; evidence continues through p. xxvi and Gardner's commentary.
42. Alabaster, *Apparatus*.
43. Ibid., pp. 228–30; Cawdrey, p. 126.
44. For documentation in art as well as literature see Tuve's *Herbert*, pp. 112–23.
45. *Batman*, Book 17, chap. 23, p. 281r.
46. See Arthur Henkel and Albrecht Schöne's reproduction of the *Mundus Symbolicus, in Emblematus Universitate*, in *Emblemata*, p. 2130.
47. See p. 4; this is handily reprinted in an appendix of Henkel and Schöne.
48. For the hexaemeral tradition of the prelapsarian rose without thorns see George W. Whiting, "And Without Thorn the Rose"; on the rose of grace see Pierio Valeriano's *Hieroglyphica*, cited in *The Poems of John Milton*, ed. John Carey and Alastair Fowler, p. 627.
49. Martz, in *English Seventeenth-Century Verse* 1:467–68.
50. Cf. the parallel terms and movement of Alabaster's sonnet 39.
51. See Caro, pp. 124–25, but particularly see the extensive catalogue and classification by Joseph Robert Miller, *The Counter-Reformation and English Poetry of the Renaissance*, pp. 177–227.
52. For Alabaster's other rainbows see sonnet 30 and suggestions in sonnet 39.
53. For Alabaster's other prominent trinities see sonnets 16, 36, 43, 45, and 59.

Chapter 3

1. For accounts of the emblem book see particularly *The Hieroglyphics of Horapollo*, ed. George Boas; Mario Praz, *Studies in Seventeenth-Century Imagery*; Robert J. Clements, *Picta Poesis*; Liselotte Dieckmann, *Hieroglyphics: The History of a Literary Symbol*; and especially Rosemary Freeman, *English Emblem Books*. For a history and analysis of specifically Protestant emblem traditions, see Barbara K. Lewalski's "Emblems and the Religious Lyric: George Herbert and Protestant Emblematics."

2. Willet, C3r.

3. Ibid., H4v.

4. Types appear sporadically in emblem literature. For instance, Robert Farlie's Christian Phoebus in *Lychnocausia* (1638) becomes yet another sun of righteousness.

5. Freeman gives the best account of emblems by Quarles, pp. 114–32, and his followers, pp. 132–47.

6. For Quarles, I quote *The Complete Works*, ed. Alexander B. Grosart.

7. Ibid., pp. 132, 134–37.

8. For Walton, I cite and quote *The Lives* introduced by George Saintsbury; this reference is from pp. 46–47.

9. Ibid., pp. 47–48.

10. For Donne, I quote and cite *The Sermons of John Donne*, ed. George R. Potter and Evelyn M. Simpson. I owe this quotation to Murray Roston, *The Soul of Wit*, pp. 63–64.

11. Walton, pp. 52, 75.

12. The literature on Donne as self-dramatist increases steadily from Pierre Legouis' *Donne, the Craftsman* (1928). Studies of influence seem to expand the contexts and intensify the sense of his personal drama. For meditation and psalmody see Martz, *Poetry of Meditation*; for love verse see Donald L. Guss' *John Donne, Petrarchist*. For Gardner see *John Donne, The Divine Poems*, p. xxxi. A sampler of assent includes Carol Marks Sicherman's "Donne's Discoveries"; Patrick Grant's "Augustinian Spirituality and the *Holy Sonnets* of John Donne"; and Richard E. Hughes' *The Progress of the Soul; The Interior Career of John Donne*, especially p. 177.

13. Testimony to how important Donne's biography is for this poem appears in the front-page coverage of a manuscript discovery by R. S. Thomson and David McKitterick, "John Donne's Kimbolton Papers," in which the authors argue for a 1610 date and conjecture that Donne was probably traveling to negotiate a possible appointment to the new King James College.

14. Friedman, pp. 418–42; Grant describes a similar movement, *Transformations*, p. 41.

15. Chambers, pp. 31–53; see addenda by Rosalie Beck, "A Precedent for Donne's Imagery in 'Goodfriday, 1613. Riding Westward'"; and Jonathan S. Goldberg, "Donne's Journey East: Aspects of a Seventeenth-Century Trope."

16. For Donne's poetry I quote *The Complete Poetry of John Donne*, ed. John T. Shawcross.

17. For Donne's *Devotions*, I quote the edition by John Sparrow; this quotation is from p. 11; see also Donne, *The Sermons*, 1:265, 8:99.

18. These conclusions are buttressed by Winfried Schleiner, *The Imagery of John Donne's Sermons*, pp. 185–200.

19. Donne, *The Sermons*, 6:62.

20. Ibid., 7:193.

21. Donne, *Devotions*, p. 113.

22. Donne, *The Sermons*, 4:226, 233; 8:351; and 9:143.

23. Ibid., 7:105, 117; 4:271; 9:234; 5:377–78; 10:141.

24. Ibid., 1:287–88; 5:136–37, 151–52; 7:349; 6:186–87, 194–96, 201.

25. Ibid., 5:110; 3:140, 142; 7:148; 8:130–31.

26. Ibid., 6:155; 2:225–26; 9:65–66; 2:180, 187–88; 7:349.

27. Ibid., 1:293, 295, 298; 7:337–38; 2:259–60; 3:297–98; 1:278–79; 1:275–79; 7:347; 6:286–91; 4:356; 8:245–46. For David, see particularly 1:275–79; 2:137–40; 5:289, 377; 9:288.
28. Ibid., 2:75; for similar statements see as well the next sermon, 2:97; and 7:51.
29. Ibid., 3:367.
30. Webber, *Contrary Music*, p. 102.
31. Donne, *The Sermons*, 4:363; Donne, *Essayes*, p. 6.
32. Mueller.
33. Donne, *Devotions*, p. 52.
34. See Gardner, p. 112.
35. In addition to *Sermons*, 2:199–200, and 3:59, see Gardner, p. 108, and Goldberg; see also Donald K. Anderson, Jr.'s contribution, "Donne's 'Hymne to God my God, in my sicknesse' and the T-in-O Maps."
36. See D. C. Allen, "John Donne's 'Paradise and Calvarie'"; Gardner, pp. 135–37; and Anderson.

Chapter 4

1. Walton, p. 63.
2. Ibid., pp. 314–15.
3. For other contemporary testimony about the efficacy of *The Temple* see Robert H. Ray, *George Herbert in the Seventeenth Century: Allusions to Him Collected and Annotated*. For a sampler see Stanley E. Fish's *The Living Temple; George Herbert and Catechizing*, pp. 49–51.
4. I quote and cite *The Works of George Herbert*, ed. F. E. Hutchinson. For similar statements see also "Employment (I)" and the first two stanzas of "Perseverance" from the Williams MS. See also Mark Taylor's discussion of a poet's duty to praise God in *The Soul in Paraphrase*, pp. 42–44.
5. Though I have benefitted from his, my theory differs from Joseph H. Summers' *George Herbert; his Religion and his Art*, pp. 80–81, in that it emphasizes Herbert's central typological pattern, his sense of the persona as a neotype (not like a type), and the gap between the persona's and our own readings of the persona's situation.
6. The first published version of my essay discussed how to read individual Herbert lyrics, in company with such other reading paradigms as the meditations applied by Louis L. Martz, *Poetry of Meditation*; the religio-aesthetic rituals posited by Rosalie L. Colie in *Paradoxia Epidemica*, pp. 190–215; the re-inventions developed by Helen Vendler into *The Poetry of George Herbert*; or the self-destructions as seen by Stanley E. Fish in his final version of "Letting Go," *Self-Consuming Artifacts*, pp. 156–223. It never purported to read *The Temple* as a whole, as say the liturgical year of Helen C. White; or the church typological of John David Walker's "The Architectonics of George Herbert's *The Temple*"; or the Christocentric aesthetic rituals of Valerie Carnes' "The Unity of George Herbert's *The Temple*: A Reconsideration"; or the I-Thou typologies of John R. Mulder's "George Herbert's *The Temple*: Design and Methodology." Since then Stanley E. Fish has united two reading approaches and a number of individual paradigms in a new context which, though related to my own as to others, accounts more explicitly, fully, and simply for much in *The Temple*. My own reading pattern continues, I believe, to be useful for a central manner in Herbert's presentation, for his neotypological lyrics, and for understanding the heritage of neotypological lyrics throughout the period.
7. See respectively Patrides, pp. 26–27; studies from Freeman through Rosalie L. Colie's *The Resources of Kind*, pp. 57–67; as extended by J. Max Patrick in "Critical Prob-

lems in Editing George Herbert's *The Temple*," *The Editor as Critic and the Critic as Editor*, with Alan Roper, pp. 3–40; and applied by Lewalski in "Emblems and the Religious Lyric"; Harnack.

8. In *George Herbert's Lyrics*, p. 121, Arnold Stein focuses on the significant personal test and affirmation, I'd say the neotypology, beyond the typology Summers notes, p. 80.

9. For the importance of Psalms see Heather Asals, "The Voice of George Herbert's 'The Church'"; and Freer.

10. Summers first suggested the parallel, p. 236.

11. On the importance for Herbert of Christian tears note particularly "The Church-porch" (415–17), "The Church-floore," "Businesse" (4–14), "The Storm," "Artillerie" (19–20), "Praise (III)," and "Grief." For further background see Miller's dissertation, particularly on Mary Magdalene weeping, pp. 187–88. The excruciating pain that Herbert feels attends such self-purgations is best expressed in the pruning necessary for a bearing tree of life in "Paradise."

12. The image is picked up again, lines 245–47.

13. Such acknowledgments extend from the opening of "Perirrhanterium" through "H. Baptisme (I)" to "Love" in the Williams MS (7–12).

14. Note the related furnace in "Longing" (25–30).

15. Purgative fires also provide the effects of "The Starre" and the second and third stanzas of "The Priesthood."

16. Cawdrey, p. 7; see also p. 11. Herbert's juxtaposition may result from the references to both fires in Malachi 3:2–3 and 4:1.

17. Montenay, pp. 350–52.

18. On this type see Tuve, *Reading*, pp. 113–17; Summers, pp. 126–28; and Mary Ellen Rickey, *Utmost Art*, pp. 156–57. Also note related eucharistic poems such as "The H. Communion," "Conscience," "The Collar," "The Invitation," "The Banquet," "Love (III)," with reemphasis on this sacrament's central value for Herbert in Elizabeth McLaughlin and Gail Thomas' "Communion in *The Temple*"; and Fish's *The Living Temple*, pp. 90–136.

19. The same dual expression in thorns appears in "The Collar" (7–9).

20. For some Herbert employments of the heart other than those discussed see "Ungratefulnesse" (25–27), "Gratefulnesse," "Praise (II)" (11–12); note also the offering of "Employment (II)" (21–25). To my knowledge the first to interpret the imagery of one of Herbert's lyrics inside the image complex of all was Fredson Bowers in "Herbert's Sequential Imagery: 'The Temper'."

21. For other examples of the heart as text see particularly "The Sinner," "Nature," "The Church-floore," and most of all, "Jesu."

22. Other prominent examples of the heart as dwelling include the end of "Nature," "Jesu," "The Starre" (5–6), the latter half of "Decay," "Sion," "Praise (II)" (19–20). The overlapping here with the other examples of heart associations is, I think, not insignificant.

23. Corroboration is offered in another triple set, that of the mediatorial office in the heart. The heart as God's house is kingship, as altar is priesthood, and as "Fleshy table" is prophet, according to Florence Sandler's "'Solomon ubique regnet': Herbert's Use of the Images of the New Covenant."

24. See "Content" (33–34), "Vanitie (I)" (22–26), "Longing" (8–9) for examples.

25. A similar general point is made by Fish in "Letting Go." I cannot agree that Christ's completion and the Christian's reception of grace negate for Herbert the Christian's individuality and ultimately his responsibility, though this last position Fish seems to abandon in *The Living Temple*.

26. In "Obedience," his most extended and interesting poem posed in contractual terms, Herbert reverses the roles to achieve the same effect. The persona deeds his bleeding heart to God only to discover that Christ's previous sacrificial purchase of the heart saves him.

27. For a discussion see Bernard Knieger's "The Purchase-Sale: Patterns of Business

Notes

Imagery in the Poetry of George Herbert," with such examples as "The Starre" (6–7), "Dialogue" (9–16), "The Bag" (24), and *Lucus IV* "In Simonem Magnum" (1–4).

28. See R. L. Montgomery, Jr.'s "The Province of Allegory in George Herbert's Verse." This essay lists a sizable group that includes most of Herbert's best-known poems.

29. For examples of this see particularly "Submission," "The Crosse," "Love (III)," and the "Affliction" series, as well as Herbert's frequent puns on the combat *topos*, such as those in "The Temper (I)" (13–14) or the last stanzas of "Artillerie."

30. Puttenham, p. 215.

31. See particularly the conclusions of "Redemption," "Jordan (II)," and "The Collar"; see also the opening of "Artillerie."

32. For examples see the frame of "Faith," the last half of "Love. II," "Mattens" (16–20), the opening of "Even-song," the center of "Ungratefulnesse," the whole of "Submission," "The Banquet" (37–48), and the enlightened union concluding "Love (III)." A related image of Christ's revelation is "The Elixir," by which God is seen in all things.

33. This identification has also been suggested by Martz, *Poetry of Meditation*, p. 309.

Chapter 5

1. For poetry, including this prose preface, I cite and quote *The Complete Poetry of Henry Vaughan*, ed. French Fogle. For prose I cite and quote *The Works of Henry Vaughan*, ed. L. C. Martin. For helpful and stimulating notes I rely on both.

2. Besides Martin's and Fogle's annotations, such studies as M. M. Mahood's *Poetry and Humanism*, particularly pp. 262–64, 286–87, 292–93; or Fern Farnham's "The Imagery of Henry Vaughan's 'The Night'"; with Robert Duvall's "The Biblical Character of Henry Vaughan's *Silex Scintillans*"; coupled with the considerations in Horace H. Underwood's "Time and Space in the Poetry of Vaughan"; and Fredson Bowers' "Henry Vaughan's Multiple Time Scheme"; to issue in the claims for typological explication of "*Isaacs* Marriage" by John R. Mulder in *The Temple of the Mind*, pp. 147–50; and by Lewalski in "Typology and Poetry" and "Typological Symbolism."

3. Vaughan, *The Works*, p. 259; the next two prose quotations follow, pp. 259–61.

4. On the importance of the tribe of Ben to Vaughan's poetic craft, see various essays by E. L. Marilla, particularly "The Secular and Religious Poetry of Henry Vaughan"; and its extension and sophistication in a most important entry to Vaughan, James D. Simmonds' *Masques of God*. For an overall assessment see Kenneth Friedenreich's *Henry Vaughan*.

5. Besides the editions see especially E. C. Pettet, who in *Of Paradise and Light* makes the largest claim for Herbert; and Mary Ellen Rickey, "Vaughan, *The Temple*, and Poetic Form," who supports it.

6. For an examination of Vaughan's reliance on Christian, especially Augustinian, tradition see Ross Garner's *Henry Vaughan, Experience and Tradition*.

7. Vaughan, *The Works*, p. 254.

8. Apparently Martz first noted this, in *The Paradise Within*, p. 4.

9. These can be summed up from F. E. Hutchinson's emphasis on Vaughan's love of nature in the Welsh terrain, *Henry Vaughan*, pp. 165–80; and Helen White's in the book of creation, *The Metaphysical Poets*, pp. 261–88; through Martz's and Simmonds' view of Vaughan presenting God through both books of God's word and God's natural world in *The Paradise Within*, especially p. 13, and in *Masques of God*, especially pp. 17–19 and 138–64; to Friedenreich's study of Vaughan's literary pastoralism in *Henry Vaughan*, pp. 46–70.

10. See especially the first central image cluster examined by R. A. Durr, *On the Mysti-*

195

cal Poetry of Henry Vaughan, pp. 29–60; and Elizabeth Holmes' *Henry Vaughan and the Hermetic Philosophy*; through L. C. Martin's notes and Richard H. Walters' "Henry Vaughan and the Alchemists"; to several essays by Alan W. Rudrum, notably "The Influence of Alchemy in the Poems of Henry Vaughan."

11. Vaughan's own poem titles and annotations, with Martin's and Fogle's supplementary ones, make many of these obvious. For analyses see the accounts of Friedenreich, pp. 60–68, and especially of Simmonds, pp. 85–116.

12. Vaughan, *The Works*, pp. 106–07.

13. Ibid., pp. 260–61.

14. Ibid., p. 176.

15. Ibid., p. 500.

16. For exemplary lists see Guild, pp. 32–35; and Mather, pp. 165–67.

17. For seventeenth-century analyses of this type see Mather, pp. 169–73; and Thomas Taylor, pp. 243–57.

18. In a number of poems Vaughan condemns biblical and seventeenth-century crowds (with typological references) for turning from and on Christ and salvation, in contrast to the true congregation. Prominent among these are "The Jews," the first "Jesus Weeping," and the concluding stanza of "The Stone."

19. For seventeenth-century support of Mulder's discussion of typological references in this poem see Thomas Taylor, pp. 147–50.

20. For the contemporary context of Puritans whom Vaughan here is satirizing and to whom he is applying types, see Simmonds, pp. 99–101.

21. For particularly good, earlier and more recent discussions of the pilgrimage in Vaughan, see Durr, pp. 60–74, and Low, pp. 183–90.

22. Cf. Low, especially p. 200, in addition to his pilgrimage discussion.

23. See Lewalski, "Typology and Poetry," pp. 57–63, 69, and "Typological Symbolism," pp. 96–99.

24. Mather, p. 98; see pp. 92–93, 97.

25. See Ainsworth's annotation or Thomas Taylor, p. 15, for examples.

26. See Simmonds' discussion, pp. 149–60, especially p. 151 as well as the paradigm on p. 62. In the longer section note as well his discussion of "The Tempest."

27. For typological commentary see Mather, pp. 92–93, 97–98.

Chapter 6

1. It causes initial surprise to realize, and later reluctance to accept that Richard Crashaw, frequently associated with the poets who wrote neotypological lyrics, is not part of my account. But he cannot be. As Low has recently argued on separate grounds, he differs essentially from the others. From Low's perspective, Crashaw's poetry does not follow the intellectual and analytic but instead the sensible mode of meditation, which rouses the affections (see pp. 128–58). From my perspective his poetry contains only a few types, and these appear only as incidental reinforcements rather than integral, not to mention dominant, features of his verse. As G. Walton Williams pointed out in *Image and Symbol in the Sacred Poetry of Richard Crashaw*: "Typology can convey extraordinarily rich connotations and levels of meaning, yet it is practically nonexistent in Crashaw's poetry," p. 5. My hunch is that in his search for mediation between God and humanity Crashaw turned away from types and toward women. Lady Denbigh, Queen Henrietta Maria, various nuns, Mary Magdalene, and most of all, St. Teresa and the Virgin Mary mediate in the place of types. Perhaps Crashaw reverted from both Reformation and Counter-Reformation inclinations

Notes

toward something nearer the means employed and the ends pursued in the affective sacred lyrics of the fourteenth- and fifteenth-century Franciscan heritage.

2. Unless noted otherwise I quote from *Thomas Traherne: Centuries, Poems, and Thanksgivings*, ed. H. M. Margoliouth; this passage appears on 1: xxx.

3. Ibid., 1: xxxi–xxxii.

4. See Carol L. Marks' "Traherne's 'Church's Year-Book'."

5. Stewart, especially pp. 86–89.

6. Ibid., pp. 95–101.

7. See Jordan, particularly pp. 108–09. Elisabeth Jefferis Bartlett, arguing that Traherne was influenced by Augustine's personal works and commentaries on Psalms, claims that Traherne merged Augustine's voice with David's, then absorbed others into his speaker. See *"All Soul and Life, an Ey most bright": A Persona Study of the Writings of Thomas Traherne*, especially pp. 122–27, but extending through p. 160.

8. See particularly Stewart, pp. 77–80; Lewalski, "Typological Symbolism," pp. 99–102; and Jordan's chapter on types. Also note Bartlett, pp. 190–92, though I would reverse her priority so as to focus more on Christ and origins in types than on the "felicitous self."

9. Traherne, *Christian Ethicks*, pp. 109–10; I use the edition and annotations by Carol L. Marks and George R. Guffey.

10. Ibid. See repetitions, pp. 113, 126–27, and especially 129–30.

11. Traherne, *Six Days of the Creation*, pp. 41–46.

12. Traherne, *Christian Ethicks*, pp. 129, 30.

13. For particulars of the *Christian Ethicks* passage see the note by editor Marks, pp. 346–47. Support includes William Chub, *Two Fruitful and godly Sermons . . . the one touching the building of Gods Temple, the other what the Temple is*; John Weemes, *The Christian Synagogue*, pp. 91–104; Thomas Taylor, *Moses and Aaron*, particularly pp. 68–71; Mather, pp. 409–51.

14. Lee, pp. [a2r], 188–92; for particularly good support see Guild, pp. 168–75. I am indebted for this reference as well as for other blueprints of the temple to Walker. For other references, applied to people and involved with catechisms, see Fish's *The Living Temple*, pp. 54–79.

15. Lee, pp. 1–6.

16. Ibid., p. 185.

17. For exemplification of this heritage see Jackson I. Cope, "Fortunate Falls as Form in Milton's 'Fair Infant'."

18. Here it is easy to see the envelopment then expansion of other sources suggested for Traherne's work, notably the *liber creatorum* proposed by Wallerstein and the hermeticism proffered by Carol L. Marks, "Thomas Traherne and Hermes Trismegistus." See further suggestive uses of the sun and its cloudy veil in "The Demonstration" and of mirrors and fountains in "The Anticipation."

19. See Margoliouth's notes; and Stewart, pp. 204–07.

20. For other examples see especially "The Salutation" (st. 6) and "The Improvment" (13–18).

21. See Clements, pp. 185–89. Another who sees this source as primary is K. W. Salter, *Thomas Traherne: Mystic and Poet*.

22. Here again an expansion through more sources can be noted. These include various kinds of efforts to recover the ideas and identities of Christianized Platonism. See Carol L. Marks' "Traherne and Cambridge Platonism"; as well as the caveat in Gerald H. Cox's "Traherne's *Centuries*: A Platonic Devotion of 'Divine Philosophy'"; and a syncretic Platonism in John E. Trimpey, "An Analysis of Traherne's 'Thoughts I.'"; note as well the Christian Platonism in Augustinian and Bonaventuran meditation described in Martz's *The Paradise Within*, pp. 35–102. On the central importance of the fall for Traherne see most obviously *Centuries* III. 8; and William H. Marshall, "Thomas Traherne and the Doctrine of Original Sin."

Notes

23. For classical as well as Christian references to man's creation in God's image, see the compendia by Poole and Pearson.
24. For more examples, see "My Spirit" (108–09), "Thoughts IV" (87–88), and especially the exulting opening of "An Hymne upon St. Bartholomews Day," *Poems from the Church's Year Book.*
25. Traherne, *Christian Ethicks,* p. 16.
26. Ibid., p. 11.
27. See also pp. 278–79, ibid.
28. Ibid., pp. 108–09.
29. For an identical, somewhat rigid scheme over consecutive poems in the Dobell MS, see Clements, especially pp. 61–62ff. For a not dissimilar four steps, see Jordan, pp. 58–73.
30. For other poems on innocent dumbness falling, see especially "Silence," but also "Solitude," "Poverty," and "Dissatisfaction." My intuition about the importance of this poem is supported by Carl M. Selkin's *The Language of Love: The Style of Thomas Traherne's Poetry.*
31. Clements, p. 113.
32. For additional mystical meanings see pp. 168–74, ibid.
33. Another similar illustrative pair is "The Person" and "The Estate."
34. For an extended reading see Clements, pp. 115–34.
35. For an entry to fortunate fall literature see Clements, pp. 108–11.
36. Among many recent accounts of the plain style, note particularly Stein's account in the opening chapter of his Herbert study, and Fish's *Self-Consuming Artifacts,* particularly pp. 1–21, 156–223, and 374–82.
37. For a suggestive exposition of this stylistic concept, see Jackson I. Cope's "Seventeenth-Century Quaker Style."
38. See Stewart, pp. 139–69, particularly 140–44, 160–64, and 184–86; also Joan Webber's *The Eloquent "I",* pp. 236–47; and most recently Carl M. Selkin's "The Language of Vision: Traherne's Cataloguing Style."
39. See Clements, especially pp. 38–44; see as well Malcolm M. Day's "'Naked Truth' and the Language of Thomas Traherne."
40. For a suggestive catalogue see Clements' fine discussion, pp. 170–74.

Chapter 7

1. See Grabo, *Edward Taylor.*
2. See Keller, *The Example of Edward Taylor.*
3. I cite and quote *The Poems of Edward Taylor,* ed. Donald E. Stanford.
4. For rather elaborate explications of the Christ-type pillar of cloud and fire see Guild, pp. 75–77; Thomas Taylor, pp. 243–57; and Mather, pp. 169–73.
5. For Taylor's own gloss on Christ's mediatorial offices of prophet, priest, and king see II. 55.
6. Taylor, *Lord's Supper,* ed. Norman S. Grabo.
7. Prominent among those who question that Taylor could have created such an aesthetic because of presumably antipoetic Puritan suppositions about the gap between the material and the immaterial are Sidney E. Lind, "Edward Taylor: A Revaluation"; Roy Harvey Pearce, "Edward Taylor: The Poet as Puritan"; and John F. Lynen, *The Design of the Present,* pp. 49–74. Those who have helped describe Taylor's aesthetic include Herbert Blau, "Heaven's Sugar Cake: Theology and Imagery in the Poetry of Edward Taylor"; Mindele Black, "Edward Taylor: Heaven's Sugar Cake"; Grabo in *Edward Taylor* and in

Notes

"Edward Taylor's Spiritual Huswifery"; Charles W. Mignon, "Edward Taylor's *Preparatory Meditations*: A Decorum of Imperfection"; E. F. Carlisle, "The Puritan Structure of Edward Taylor's Poetry"; Donald Junkins, "'Should Stars Wooe Lobster Claws?': A Study of Edward Taylor's Poetic Practice and Theory"; Kathleen Blake, "Edward Taylor's Protestant Poetic: Non-transubstantiating Metaphor"; and William J. Scheick, *The Will and the Word: Conversion in the Poetry of Edward Taylor*, which includes his earlier "Nonsense from a Lisping Child: Edward Taylor on the Word as Piety," and "Typology and Allegory: A Comparative Study of George Herbert and Edward Taylor"; and Keller, *Example*.

8. See Stanford's glossary and p. 536; Karen E. Rowe's *Puritan Typology and Allegory as Metaphor and Conceit in Edward Taylor's "Preparatory Meditations,"* which supplies convincing parallels to Taylor's poems from Mather, pp. 51–54, 80–84, and Appendix A on pp. 236–44; and Charles W. Mignon's "The Nebraska Edward Taylor Manuscript: 'Upon the Types of the Old Testament'." Typology has proved to be a prominent, popular, and enlightening approach to Taylor's verse. Among the most helpful studies are the chapter in Ursula Brumm's *American Thought and Religious Typology*; Peter Nicolaisen, *Die Bildlichkeit in der Dichtung Edward Taylors*, especially pp. 110–37; Thomas M. Davis, "Edward Taylor and the Tradition of Puritan Typology"; Robert E. Reiter, "Poetry and Typology: Edward Taylor's *Preparatory Meditations*"; Karl Keller, "'The World Slickt up in Types': Edward Taylor as a Version of Emerson"; and the provocative Taylor chapter in Albert Gelpi's *The Tenth Muse*. Bercovitch's collection reprints several of these with other useful essays.

9. Taylor, *Lord's Supper*, pp. 10, 135.

10. Taylor, *Christographia*, p. 6.

11. Ibid., pp. 210, 421.

12. Ibid., pp. 269–70; see also the peroration, pp. 294–96.

13. Ibid., pp. 458–62, with pp. 422–24.

14. Full exemplification of types in the *Meditations* would require a catalogue. Davis' confessedly partial, at times loosely allegorical, listing is available for the second series, note 18, pp. 46–47; Rowe's appendices A and B, pp. 236–55, are also helpful.

15. For man see especially II. 35.

16. See as well the related pair of meditations of the same form, II. 157 A. and B.

17. See Brumm, *Religious Typology*; and Reiter, with expansions in Davis and Rowe, particularly her fourth chapter, on "antitypal image clusters."

18. See Brumm, "The 'Tree of Life' in Edward Taylor's Meditations"; in answer to Johannes Hedberg, "Meditations, Linguistic and Literary. On Meditation Twenty-Nine by Edward Taylor"; and Cecelia L. Halbert, "Tree of Life Imagery in the Poetry of Edward Taylor."

19. "Edward Taylor and the Poetic Use of Religious Imagery," in Bercovitch, pp. 191–206, subsumes Kathy Siebel and Thomas M. Davis' "Edward Taylor and the Cleansing of *Aquae Vitae*."

20. Bercovitch, p. 182.

21. Taylor, *Lord's Supper*, p. 43.

22. Taylor, *Christographia*, p. 291; see pp. 260–96. Cf. Mignon's emphasis on "But Grace excells all Metaphors," which he quotes from p. 253 on p. 1425; and the implications in Nicolaisen's discussion about the diminished importance of types since Christ has been manifested, pp. 124–26. For a similar hypothesis derived from Puritan exegesis (but one that neglects interests beneath the spiritual) see Rowe, especially pp. 9–15, 159–60, and chapter 4.

23. In addition to Mignon see Carlisle, especially Blake, and the implications of Clark Griffith, "Edward Taylor and the Momentum of Metaphor." I wish to add one more effect to Mignon's fine catalogue and at the same time to imply that his first effect, true poetry is written only in heaven, should be modified by the possibility for Taylor of an infusion of Christ's grace on earth. This is suggested as well, with emphasis on the conditional mode, by Michael D. Reed in "Edward Taylor's Poetry: Puritan Structure and Form."

24. Good examples of the transfer being effected appear in II. 46, 67 [A] and 68 [A], the latter two based on the sun of righteousness. Particularly interesting examples, which extend into contemporary failures and sins of the flesh, appear in I. 40 and II. 18.

25. The best early description appears on pp. 366–67 of Austin Warren's "Edward Taylor's Poetry: Colonial Baroque." This has been expanded in Grabo's discussion of Taylor's style, *Edward Taylor*, pp. 141–49, and elaborated in Keller's discussion of Taylor's primitivism, *Example*, pp. 246–59.

26. Other outstanding repetitions include the *sweetness* of ointment in I. 3, the *crown* of life and righteousness in I. 43–45, Christ as *head* of the mystical body of believers in II. 36–37, *life* in II. 47, *golden* and *ring*, *orb*, *sphere* of grace in II. 118 and 122, *glory* in II. 73 and 158.

27. See Grabo's *Edward Taylor*, p. 91.

28. For similar series see the opening stanzas of I. 34 and II. 158. For an important discussion of the relationship between the Word and Taylor's words (though its stress falls opposite to mine, on human mediation, integration, and unity as against severance repaired solely by Christ), see William J. Scheick, "Tending the Lord in All Admiring Style: Edward Taylor's *Preparatory Meditations*," reprinted in *The Will and the Word*.

29. For explications of Jacob's ladder as a type signifying Christ's duality, see particularly Guild, pp. 32–35; and Mather, pp. 165–67.

30. See Bercovitch, pp. 191–206, and 180, respectively.

31. See Grabo's *Edward Taylor*, pp. 151–54; note also Taylor's gathering of shards into tabernacles and temples from II. 20 through II. 24.

32. Grabo provides important discussions of Taylor's cloth imagery from early poems (which borrow from childhood backgrounds in the cloth-producing regions of England) to late meditations (which seem to expand the "wedden garment" in the Puritan controversy over the lord's supper to a mystical sense of the believer's soul uniting with God) in *Edward Taylor*, pp. 95–100, "Huswifery," and the introduction to *Treatise*. For other views relating his sermons and poems see Robert M. Benton's "Edward Taylor's Use of his Text"; and Donald Junkins' "Edward Taylor's Creative Process."

33. Another series expanding on this emblem, which is pervasive throughout the *Meditations*, begins with I. 20.

34. Mather, p. 628; see pp. 627–53.

35. Ibid., p. 630.

36. For Guild see p. 69; for Thomas Taylor, pp. 114–28.

37. For the latter see Grabo's "Huswifery."

38. See Blake.

39. Compare Taylor's use of *adjuncts* in II. 101.

Bibliography

Primary Works Cited

Adam of St. Victor. *The Liturgical Poetry*. Edited by Digby S. Wrangham. 3 vols. London, 1881.

————. *Oeuvres Poétiques*. Edited by León Gautier. 3rd ed. Paris, 1894.

————. *Le Proses*. Edited by Pierre Aubry and E. Misset. Paris, 1900.

Ainsworth, Henry. *Annotations upon the Five Bookes of Moses*. London, 1626.

Alabaster, William. *Apparatus in Revelationem Jesu Christi*. Antwerp, 1607.

————. *The Sonnets of William Alabaster*. Edited by G. M. Story and Helen Gardner. Oxford: Oxford University Press, 1959.

Anon. *Apollo Christian: or Helicon Reformed*. London, 1617.

Barnes, Barnabe. *A Divine Centvrie of Spirituall Sonnets*. London, 1595.

Bartolomaeus. *Batman uppon Bartholome*. London, 1582.

Beaumont, Joseph. *The Complete Poems*. Edited by Alexander B. Grosart. 2 vols. St. George's, 1880.

Bernard, Richard. *The faithfull shepheard*. London, 1621.

Braidshaigh, John. *Virginalia, or Spirituall Sonnets*. Rouen, 1632.

Calvin, John. *A Commentarie upon the Epistle of Saint Paul to the Romanes*. Translated by Christopher Rosdell. London, 1583.

————. *Institutes of the Christian Religion*. Edited by John T. McNeill. Translated by Ford Lewis Battles. 2 vols. Philadelphia: Westminster Press, 1960.

————. *The psalmes of David and others with J. Calvins Commentaries*. Translated by Arthur Golding. London, 1571.

Cawdrey, Robert. *A Treasvrie or Storehouse of Similies*. London, 1600.

Chub, William. *Two Fruitful and godly Sermons . . . the one touching the building of Gods Temple, the other what the Temple is*. London, 1585.

Day, Richard. *A Booke of Christian Prayers*. London, 1579.

Diodati, John. *Pious and Learned Annotations Upon the Holy Bible*. Translated by R. G. 3rd ed. London, 1651.

Donne, John. *The Complete Poetry of John Donne*. Edited by John T. Shawcross. Garden City, N.Y.: Anchor Books, 1967.

————. *The Divine Poems*. Edited by Helen Gardner. Oxford: Clarendon Press, 1952.

————. *Devotions upon Emergent Occasions*. Edited by John Sparrow. Cambridge: Cambridge University Press, 1923.

201

Bibliography

————. *Essayes in Divinity.* Edited by Evelyn Simpson. Oxford: Clarendon Press, 1952.

————. *The Sermons of John Donne.* Edited by George R. Potter and Evelyn M. Simpson. 10 vols. Berkeley: University of California Press, 1953–62.

Drummond, William, of Hawthornden. *Poems.* Edited by William C. Ward. London, n.d.

Everard, John. *The Gospel-Treasury Opened.* London, 1657, 1659.

Farlie, Robert. *Lychnocavsia.* London, 1638.

Ferguson, Robert. *The Interest of Reason in Religion.* London, 1675.

Fitz-Geffrey, Charles. *The Blessed Birth-day, Celebrated.* 2nd ed., enl. Oxford, 1636.

Fletcher, Joseph. *Christes Bloodie Sweat.* London, 1613.

The Geneva Bible; A facsimile of the 1560 edition. Introduction by Lloyd E. Berry. Madison: University of Wisconsin Press, 1969.

Guild, William. *Moses Vnuailed.* London, 1620.

Guiney, Louise Imogen. *Recusant Poets.* New York: Sheed and Ward, 1939.

Hall, John. *The Court of Virtue.* Edited by Russell A. Fraser. London: Routledge and K. Paul, 1961.

Harvey, Christopher. *The Complete Poems.* Edited by Alexander B. Grosart. London: Fuller Worthies' Library, 1874.

Henkel, Arthur, and Schöne, Albrecht. *Emblemata.* Stuttgart: J. B. Metzler, 1967.

Herbert, George. *The English Poems of George Herbert.* Edited by C. A. Patrides. London: Rowman and Littlefield, 1974.

————. *The Works of George Herbert.* Edited by F. E. Hutchinson. Oxford: Clarendon Press, 1941.

Horapollo. *The Hieroglyphics of Horapollo.* Edited by George Boas. New York: Pantheon Books, 1950.

Hume, Alexander. *Hymnes, or sacred songs . . . and certaine precepts.* Edinburgh, 1599.

Hunnis, William. *Seven Sobs of a Sorrowful Sovle for Sinne.* London, 1600.

Jenner, Thomas. *The Soules Solace, or Thirtie and one Spiritual Emblems.* London, 1626.

Lapide, Cornelius à. *Commentaria.* 11 vols. Lyons, 1714–40.

Lee, Samuel. *Orbis Miraculum, or the Temple of Solomon.* London, 1659.

Lever, Christopher. *A Crucifixe; or, a meditation upon repentance and the holie Passion.* London, 1607.

Lok, Henry. *Sundry Christian Passions, Contained in 200 Sonnets* (1593), *Miscellanies of the Fuller Worthies' Library.* Edited by Alexander B. Grosart. St. George's, 1871.

Martz, Louis L., ed. *English Seventeenth-Century Verse* I. 2 vols. rev. ed. New York: W. W. Norton, 1973.

Mather, Samuel. *The Figures or Types of the Old Testament.* Dublin, 1685.

Milton, John. *The Poems of John Milton.* Edited by John Carey and Alastair Fowler. London: Longmans, 1968.

Miscellanies of the Fuller Worthies' Library. Edited by Alexander B. Grosart. 4 vols. St. George's, 1871.

Montenay, Georgette de. *Monumenta emblematum Christianorum Virtutem or A Booke of armes or remembrance, wherein ar one hundred godly emblemata.* Frankfort, 1619.

The Paradise of Dainty Devices (1576–1606). Edited by Hyder E. Rollins. Cambridge, Mass.: Harvard University Press, 1927.

Pearson, John. *Critici Sacri.* 8 vols. Amsterdam, 1698.

Perkins, William. *Works.* 2 vols. Cambridge, 1609.

Poole, Matthew. *Synopsis Criticorum.* 5 vols. London, 1669–76.

Puttenham, George. *The Arte of English Poesie.* Edited by Gladys Doidge Willcock and Alice Walker. Cambridge: Cambridge University Press, 1936.

Quarles, Francis. *The Complete Works.* Edited by Alexander B. Grosart. 3 vols. St. George's, 1880–81.

Richards, Nathanael. *Poems Sacred and Satyricall.* London, 1641.

Bibliography

Roberts, Francis. *Clavis Bibliorum*. 2 vols. 2nd ed. London, 1649.

Rowlands, Richard. *Odes, in Imitation of the Seaven Penitential Psalmes*. Antwerp, 1601.

Sandys, George. *A Paraphrase upon the Divine Poems*. London, 1638.

Smith, John. *The Mysterie of Rhetorique Unvail'd*. London, 1657.

Southwell, Robert. *An Epistle of Comfort, to the Reverend Priests, and to the Honourable, Worshipfull, & other of the Lay sort, restrayned in durance for the Catholike Faith*. London, 1616.

———. *The Poems of Robert Southwell, S. J.* Edited by James H. McDonald and Nancy Pollard Brown. Oxford: Clarendon Press, 1967.

———. *Spiritual Exercises and Devotions of Blessed Robert Southwell, S. J.* Edited by J.-M. de Buck, S. J. Translated by Mgr. P. E. Hallett. London: Sheed and Ward, 1931.

———. *Two Letters and Short Rules of a Good Life*. Edited by Nancy Pollard Brown. Charlottesville: University Press of Virginia, 1973.

Sternhold and Hopkins, trans. *The Whole Booke of Davids Psalms*. London, 1582.

Taylor, Edward. *Christographia*. Edited by Norman S. Grabo. New Haven: Yale University Press, 1962.

———. *Edward Taylor's Treatise Concerning the Lord's Supper*. Edited by Norman S. Grabo. East Lansing: Michigan State University Press, 1966.

———. *The Poems of Edward Taylor*. Edited by Donald E. Stanford. New Haven: Yale University Press, 1960.

Taylor, Thomas. *Christ Revealed: or the Old Testament Explained*. London, 1635.

———. *Moses and Aaron*. London, 1653.

Traherne, Thomas. *Christian Ethicks*. Edited by Carol L. Marks and George R. Guffey. Ithaca: Cornell University Press, 1968.

———. *Meditations on the Six Days of Creation*. Edited by George R. Guffey. The Augustan Reprint Society, no. 119. Los Angeles: University of California, 1966.

———. *Thomas Traherne: Centuries, Poems, and Thanksgivings*. Edited by H. M. Margoliouth. 2 vols. Oxford: Clarendon Press, 1958.

Tyndale, William. *Doctrinal Treatises and Introductions to Different Portions of the Holy Scriptures by William Tyndale, Martyr, 1536*. Edited by H. Walter. Cambridge, 1848.

Vaughan, Henry. *The Complete Poetry of Henry Vaughan*. Edited by French Fogle. Garden City, N.Y.: Anchor Books, 1964.

———. *The Works of Henry Vaughan*. Edited by L. C. Martin. 2nd ed. Oxford: Clarendon Press, 1957.

Walpole, A. S. and Mason, A. J., eds. *Early Latin Hymns*. Cambridge: Cambridge University Press, 1922.

Walton, Izaak. *The Lives*. Introduction by George Saintsbury. Oxford: Oxford University Press, 1927.

Washbourne, Thomas. *Divine Poems*. Edited by Alexander B. Grosart. n.p., Fuller Worthies' Library, 1868.

Weemes, John. *The Christian Synagogue*. London, 1623.

———. *An Explication of the Iudiciall Lawes of Moses*. London, 1632.

Westminster Assembly. *Annotations Upon All the Books of the Old and New Testament*. 2 vols. 3rd ed., enl. London, 1657.

Whitaker, William. *A Disputation on Holy Scripture against the Papists*. Edited and translated by William Fitzgerald. Cambridge, 1847.

Willet, Andrew. *Sacrorum emblematum centuria una*. n.p., n.d.

Wither, George. *Halelviah or Britans Second Remembrancer*. Spenser Society Reprints, no. 30. London, 1881.

———. *Hymns and Songs of the Church*. Spenser Society Reprints, nos. 26–27. London, 1879.

Wyatt, Sir Thomas. *The Collected Poems of Sir Thomas Wyatt*. Edited by Kenneth Muir and Patricia Thomson. Liverpool: Liverpool University Press, 1969.

Bibliography

List of Abbreviations

AL	American Literature
AQ	American Quarterly
DAI	Dissertation Abstracts International
EAL	Early American Literature
EIC	Essays in Criticism
ELH	Formerly Journal of English Literary History
ELN	English Language Notes
ELR	English Literary Renaissance
ELWIU	Essays in Literature
EM	English Miscellany
Hebrew Univ. Stud. in Lit.	Hebrew University Studies in Literature
HLQ	Huntington Library Quarterly
JEGP	Journal of English and Germanic Philology
KR	The Kenyon Review
Lang&S	Language and Style
MLN	Formerly Modern Language Notes
MLQ	Modern Language Quarterly
MP	Modern Philology
MSpr	Moderna Sprak
NEQ	New England Quarterly
PBSA	Papers of the Bibliographical Society of America
PCP	Pacific Coast Philology
PLL	Papers on Language and Literature
PMLA	Publications of the Modern Language Association
PQ	Philological Quarterly
RES	Review of English Studies
RN	Renaissance News (now Renaissance Quarterly)
RPh	Romance Philology
SAQ	South Atlantic Quarterly
SCN	Seventeenth-Century News
SEL	Studies in English Literature, 1500–1900
SP	Studies in Philology
Stud. in the Ren.	Studies in the Renaissance
TLS	Times Literary Supplement (London)
TSLL	Texas Studies in Literature and Language
UTQ	University of Toronto Quarterly

Bibliography

Secondary Works Cited

Allen, D. C. "John Donne's 'Paradise and Calvarie'." *MLN*, 60 (1945):398–400.

Anderson, Donald K., Jr. "Donne's 'Hymne to God my God, in my sicknesse' and the T-in-O Maps." *SAQ*, 71 (1972):465–72.

Armstrong, Louise A. *The Medieval Latin Hymn: A Study of a Literary Genre as It Developed in a Dying Language.* Ph.D. dissertation, Johns Hopkins University, 1951.

Asals, Heather. "The Voice of George Herbert's 'The Church'." *ELH*, 36 (1969):511–28.

Auerbach, Erich. "Dante's Prayer to the Virgin (Paradiso, xxxiii) and Earlier Eulogies." *RP*, 3 (1949):1–26.

———. "Figura," In *Scenes from the Drama of European Literature*, translated by Ralph Manheim, pp. 11–76. New York: Meridian Books, 1959.

Bartlett, Elisabeth Jefferis. *"All Soul and Life, an Ey most bright": A Persona Study of the Writings of Thomas Traherne.* Ph.D. dissertation, Brown University, 1976.

Beck, Rosalie. "A Precedent for Donne's Imagery in 'Goodfriday, 1613. Riding Westward'." *RES*, 19 (1968):166–69.

Benton, Robert M. "Edward Taylor's Use of his Text." *AL*, 39 (1967):31–41.

Bercovitch, Sacvan, ed. *The American Puritan Imagination: Essays in Revaluation.* Cambridge: Cambridge University Press, 1974.

———. ed. *Typology and Early American Literature.* Amherst: University of Massachusetts Press, 1972.

Black, Mindele. "Edward Taylor: Heaven's Sugar Cake." *NEQ*, 29 (1956):159–81.

Blake, Kathleen. "Edward Taylor's Protestant Poetic: Nontransubstantiating Metaphor." *AL*, 43 (1971):1–24.

Blau, Herbert. "Heaven's Sugar Cake: Theology and Imagery in the Poetry of Edward Taylor." *NEQ*, 26 (1953):337–60.

Blench, J. W. *Preaching in England in the Late Fifteenth and Sixteenth Centuries.* Oxford: Basil Blackwell, 1964.

Bowers, Fredson. "Henry Vaughan's Multiple Time Scheme." *MLQ*, 23 (1962):291–96.

———. "Herbert's Sequential Imagery: 'The Temper'." *MP*, 59 (1962):202–13.

Bowers, R. H. *The Legend of Jonah.* The Hague: Martinus Nijhoff, 1971.

Brumm, Ursula. *American Thought and Religious Typology.* Translated by John Hoaglund. New Brunswick: Rutgers University Press, 1970.

———. "The 'Tree of Life' in Edward Taylor's Meditations." *EAL*, 3 (1968):72–87.

Campbell, Lily Bess. *Divine Poetry and Drama in Sixteenth-Century England.* Berkeley: University of California Press, 1959.

Cannon, Charles K. "William Whitaker's *Disputatio de Sacra Scriptura*: A Sixteenth-Century Theory of Allegory." *HLQ*, 25 (1962):129–38.

Carlisle, E. F. "The Puritan Structure of Edward Taylor's Poetry." *AQ*, 20 (1968):147–63.

Carnes, Valerie. "The Unity of George Herbert's *The Temple*: A Reconsideration." *ELH*, 35 (1968):505–26.

Caro, Robert V. *Rhetoric and Meditation in the Sonnets of William Alabaster.* Ph.D. Dissertation, University of Washington, 1977.

Chambers, A. B. "'Goodfriday, 1613. Riding Westward.' The Poem and the Tradition." *ELH*, 28 (1961):31–53.

Clark, Ira. "'Lord, in thee The *beauty* lies in the *discovery*': 'Love Unknown' and Reading George Herbert." *ELH*, 39 (1972):560–84.

Clements, A. L. *The Mystical Poetry of Thomas Traherne.* Cambridge, Mass.: Harvard University Press, 1969.

Clements, Robert J. *Picta Poesis.* Rome: Edizióni di Storia e litteratura, 1960.

Colie, Rosalie L. *Paradoxia Epidemica.* Princeton: Princeton University Press, 1966.

———. *The Resources of Kind.* Berkeley: University of California Press, 1973.

205

Bibliography

Cope, Jackson I. "Fortunate Falls as Form in Milton's 'Fair Infant'," *JEGP*, 62 (1964): 660–74.

——. "Seventeenth-Century Quaker Style." *PMLA*, 71 (1956): 725–54.

Cox, Gerald H. "Traherne's *Centuries*: A Platonic Devotion of 'Divine Philosophy'." *MP*, 69 (1971): 10–24.

Danielou, Jean. *From Shadows to Reality*. London: Burns & Oates, 1960.

Davies, Horton. *Worship and Theology in England: From Andrewes to Baxter and Fox, 1603–1690*. Princeton: Princeton University Press, 1975.

——. *Worship and Theology in England: From Cranmer to Hooker, 1534–1603*. Princeton: Princeton University Press, 1970.

Davis, Thomas M. "Edward Taylor and the Tradition of Puritan Typology." *EAL*, 4 (1969): 27–47.

Day, Malcolm M. "'Naked Truth' and the Language of Thomas Traherne." *SP*, 68 (1971): 305–25.

Dronke, Peter. *The Medieval Lyric*. London: Hutchinson, 1968.

Durr, R. A. *On the Mystical Poetry of Henry Vaughan*. Cambridge, Mass.: Harvard University Press, 1962.

Duvall, Robert. "The Biblical Character of Henry Vaughan's *Silex Scintillans*." *PCP*, 6 (1971): 13–19.

Evans, Maurice. "Metaphor and Symbol in the Sixteenth Century." *EIC*, 3 (1953): 267–84.

Fairbairn, Patrick. *The Typology of Scripture*. 2 vols. New York: Funk, 1900.

Farnham, Fern. "The Imagery of Henry Vaughan's 'The Night'." *PQ*, 38 (1959): 425–35.

Fish, Stanley E. *The Living Temple; George Herbert and Catechizing*. Berkeley: University of California Press, 1978.

——. *Self-Consuming Artifacts*. Berkeley: University of California Press, 1972.

Freeman, Rosemary. *English Emblem Books*. London: Chatto & Windus, 1948.

Freer, Coburn. *Music for a King*. Baltimore: Johns Hopkins University Press, 1972.

Friedenreich, Kenneth. *Henry Vaughan*. Boston: Twayne, 1978.

Friedman, Donald M. "Memory and the Art of Salvation in Donne's Good Friday Poem." *ELR*, 3 (1973): 418–42.

Galdon, Joseph A. *Typology and Seventeenth-Century Literature*. Ph.D. Dissertation, Columbia University, 1965; rev. for The Hague: Mouton, 1975.

Garner, Ross. *Henry Vaughan: Experience and Tradition*. Chicago: University of Chicago Press, 1959.

Gelpi, Albert. *The Tenth Muse*. Cambridge, Mass.: Harvard University Press, 1975.

Goldberg, Jonathan S. "Donne's Journey East: Aspects of a Seventeenth-Century Trope." *SP*, 68 (1971): 470–83.

Grabo, Norman S. *Edward Taylor*. New York: Twayne, 1961.

——. "Edward Taylor's Spiritual Huswifery." *PMLA*, 79 (1964): 554–60.

Grant, Patrick. "Augustinian Spirituality and the *Holy Sonnets* of John Donne." *ELH*, 38 (1971): 542–61.

——. *The Transformation of Sin*. Amherst: University of Massachusetts Press, 1974.

Gray, Douglas. *Themes and Images in the Medieval English Religious Lyric*. London: Routledge and K. Paul, 1972.

Griffith, Clark. "Edward Taylor and the Momentum of Metaphor." *ELH*, 33 (1966): 448–60.

Guss, Donald L. *John Donne, Petrarchist*. Detroit: Wayne State University Press, 1966.

Halbert, Cecelia L. "Tree of Life Imagery in the Poetry of Edward Taylor." *AL*, 38 (1966): 22–34.

Halewood, William H. *The Poetry of Grace*. New Haven: Yale University Press, 1970.

Haller, William. *The Rise of Puritanism*. New York: Columbia University Press, 1938.

Hanson, R. P. C. *Allegory and Event*. London: Knox Press, 1959.

Harnack, H. Andrew. "George Herbert's 'AARON': The Aesthetics of Shaped Typology." *ELN*, 14 (1976): 25–32.

Bibliography

Harris, Victor. "Allegory to Analogy in the Interpretation of the Scriptures During the Middle Ages and the Renaissance." *PQ*, 45 (1966):1–23.

Hedberg, Johannes. "Meditations, Linguistic and Literary. On Meditation Twenty-Nine by Edward Taylor." *MSpr*, 54 (1960):253–70.

Holmes, Elizabeth. *Henry Vaughan and the Hermetic Philosophy*. Oxford: Russell & Russell, 1932.

Hudson, George C., Jr. *The Heart of Stone: An Image of the Spiritual Condition of Man in Seventeenth-Century Poetry*. Ph.D. Dissertation, University of Minnesota, 1972.

Hughes, Richard E. *The Progress of the Soul; The Interior Career of John Donne*. New York: W. Morrow, 1968.

Hutchinson, F. E. *Henry Vaughan*. Oxford: Clarendon Press, 1947.

Janelle, Pierre. *Robert Southwell, the Writer*. London: Sheed & Ward, 1935.

Jordan, Richard D. *The Temple of Eternity*. Port Washington, N.Y.: Kennikat Press, 1972.

Junkins, Donald. "Edward Taylor's Creative Process." *EAL*, 4 (1969):67–78.

———. "'Should Stars Wooe Lobster Claws?': A Study of Edward Taylor's Poetic Practice and Theory." *EAL*, 3 (1968):88–117.

Kaufmann, U. Milo. *The Pilgrim's Progress and Traditions in Puritan Meditation*. New Haven: Yale University Press, 1966.

Keller, Karl. *The Example of Edward Taylor*. Amherst: University of Massachusetts Press, 1975.

———. "'The World Slickt up in Types': Edward Taylor as a Version of Emerson." *EAL*, 5 (1970):124–40.

Knieger, Bernard. "The Purchase-Sale: Patterns of Business Imagery in the Poetry of George Herbert." *SEL*, 6 (1966):111–24.

Legouis, Pierre. *Donne, the Craftsman*. Paris: Henri Didier, 1928.

Lewalski, Barbara K. *Donne's 'Anniversaries' and the Poetry of Praise*. Princeton: Princeton University Press, 1973.

———. *Milton's Brief Epic*. Providence: Brown University Press, 1966.

———. *Protestant Poetics and the Seventeenth-Century Religious Lyric*. Princeton: Princeton University Press, 1979.

———. "*Samson Agonistes* and the 'Tragedy' of the Apocalypse." *PMLA*, 85 (1970): 1050–62.

———. "Typological Symbolism and the 'Progress of the Soul' in Seventeenth-Century Literature." In *Literary Uses of Typology from the Late Middle Ages to the Present*, edited by Earl Miner, pp. 79–114. Princeton: Princeton University Press, 1977.

———. "Typology and Poetry: A Consideration of Herbert, Vaughan, and Marvell." In *Illustrious Evidence*, edited by Earl Miner, pp. 41–69. Berkeley: University of California Press, 1975.

Lind, Sidney E. "Edward Taylor: A Revaluation." *NEQ*, 21 (1948):518–30.

Low, Anthony. *Love's Architecture: Devotional Modes in Seventeenth-Century English Poetry*. New York: New York University Press, 1978.

Lubac, Henri de. *Exégèse Médiévale*. 4 vols. Paris: Aubier, 1959.

Lynen, John F. *The Design of the Present*. New Haven: Yale University Press, 1969.

MacCallum, H. R. "Milton and Figurative Interpretation of the Bible." *UTQ*, 31 (1962): 397–415.

Madsen, William G. *From Shadowy Types to Truth*. New Haven: Yale University Press, 1968.

Mahood, M. M. *Poetry and Humanism*. London: Cape, 1950.

Manning, Stephen. *Wisdom and Number*. Lincoln: University of Nebraska Press, 1962.

Marilla, E. L. "The Secular and Religious Poetry of Henry Vaughan." *MLQ*, 9 (1948): 394–411.

Marks, Carol L. "Thomas Traherne and Hermes Trismegistus." *RN*, 19 (1966):118–31.

———. "Traherne and Cambridge Platonism." *PMLA*, 81 (1966):521–34.

———. "Traherne's 'Church's Year-Book'." *PBSA*, 60 (1966):31–72.

Bibliography

Marshall, William H. "Thomas Traherne and the Doctrine of Original Sin." *MLN*, 73 (1958):161–65.

Martz, Louis L. *The Paradise Within*. New Haven: Yale University Press, 1964.

———. *The Poetry of Meditation*. rev. ed. New Haven: Yale University Press, 1962.

Mason, H. A. *Humanism and Poetry in the Early Tudor Period*. London: Routledge and K. Paul, 1959.

McLaughlin, Elizabeth and Gail Thomas. "Communion in *The Temple*." *SEL*, 15 (1975): 111–24.

Messenger, Ruth Ellis. *The Medieval Latin Hymn*. Washington, D.C.: Capitol Press, 1953.

Mignon, Charles W. "Edward Taylor's *Preparatory Meditations*: A Decorum of Imperfection." *PMLA*, 83 (1968):1423–28.

———. "The Nebraska Edward Taylor Manuscript: 'Upon the Types of the Old Testament'." *EAL*, 12 (1978):296–301.

Miller, Perry. *The New England Mind: The Seventeenth Century*. New York: Macmillan Company, 1939.

Miller, Joseph Robert. *The Counter-Reformation and English Poetry of the Renaissance*. Ph.D. Dissertation, Princeton University, 1977.

Montgomery, R. L., Jr. "The Province of Allegory in George Herbert's Verse." *TSLL*, 1 (1960):457–72.

Mueller, Janel M. "The Exegesis of Experience: Dean Donne's *Devotions upon Emergent Occasions*." *JEGP*, 67 (1968):1–19.

Mulder, John R. "George Herbert's *The Temple*: Design and Methodology." *SCN*, 31 (1973):37–45.

———. *The Temple of the Mind*. New York: Pegasus, 1969.

Nicolaisen, Peter. *Die Bildlichkeit in der Dichtung Edward Taylors*. Neümunster, 1966.

Ong, Walter J. "Wit and Mystery: A Revaluation in Medieval Latin Hymnody." *Speculum*, 22 (1947):310–41.

Patrick, J. Max. "Critical Problems in Editing George Herbert's *The Temple*." In *The Editor as Critic and the Critic as Editor*, pp. 3–40. Los Angeles: William Andrews Clark Memorial Library, 1973.

Pearce, Roy Harvey. "Edward Taylor: The Poet as Puritan." *NEQ*, 23 (1950):31–46.

Pelikan, Jaroslav. *Luther the Expositer*. St. Louis: Concordia Publishing House, 1959.

Pettet, E. C. *Of Paradise and Light*. Cambridge: Cambridge University Press, 1960.

Praz, Mario. *Studies in Seventeenth-Century Imagery*. 2 vols. London: University of London, 1939, 1947.

Preus, James Samuel. *From Shadow to Promise*. Cambridge, Mass.: Harvard University Press, 1969.

Quinn, Dennis B. "John Donne's Principles of Biblical Exegesis." *JEGP*, 61 (1962):313–29.

Raby, F. J. E. *A History of Christian-Latin Poetry From the Beginnings to the Close of Middle Ages*. 2nd ed. Oxford: Clarendon Press, 1953.

Ray, R. H. *George Herbert in the Seventeenth Century: Allusions to Him Collected and Annotated*. Ph.D. Dissertation, University of Texas, 1977.

Reed, Michael D. "Edward Taylor's Poetry: Puritan Structure and Form." *AL*, 46 (1974): 304–12.

Reiss, Edmund. *The Art of the Middle English Lyric*. Athens: University of Georgia Press, 1972.

Reiter, Robert E. *In Adam's Room*. Ph.D. Dissertation, University of Michigan, 1964.

———. "Poetry and Typology: Edward Taylor's *Preparatory Meditations*. Second Series, Nos. 1–30." *EAL*, 5 (1970):111–23.

Rickey, Mary Ellen. *Utmost Art*. Lexington: University of Kentucky Press, 1966.

———. "Vaughan, *The Temple*, and Poetic Form." *SP*, 59 (1962):162–70.

Roberts, John R. "The Influence of *The Spiritual Exercises* of St. Ignatius on the Nativity Poems of Robert Southwell." *JEGP*, 59 (1960):450–56.

Bibliography

Roston, Murray. *Biblical Drama in England*. Evanston: Northwestern University Press, 1968.

———. *The Soul of Wit*. Oxford: Clarendon Press, 1974.

Rowe, Karen E. *Puritan Typology and Allegory As Metaphor and Conceit in Edward Taylor's "Preparatory Meditations."* Ph.D. Dissertation, Indiana University, 1971.

Rudrum, Alan W. "The Influence of Alchemy in the Poems of Henry Vaughan." *PQ*, 49 (1970):469–80.

Salter, K. W. *Thomas Traherne: Mystic and Poet*. New York: Barnes and Noble, 1964.

Sandler, Florence. "'Solomon ubique regnet': Herbert's Use of the Images of the New Covenant." *PLL*, 8 (1972):147–58.

Scheick, William J. "Nonsense from a Lisping Child: Edward Taylor on the Word as Piety." *TSLL*, 13 (1971):39–53.

———. "Tending the Lord in All Admiring Style: Edward Taylor's *Preparatory Meditations*." *Lang & S*, 4 (1971):163–87.

———. "Typology and Allegory: A Comparative Study of George Herbert and Edward Taylor." *EIL*, 2 (1975):76–86.

———. *The Will and the Word: Conversion in the Poetry of Edward Taylor*. Athens: University of Georgia Press, 1973.

Schleiner, Winfried. *The Imagery of John Donne's Sermons*. Providence: Brown University Press, 1970.

Schten, Carolyn A. "'Christs Bloody Sweat': A Meditation on the Mass." *EM*, 20 (1969):75–80.

Selkin, Carl M. *The Language of Love: The Style of Thomas Traherne's Poetry*. Ph.D. Dissertation, SUNY Binghamton, 1973; *DAI*, 34 (1974):7722A.

———. "The Language of Vision: Traherne's Cataloguing Style." *ELR*, 6 (1976):92–104.

Sicherman, Carol Marks. "Donne's Discoveries." *SEL*, 11 (1971):69–88.

Siebel, Kathy and Thomas M. Davis. "Edward Taylor and the Cleansing of *Aquae Vitae*." *EAL*, 4 (1969):102–09.

Simmonds, James D. *Masques of God*. Pittsburgh: University of Pittsburgh Press, 1972.

Sizemore, Christine W. "The Authorship of *The Mystery of Rhetoric Unveiled*." *PBSA*, 69 (1975):79–81.

Smalley, Beryl. *The Study of the Bible in the Middle Ages*. 2nd ed. Oxford: Clarendon Press, 1952.

Smith, Hallett. "English Metrical Psalms in the Sixteenth Century and their Literary Significance." *HLQ*, 9 (1946):249–71.

Spitzer, Leo. *Essays on English and American Literature*. Princeton: Princeton University Press, 1962.

Stein, Arnold. *George Herbert's Lyrics*. Baltimore: Johns Hopkins University Press, 1968.

Stewart, Stanley. *The Expanded Voice: The Art of Thomas Traherne*. San Marino, Cal.: Huntington Library, 1970.

Summers, Joseph H. *George Herbert; his Religion and his Art*. Cambridge, Mass.: Harvard University Press, 1954.

Taylor, Mark. *The Soul in Paraphrase*. The Hague: Mouton, 1974.

Trimpey, John E. "An Analysis of Traherne's 'Thoughts I'." *SP*, 68 (1971):88–104.

Tuve, Rosemond. *A Reading of George Herbert*. Chicago: University of Chicago Press, 1952.

———. "Sacred 'Parody' of Love Poetry, and Herbert." *Stud. in the Ren.*, 8 (1961):249–90.

Twombley, Robert G. "Thomas Wyatt's Paraphrases of the Penitential Psalms of David." *TSLL*, 12 (1970):345–80.

Underwood, Horace H. "Time and Space in the Poetry of Vaughan." *SP*, 69 (1972):231–41.

Vendler, Helen. *The Poetry of George Herbert*. Cambridge, Mass.: Harvard University Press, 1975.

Bibliography

Walker, John David. "The Architectonics of George Herbert's *The Temple*." *ELH*, 29 (1962):289–305.

Walters, Richard H. "Henry Vaughan and the Alchemists." *RES*, 23 (1947):107–22.

Wardropper, Bruce W. "The Religious Conversion of Profane Poetry." In *Studies in the Continental Background of Renaissance English Literature*, edited by Dale B. J. Randall and George Walton Williams, pp. 203–21. Durham: Duke University Press, 1977.

Warren, Austin. "Edward Taylor's Poetry: Colonial Baroque." *KR*, 3 (1941):355–71.

Webber, Joan. *Contrary Music*. Madison: University of Wisconsin Press, 1963.

————. *The Eloquent "I"*. Madison: University of Wisconsin Press, 1968.

Weber, Sarah Appleton. *Theology and Poetry in the Middle English Lyric*. Columbus: Ohio State University Press, 1969.

White, Helen C. *English Devotional Literature, 1600–1640*. Madison: University of Wisconsin Press, 1931.

————. *The Metaphysical Poets*. New York: Macmillan Company, 1936.

Whiting, George W. "And Without Thorn the Rose." *RES*, n.s. 10 (1959):60–62.

Williams, Arnold L. *The Common Expositor*. Chapel Hill: University of North Carolina Press, 1948.

Williams, G. Walton. *Image and Symbol in the Sacred Poetry of Richard Crashaw*. Columbia: University of South Carolina Press, 1964.

Woollcombe, K. J. and G. W. H. Lampe. *Essays on Typology*. Naperville, Ill.: A. R. Allenson, 1957.

Zwicker, Steven N. *Dryden's Political Poetry: The Typology of King and Nation*. Providence: Brown University Press, 1972.

Index

Aaron, 140, 165, 180, 182. *See also works by individual authors*

Abel, 88, 128–29

Abraham, 7, 10, 20, 22, 75, 115, 122, 127, 165, 167. *See also* Gal. **4:21–31**

Absalom, 53

Acts **10**, 47; **17:27–28**, 125

Adam, 2, 4, 7, 18, 23, 49, 54, 70, 75, 78, 85, 87, 89, 134, 136, 138–40 passim, 145–53 passim, 185, 190n18; sweat of, 78. *See also* Rom. **5:10–17**; 1 Cor. **15:21–22**, 45–47; *works by individual authors*

Adam of St. Victor, 21, 42, 189n51

Ainsworth, Henry: *Annotations upon the Five Bookes of Moses*, 89, 115–16, 188n31, 196n25–26

Alabaster, William, x, 3, 30, 64, 68, 126, 128, 160, 185, 191n40; conversion to Catholicism, 51–52; identification with Christ's sacrifice, 52; association with David, 52–59 passim, 62; psalmody, 52–59 passim, 62; definition and use of types, 53–56; meditation, 56; Petrarchism, 56–59, 62

—*Apparatus in Revelationem Jesu Christi*, 53, 191n42–43

—*Divine Meditations*, 51–63

—sonnets: Sonnet 1, 52; Sonnet 2, 52–53; Sonnet 3, 55; Sonnet 4, 57; Sonnet 9, 51; Sonnet 12, 57; Sonnet 15, 56; Sonnet 16, 191n53; Sonnet 18, 57–58; Sonnet 20, 54; Sonnet 21, 61; Sonnet 26, 51, 54; Sonnet 30, 191n52; Sonnet 32, 53–54; Sonnet 33, 56; Sonnet 36, 191n53; Sonnet 37, 54; Sonnet 39, 191n50, 191n52; Sonnet 40, 52; Sonnet 41, 52; Sonnet 43, 191n53; Sonnet 45, 191n53; Sonnet 48, 56; Sonnet 52, 56; Sonnet 59, 191n53; Sonnet 68, "A Morning Meditation (I)," 59; Sonnet 69, "Of the Motions of the Fiend," 56–57; Sonnet 70, "A Morning Meditation (2)," 59–62; Sonnet 71, "The Difference 'twixt Compunction and Cold Devotion in Beholding the Passion of Our Saviour," 58–59; Sonnet 76, 51

Alciati, Andreas: *Emblematum Liber*, 65

allegory: Catholic, 9–15 (*see also* Mary); Judaic, relationship to typology, 7–8; medieval fourfold, 9–11

Allen, D. C., 193n36

Ambrose, 60–61, 71

Amos **5:26**, 6

Anderson, Donald K. Jr., 193n35–36

Anglicans, xi, xii. *See also* typology, Anglican

Apollo Christian, 23, 189n59

Apostles' Creed, 33

aquae vitae, 167, 187n2, 199n19. *See also*

Author's Note: Only primary works appear in this index, many cited by short title. Most appear under their authors, probable authors, or pseudonymous authors. Books of the Bible appear individually, chapter and verse numbers in boldface type.

Index

118, 123; "The Search," 124–25; "The Seed growing secretly," 126; "The Stone," 111–12, 196n18; "The Storm," 124; "The Tempest," 130, 196n26; "The Timber," 126; "To the Holy Bible," 110; "Trinity-Sunday," 114; "Vanity of Spirit," 125, 126; "White Sunday," 113; "The World," 125
Vendler, Helen, 193n6
Verstegan, Richard. *See* Rowlands, Richard
Victorines, 9. *See also* Adam of St. Victor
vine, 3, 54, 144, 167, 187n2. *See also* John **15:1–8**
Vives, Juan Luis, 21

Walker, John David, 193n6, 197n14
Wallerstein, Ruth, 197n18
Walpole, A. S., 189n51
Walter, H., 188n12
Walton, Izaak: *Lives*, 71–72, 80–81, 192n8–9, 192n11, 193n1–2
Ward, William C., 189n55
Wardropper, Bruce W., 191n32
Warren, Austin, 200n25
Washbourne, Thomas, 25, 185; *Divine Poems*, 2–4; "The Rock," 3–4; "A Colloquy upon the Ascension," 187n2; "The Fountain," 187n2; "The Vine Wasted," 187n2
water: as cleansing (*see* fountain: tears); with blood, wine (*see* blood, and water; John **19:34**)
Webber, Joan, 76, 193n30, 198n38
Weber, Sarah Appleton, 189n53

Weemes, John: *The Christian Synagogue*, 197n13; *An Explication*, 19, 189n43
well, 177. *See also* fountain
Westminster Assembly: *Annotations upon . . . the Old and New Testament*, 92, 181, 189n44
Whitaker, William: *Disputatio De Sacra Scriptura*, 12–15, 188n22–28
White, Helen C., xi, 189n50, 193n6, 195n9
Whiting, George W., 191n48
Willet, Andrew: *Sacrorum emblematum centuria una*, 65–66, 192n2–3; "Emblemata Typica sive Allegorica," 65; Emblem 8, 65–66; Emblem 18, 65; Emblem 19, 91; Emblem 41, 65; Emblem 63, 65; Emblem 72, 66
Williams, Arnold L., 15, 188n30
Williams, G. Walton, 196n1
Wither, George, 188n60, 189n61–63; *Haleluiah*, "For Saterday," 24–25; *Hymns and Songs of the Church*, 24–25
Woolcombe, K. J., 187n3, 187n5
Word, the, 62, 143, 151, 153, 154–58, 174–76, 178, 183–84, 200n28
Wrangham, Digby S., 189n51
Wyatt, Sir Thomas, 30–31, 190n6, 190n8; "I fynde no peace and all my warr is done," 43; "My galy charged with forgetfulnes," 43; "My Lute, awake," 33; Psalm **102**, 31

Zacchaeus, 49
Zechariah **3:4**, 180; **4:3**, 65; **13**, 187n2; **13:1**, 26; **14:20–21**, 93
Zwicker, Steven N., xi, 187n3

UNIVERSITY OF FLORIDA MONOGRAPHS
Humanities